POETRY AND DRAMA
1570–1700

ESSAYS IN HONOUR OF
HAROLD F. BROOKS

HAROLD F. BROOKS

POETRY AND DRAMA
1570–1700

ESSAYS IN HONOUR OF
HAROLD F. BROOKS

edited by
Antony Coleman
and
Antony Hammond

METHUEN

LONDON & NEW YORK

First published in 1981 by
Methuen & Co. Ltd
11 New Fetter Lane, London EC4P 4EE
Published in the USA by
Methuen & Co.
in association with Methuen, Inc.
733 Third Avenue, New York, NY 10017

Photoset by
Rowland Phototypesetting Ltd
Bury St Edmunds, Suffolk
Printed in Great Britain by
St Edmundsbury Press, Bury St Edmunds
Suffolk

British Library Cataloguing in Publication Data

Poetry and drama 1570–1700.
1. English prose literature – History and criticism
I. Title   II. Brooks, Harold F.
III. Coleman, Antony   IV. Hammond, Antony
828'.08   PR751
ISBN 0-416-74470-2

CONTENTS

Preface   vii

Abbreviations   viii

1   Harold F. Brooks   1
Arthur Johnston

2   'The Vice' and the popular theatre 1547–80   13
Peter Happé

3   'The very temple of delight':   32
the twin plots of *Much Ado About Nothing*
David Cook

4   Torch, cauldron and taper: 47
light and darkness in *Macbeth*
William A. Armstrong

5   The politics of pageantry: 60
social implications in Jacobean London
M. C. Bradbrook

6   The role of Livia in *Women Beware Women*   76
Kenneth Muir

7   The Restoration: age of faith, age of satire   90
Earl Miner

8 Oldham's versions of the classics 110

Raman Selden

9 The art of adaptation: 136
some Restoration treatments of Ovid

Harold Love

10 Securing a repertory : 156
plays on the London stage 1660–5

Robert D. Hume

11 The 'Greatest Action': 173
Lee's *Lucius Junius Brutus*

Antony Hammond

12 Congreve as a Shakespearean 186

T. W. Craik

13 The future of Dryden bibliography 200

W. J. Cameron

*A list of the published writings
and the recordings of Harold F. Brooks
compiled by Antony Coleman 233*

Index 239

PREFACE

In this collection of essays by friends, colleagues and former students, we honour one aspect of Harold Brooks's large achievement – his contribution to our understanding and appreciation of poetry and drama from Shakespeare to Dryden. As critic, scholar and teacher his range is ample, and his mastery has been demonstrated in studies extending from Chaucer to T. S. Eliot. Such rich diversity imposed a restriction of focus on us and we regret that this has precluded contributions from many who would otherwise have found a place. Within the defined limits, contributors were free to nominate their topics and we are happy that this freedom has resulted in essays which consider several subjects of especial interest to him, notably Shakespeare, Jacobean and Restoration drama, the art of satire, and bibliography. The essays also exploit variety of approach, from analysis of a single text to the discussion of general principles, a variety which has distinguished Harold Brooks's scholarly and critical activity. We hope, too, that they reflect something of his own meticulous and enthusiastic spirit.

A.C.
A.H.

ABBREVIATIONS

EETS   Early English Text Society
ELH   *English Literary History*
JEGP   *Journal of English and Germanic Philology*
MLN   *Modern Language Notes*
MLR   *Modern Language Review*
N&Q   *Notes and Queries*
OED   *Oxford English Dictionary*
PMLA   *Publications of the Modern Language Association*
RECTR *Restoration and Eighteenth Century Theatre Research*
RES   *Review of English Studies*
SEL   *Studies in English Literature*

HAROLD F. BROOKS

Arthur Johnston

Harold Fletcher Brooks was born in King Cross, a suburb of Halifax, on 1 May 1907, the only child of the Reverend Joseph Barlow Brooks and his wife Jenny. All those who know Harold Brooks will recognize that it is not the mere acceptance of a biographical convention that prompts an account of his family; his debt to and his love for his family are well known. So also is his conscious pride in the two strands which united to create the formative background in which he grew up. From his mother's family came that public-spirited middle-class sense of service to communities and in particular to education, which in Harold Brooks has been manifested for half a century in his unsparing work as teacher, examiner or governor, not only for his university and its students, but also for colleges of education, extramural and WEA classes, and sixth form conferences. Jane Johnson was the elder daughter of George Johnson, 'the little alderman', a quiet but forceful retired draper, who was twice mayor of Jarrow, a freeman of the city, and for thirty years chairman of its education committee. She was herself a B.Litt. of Durham University and a certificated teacher, and supervised Harold's education at home until his twelfth year. Her unmarried sisters were, until their deaths in 1955 and 1959, of great importance in Harold's life: Lillie was Medical Inspector of Schools for Northumberland and later Durham, and had a keen interest in botany, drama and theatre; Kathie looked after her father and sister, was mayoress during her father's second mayoralty, and became a JP. She sang in W. G. Whittaker's Newcastle Bach Choir. Their brother George became Town Clerk of Jarrow.

From his father's family Harold inherited the traditions of the intellectual and radical working class. His father's mother (Ann Fletcher) was left a widow with two small sons, Samuel and Joseph, in 1880, and for most of her life earned her living as a weaver in the Red Bank Mill at Radcliffe, just north of Manchester. The boys became part-timers in the mill as soon as they were ten. But Joseph progressed to pupil-teacher, and later to the Methodist New Connexion College at Ranmoor. It was as a probationary preacher in Jarrow that Joseph Barlow Brooks met the daughter of the treasurer of the New Connexion Chapel there, and they were married in 1904. He had been ordained at Hanley in 1901. The couple settled in King Cross, but in 1909 moved to Connah's Quay, on the Dee estuary, for ten happy years.

It was a strange coincidence that the Methodist New Connexion in Radcliffe had been started by Joseph Brooks's grandmother, and in Jarrow by Jane Johnson's grandmother. Both families, though one was that of a widowed weaver and the other that of a relatively affluent alderman, were still active, in their sturdy and independent manner, in their chapels and Sunday Schools. Harold Brooks is very much the product of this background; those who know him are conscious of his happy memories of his boyhood, first in Connah's Quay, then from 1919 to 1923 in Blackburn, and from 1923 in Middlesborough. These memories are always intermingled with those of 'Albert Road', the family home in Jarrow, where he spent holidays with his maiden aunts, and where in his late teens, when at the Royal Grammar School, Newcastle, from 1923–6, he lived in term-time.

When the young family moved to Connah's Quay in 1909, Mrs Brooks took Harold, aged 2, to Newcastle for his first operation for mastoiditis. He had contracted tuberculosis of the glands; his fifth and last operation was when he was eleven. Thus his memories of early childhood are of pain, and of his education at home, largely by his mother; but they are also of a leisured boyhood by the estuaries of the Dee and Tyne, with sailing-ships and ferry-boats; retired schooner-captains singing hymns loudly in his father's chapel; holidays with his parents and aunts, walking, farmers' dog-carts and horsedrawn coaches in the Lake District; his mother's evening readings, and wide reading of his own, much facilitated by the library of the Newcastle Literary and Philosophical Society; of his family's pacifism, and his father's service on the local tribunal which heard appeals, on other than conscientious grounds, against military call-up.

It was a boyhood spent almost entirely in the company of forceful adults, to retain whose constant approval mattered to him enormously, and whose activities, intellectual and practical, were very varied. He absorbed from his mother a care for precise detail: Harold Brooks's strength as a critic and as a scholar lies in his patient attention to every detail of a text. And from her he also learned how to read aloud from literary works, so as to bring out to his listeners the emotional impact intended. Those who have attended his lectures will know how significant this is for him. In his inaugural lecture delivered just before his retirement, there is a passage in which he describes 'the final abuse of criticism', which is 'to put its analysis in the place of the experience of art itself'. Behind the passage there is not only half a century of intense interest in Shaw and Hardy and Yeats, and almost as long as a lecturer on English literature, but the memory of his mother's reading voice.

At four o'clock in the morning, when, as in Yeats's poem, the Man is confronted by the Echo, and I wonder if as critic and teacher I have done more harm than good, I am haunted by Bernard Shaw's indictment: 'The secret of the absurd failure of our universities . . . to produce any real change in the students who are constantly passing through them is that their method is invariably to attempt to lead their pupils to feeling by way of thought. . . .' With scant justice to the education of the intellect, he continues: 'All education, as distinct from technical instruction, must be education of the feelings.' He has put his finger, however, on the weak spot. We know a great deal, and do a great deal, about the education of the intellect; we know and do much less about the education of the feelings. In my teaching, at least, I have quoted freely – the literature-teacher's means of inviting his students to respond directly to pieces, if not more, of literary art. Sometimes one plans beforehand to make, in the course of quoting, a particular effect. But I prefer to recall an occasion when I was taken by surprise, and was left admiring the greatness of the artist, and the responsiveness of an audience worthy of him. I was reading Hardy's description of Norcombe Hill, which evokes a sense of geological time and the cosmic space of the starry heavens. Then comes – the one human touch –

the sound of shepherd Oak's flute. When I reached that, my Birkbeck listeners audibly drew in their breath. I had a moment of marvellous delight, and of humility and gratitude towards the artist who, being lent my voice, had given those men and women, and with them myself, so moving an experience; a heightened feeling of what it is to be human, when the man is so small, yet worth so much, in the vast unconscious Hardeian universe.

During those early years and for long afterwards Harold was observing and admiring his father, and particularly his father in the pulpit, with his literary and dramatic imagination, his power of public exposition, expressiveness of voice and skilful ordering of material. His father's preaching was more; it was, for Harold, an education in ethical and emotional discrimination. This education in sensitive discrimination is seen constantly in Harold Brooks whenever he speaks or writes on characters in plays or novels.

When, at the age of 12, Harold moved with his parents to Blackburn and went for the first time to school – Blackburn Grammar School, with its excellent headmaster, Arthur Holden – he was precocious and serious, conscious of his physical disabilities and fearful of the rough-and-tumble of a school. But, though he set such store by the approval of his family, he was accustomed as the only child to being in a minority of one. His family experience was of belonging to minority groups. As a member of a Nonconformist minister's family (the Methodism of the New Connexion being in itself only a small breakaway from Wesleyanism), as one of a family known for its anti-war stance throughout the 1914–18 war, as one of a family of teetotallers, and as a supporter of working-class radicalism, which is always in opposition, Harold was aware that his desire for approval was not indiscriminate. There were many matters then, and ever afterwards, on which Harold was going to find himself in a minority. He would have been disturbed not to be. The deep conviction and courage on political, social and ethical matters which we have known in the man were clearly there in the boy going with trepidation to his first school at twelve. So also was the determination to succeed, by hard work and attention to detail, academically and socially.

Harold's years at school in Blackburn were happy and successful; he played cricket and soccer, learned French and some Latin, took

School Certificate, wrote poetry and continued to read widely. When, in the sixth form, he moved to the Royal Grammar School in Newcastle (living with his aunts in Jarrow in term-time), his success in winning the prizes for poetry, reading aloud, essay writing and debating, and his admiration for his history and English master, Sydney Middlebrook, and gratitude to another teacher of history, Thompson, who took generous pains with his Latin, meant continued development. In 1926, declaring himself a socialist and Unitarian, he went to Merton College, Oxford, with an Open Exhibition in history of £60 per annum.

The Unitarianism he had imbibed from his aunts, and he had even, at the age of 16, begun his career as a public speaker when he preached from a Unitarian pulpit in Jarrow. But he also helped his father to take Methodist services, and preached from Methodist pulpits. At Oxford he read history, and was awarded his colours as goal-keeper for his college hockey team. Oxford cemented a life-long friendship, begun at his father's Bradford chapel, with Harold Watkins Shaw, afterwards chosen by E. H. Fellowes to succeed him at Tenbury, and author of a celebrated edition of Handel's *Messiah*. At Oxford, too, aware that he knew nothing of young women, Harold was determined to remedy the defect. He is accustomed to say: 'Without close women-friends, how can a man obtain binocular vision?' One of those he made, when a member of a play-reading group, was his life-long friend Eleanor Shaw. She introduced him to the works of Jung, which led to an (unpublished) study of the parallels between Blake and Jung, and the reasons for them, and to the abiding influence of Jung on Harold's thought.

On obtaining a Class II in his degree in 1929, and failing to obtain a lectureship in history at Lampeter, he spent two years reading for his degree in English. These were years when high unemployment made it difficult to begin the obvious career for many graduates. Harold was lucky in that his family encouraged him to spend the next three years in preparing, for his B.Litt. thesis, an edition of John Oldham's *Satyrs upon the Jesuits*. The course which, for B.Litt. and D.Phil. candidates, accompanied their first year of research gave him a thorough grounding in the resources available to a scholar and in scholarly techniques.

His supervisor, H. F. B. Brett-Smith, showed the thesis to Sir Charles Firth, the Regius Professor of Modern History, who said that he had not seen a better presented for the degree. For the next two years, until Firth's death in 1936, Harold acted as his part-time literary assistant, while continuing to work on his D.Phil. thesis, a complete critical and textual study of the works of Oldham, with a biography. When this was presented in 1939, C. H. Wilkinson, who was one of the examiners, regarded Harold as 'one of the foremost living authorities on the literature of the Restoration period'. But still there was no job, and Harold was now 32. He was living with his parents in Headington, where his father had retired in 1936. He had taught extramural and WEA classes around Oxford since 1935, on international affairs of the day as well as on English literature. Then, with the start of the Second World War, Harold was offered an assistant lectureship at the Queen's University of Belfast. This he took up in January 1940; it was to last until 1945, when he began his twenty-nine-year association with Birkbeck College in the University of London. For one more year he was an assistant lecturer. Then Professor Geoffrey Tillotson promoted him, at the age of 39, to lecturer. He became a senior lecturer in 1961, reader in 1962, and professor in January 1970, retiring in 1974.

When Harold joined the English department at Birkbeck College at the end of the war, Geoffrey Tillotson had recently become professor and head of the department, and the College had just changed from its wartime expedient of weekend teaching to evening lectures. The mature student, strongly motivated to study and seeking for a second chance, found in Harold Brooks a complete sympathy. Harold enjoyed teaching these students for their responsiveness, and they invariably enjoyed his teaching for its thoroughness, its range, and its mingling of severe scholarship and human understanding. Harold admired and loved his colleagues, and found in Geoffrey Tillotson a man whose leadership he could support with complete loyalty. Geoffrey expected only the highest quality of teaching, research, and supervision of research, to match what he himself gave. Those of us who later joined the department found that Geoffrey, Harold and Rosemary Freeman gave it a powerful centre that would not have been easy to match elsewhere. For twenty-nine years Harold served the department as it grew and flourished under Geoffrey Tillotson and later under Barbara Hardy. Undergraduate and postgraduate students remember vividly the extensive annotation of their essays and draft chapters, in Harold's thick-nibbed handwriting.

The depth and range of Harold's knowledge about English literature have impressed undergraduates, postgraduates and fellow scholars for more than thirty years. The foundations of his learning were laid in those years before the war spent in the Bodleian library. Although John Oldham's life was brief, and his literary output comparatively small in the seven years during which he wrote and published, it required a thorough and detailed knowledge of the history and literature of the period, and its antecedents, in order to annotate his poems. Harold became an expert in biographical research in the late seventeenth century, in descriptive and analytical bibliography, in seventeenth-century manuscripts, in textual criticism, in literary genres, as well as in political and social minutiae, and on this basis he has built and extended over the years. As each of these aspects of study has been advanced by later scholars, Harold has kept up with the new approaches. It was not common in the 1930s, for example, to analyse the printing of a book to see whether it was printed seriatim or by formes, nor to identify compositors by their favoured spellings; but, when these techniques were developed, Harold returned to his Oldham to see what new light could be shed on the text of his author. In those early days he published very little from his thesis; his bibliography of Oldham in 1936 had some additions and corrections in the reprint of 1969, but his detailed study of the substantive editions, based on later work, did not appear until 1974. But his article, in *RES* (1949), on 'Imitation in English poetry, especially in formal satire, before the age of Pope', was a seminal essay on this topic. In retirement, returning to his biography of Oldham for an intended separate publication, he has been delighted to track the right John Shepherd of Wadham to Whitgift School when Oldham was usher there, and so correct a small part of his original biography.

On the basis of his work on Oldham (which had extended over eight years) he began to enlarge his range of authors and periods. This was commonly in response to requests that he teach an author to undergraduates. In response to each request he began to work to know the texts well, and completely; to know the background and the relevant historical and political information; to know the biography and its implications; and to know the best critics and commentators. Many of those reading this memoir will have known Harold, as I have, for about thirty years, and will realize that there has not been a time when they were not astonished at the ready recall which Harold has, not of the writers of a single period, but of most of the major and many minor writers from Chaucer to T. S. Eliot. He would never regard himself as a medievalist, yet it was he who lectured at Birkbeck on Chaucer and Langland and medieval drama and the ballads. He absorbed and used what medieval scholars had written, but how fresh and original his lectures were can be seen in his published study of the artistic order of the portraits in the Prologue to *The Canterbury Tales* (1962). The series of six lectures on an author, and sometimes on a single text such as a Shakespeare play, given over a period of two weeks, was the pattern used in the English department at Birkbeck. The two-year cycle meant that a revised form of the six lectures would soon be needed. Over the years, Harold's revised lecture courses became possible books in many instances. Certainly his work on Dryden and T. S. Eliot has developed to such a state. But Harold lectured on Tudor and Elizabethan drama and Shakespeare authoritatively, as well as on Yeats and T. S. Eliot, on Hardy and Virginia Woolf and Bernard Shaw. He supervised and examined research degrees in seventeenth-, nineteenth- and twentieth-century literature, and many a Birkbeck postgraduate is deeply and gladly indebted to him, not merely for assistance in finding a good research topic, but for the careful reading and annotation of drafts, and advice on sources for material. His interest in and help for his postgraduate students extended long after the completion of a thesis into help with publication and career.

This willingness to offer his time, his energy and advice, and above all his knowledge, to young scholars beginning their re-search, has always been a source of surprise and delight, since Harold has always been fully committed as a teacher – not only of Birkbeck students but of students in colleges of education and schools – and as an examiner, for initial and postgraduate degrees, in many British universities. He has loved the theatre and opera, talking with his friends, and maintaining a very extensive corre-spondence with friends and scholars. The delicate child grew into a man who, though he can say that since 1954 he has not known a day without discomfort – not pain, but discomfort – has not allowed this to interrupt his consistent hard work. During the period since he joined Geoffrey Tillotson, Rosemary Freeman and Marjorie Daunt at Birkbeck, and developed the rich life of scholar-ship and teaching, Harold has known the sadness of the deaths of his father and his aunts, and of the failure of his first marriage. The cumulative effect of these events made 1954–5 an unhappy and difficult year for him; but his recovery was completed by his marriage in 1958 to Jean Rylatt Lee, a fellow scholar and teacher with whom he has happily shared his interests in theatre, music, literature and teaching. Jean 'changed the colour of the sky' for him.

Just as Harold was settling to his life at Birkbeck College with colleagues he admired, his meticulousness and his experience as an editor were called on by Professor Una Ellis-Fermor. In 1952 she asked him to be advisory editor, concerned with textual matters, to the New Arden Shakespeare, of which she was general editor. He himself took on the editorship of *Richard III*, a play with as difficult a textual history as any. His application to the textual problems of each of the plays was at once noticeable in the editions that went through his hands, and he extended his comments on editors' manuscripts to all aspects of the introductions and annotations. On the death of Professor Ellis-Fermor in 1958, Harold became joint general editor with Professor Harold Jenkins. In order to advise individual editors at all stages of their work, Harold undertook research into every aspect of Shakespeare scholarship – text, sources, and critical commentary. His own publications, which had never been numerous, and never approaching the range and depth of his learning, almost ceased under the weight of this new research. But editors recorded, in the Arden editions published, their debt to his 'rich and subtle scholarship', as twenty-nine volumes appeared. Sometimes a whole appendix to an Arden volume would be contributed by Harold; he published critical articles on *Two Gentlemen* and *Comedy of Errors*. His notes of guidance for editors were themselves an indication of how thoroughly and confidently he had mastered the problems of Shakespearean editing. As the series began to be appreciated, Professor J. G. MacManaway said, 'Before the Arden got going, I had concluded that the centre of Shakespeare studies had left England for America: I would not say that now.'

Harold's own work on *Richard III* progressed slowly, though pieces of his work on it have appeared in print. But he could never reach a conclusion that satisfied him about the text of the play. Harold is a perfectionist in scholarship and needs to feel that he has reached a conclusion, from all the evidence, that is reasonable and can stand. He was, therefore, eager to give up *Richard III* and take on the play for which he has most affection, *A Midsummer Night's Dream*. This play, in Granville Barker's famous production with the golden fairies, he saw with his aunts when he was seven, and so began his delight in the theatre, in plays as acted on the stage. So, with great speed, once he began to edit the play, he wrote his 50,000-word introduction and the textual and critical apparatus, completing his own manuscript by August 1978. This edition is the high-water mark of his achievement so far; it is so complete a survey of the play, and of previous work on the play, that there are hardly more than half a dozen tiny points remaining to be solved. Perhaps some day someone will explain the allegory of the mermaid and the stars. And perhaps Harold will himself supply what he was forced to omit – a theatre history of the play. For though Harold has spent so much of his energy as scholar, critic and teacher of drama, in establishing texts, annotating allusions, tracing sources and references, analysing themes and describing complex literary structures, he has never ceased to delight in the theatre and to stress this in his writing. In Belfast he was president of the Queen's University Dramatic Society, responsible for productions of *Twelfth Night* and *You Never Can Tell*. Shortly before completing the edition of *A Midsummer Night's Dream*, he delivered the annual Shakespeare lecture at the British Academy, on *The Tempest*. His masterly analysis of the theme of sovereignty in the play presents us with a drama of ideas 'remarkable for its concentration and dramatic unity'. 'Yet', he goes on, 'it is not the themes and interpretation of life, abstracted from the drama, which are rich and moving. They are rich and moving as we meet them in the drama: that, alone, makes them speak to us in all their living complexity; that, alone, makes them not an expositor's despair, but a theatre-audience's delight.'

In retirement Harold has turned to reap a late harvest, publishing as he was never able to do when responding to all the demands on him as a teacher in Birkbeck. He was delighted to record some of his lectures for the Audio Visual Centre in London; to revise his edition of the works of Oldham, completed forty years ago, for publication by the Clarendon Press; to work on his book on Dryden and the vogue of satire, and his book on T. S. Eliot as poet, dramatist and critic; to collect and expand some published pieces for a volume on approaches to criticism and scholarship; and to continue working on his 'Progressions and resolutions: archetypal themes and musical structure in four twentieth-century master-pieces – "The Tower", *The Waves, Four Quartets, Major Barbara*'. He now seeks and accepts fewer invitations to lecture or to examine, so that these ventures he trusts he may complete, as he guides the editors of the remaining New Arden volumes.

What Harold Brooks most admires in a fellow-scholar is what he most surely possesses himself – a combination of scholarship, literary judgement and mastery of a wide range of literature, in many periods and in more than one culture. It is inevitable that he should single out W. P. Ker for his highest esteem. But it is interesting to note how often he refers in his writing to Hazlitt and to G. B. Shaw. Shaw has been the writer – as dramatist, as critic and as thinker on social and political problems – to whom Harold has most frequently turned. There is obvious pleasure to Harold Brooks the scholar, the critic and the experienced theatre-goer, when, in a footnote to I.i.136–40 of *A Midsummer Night's Dream*, he quotes Shaw on Hermia and Lysander speaking in alternate lines 'with an effect which sets the whole scene throbbing with their absorption in one another'. Harold himself feels that the use of stichomythia here is not mere flat rigidity; to be able to quote Shaw in support is a pleasure to him and an added surprise to the reader of the note. But more important than the detailed insight of Shaw has been Shaw's general position, that 'time is open-ended, with limit-less scope for man or his successors to evolve perhaps beyond the trammels of matter altogether, but certainly to a higher civilization'. In his essay on the structure and themes of the *Four Quartets*, Harold cannot avoid stating his own need to think of the present 'as capable in itself of timeless value; and as valuable also because there runs through it the creative effort, divinely inspired, towards a far better future'.

Harold Brooks has always presented to us the image of the dedicated scholar, working hard and with never-waning enthusiasm for literary study, giving the results of his own labours and critical insight with amazing generosity. He surprised us often as a pacifist with an extensive knowledge of naval vessels and naval warfare; as a Londoner by adoption who always sees himself as a northener – both a Lancastrian and a Tynesider. He has never shown any interest in material possessions; his collection of books is a working scholar's library, the volumes likely to be covered in his annotations; his collection of early Oldham editions he regarded as valuable for establishing the text, and, now that is done, as best deposited in Oldham's college, St Edmund Hall. He is notable, in his conversation, for his power of appreciating other men and women, and their works; from Harold Brooks one learns of their successes, their knowledge, their virtues, never of their failures, their ignorance, their vices. He has known suffering himself, and in those close to him; he has known the pain of the two world wars, the unemployment in Jarrow, and 'the grim modern reminders of the depravity possible to human nature'. But even in the darkest times he affirms his optimism. However hideous the world looks, Harold will see the first characteristic of mankind as its beauty: 'How beauteous mankind is'. *The Tempest* was an inevitable choice of play for his British Academy lecture, since this play is a mature affirmation of the redressing of the troubles of the old world in the generation of the new, in which is reborn that sense of 'How beauteous mankind is'.

We who have known Harold Brooks have not only become more learned by knowing him; we have learned to feel better about ourselves and about the world. When I look for Harold's own statement of his alert and invigorating attitude, I find it at its clearest in his essay on the *Four Quartets*, when he is expounding the message of T. S. Eliot.

> History . . . has its significance in the opportunity it offers for the lifetime of disinterested, right action. On the temporal plane, it is because we have gone on trying to live such a life that we may hope to have done our part to enrich temporal existence by a contribution . . . not too remote from the true, central, human tradition; a contribution that will help to maintain the meaning of history, and so to keep it a 'significant soil' for other fertile lives.

2

'THE VICE' AND THE POPULAR THEATRE, 1547–80

Peter Happé

I

In this essay I want to deal with some of the most evanescent elements in theatre criticism, those relating to the actual theatrical experience as distinct from matters which can be dealt with specifically and solely from text. The problem is that all we have left of the dramatic figure called 'the Vice' is in the texts of interludes and a few contemporary or retrospective comments. We cannot see or hear him, and we cannot experience in real life the impact he had upon his audiences. Yet he was a theatrical reality, unmistakable, pungent, and effective enough to be almost indispensable to writers for about thirty years in the second half of the sixteenth century.

In his pioneering work, *From 'Mankind' to Marlowe*,[1] David Bevington set out to establish criteria of the popular drama in Tudor times, concentrating upon the professionalism of the troupes. He showed the importance of doubling as a technique in a context of small itinerant companies who had to make an immediate impact upon their audiences in an unlocalized playing area in order to secure an adequate income. He mentioned briefly their need to appeal to all classes and, more extensively, he showed how the interludes were structured to this end. But the emphasis of his work is less upon the Vice than upon the troupe as a whole, and it seems worth enquiring more fully into the conventions embodied in this role which were, I suggest, dependent upon the context of popular theatre. In other words, I should like to shift the emphasis from considerations of troupe organization and dramatic structure to material related specifically to the theatrical context of popular drama. This implies an attempt to describe popular drama as a form of entertainment, rather than as a matter of organization.

Such a task, though beyond the scope of this essay in its fullest sense, is particularly interesting in the context of the modern western theatre, which has for a hundred years been in a period of continuing innovation, and indeed success. But against the achievements of Ibsen, Chekhov and Strindberg there remains an uneasiness about the impact of the theatre upon society at large, and the fear that it remains the plaything of the rich, or the self-defining indulgence of the intelligentsia. In practical terms this concern led to Brecht's attempt to use theatre to make political ideas open to all, and he has been followed by a wide range of politically committed writers, actors and directors. It has led to Joan Littlewood's Theatre Workshop, which set out specifically to reach working-class audiences.[2] The interests of Yeats, Rolland and Piscator[3] in the development of popular theatre all betray political criteria and, more significantly, a predisposition to impose a doctrine of theatre upon 'the people' – by whom they mean the members of a social class which they themselves view from the standpoint of the intellectual, the mentor or the prophet. A didactive objective is not incompatible with popular theatre, but an attempt to impose it from outside probably is. Recent academic criticism has begun to create a theoretical discipline for popular theatre, and this approach perhaps offers some help in defining the context of the Vice's activities on the Tudor stage.[4]

I take 'popular' to be a loose description for society at large, with a particular emphasis upon the majority who do not have and who do not seek access to the international learned and cultural tradition represented by literature, philosophy and other cultivated activities. A useful model is found in Robert Redfield's division of society into the great tradition, which embodies such learned activities and is cultivated in schools or temples, and the little tradition, which operates in village communities.[5] Such a model is bound to suffer from oversimplification, but it should be remembered that English society of the sixteenth century was largely rural. Indeed, recent work on the kinds of drama found in the villages of rural England suggests that the folk drama rather than the mystery or morality play was by far the more common form of popular dramatic entertainment.[6]

Popular theatre as here conceived does not depend entirely or even primarily upon text, but upon a scenario in which things happen in a recognizable pattern. The scenario holds the material together and perhaps imposes a sequential discipline. Within a given set of conventional events, there is possible a wide variety of tactical decisions about the content of the entertainment. Sometimes, as in the *commedia dell' arte*, this involves improvisation. Since the mode of entertainment is not purely verbal, there is scope for a variety of items which please and divert. Theatre is always a visual art, but in popular entertainment what is seen takes on an added potency. This may have to do with the grotesque, the unfamiliar, the exotic. We must be able to recognize Chaplin or Punch as soon as we see them, and the pleasure of participating in their performances depends partly upon our responses to visual stimuli like the cane or the nose. Events of a particular physical nature also play a large part, especially a visual one. There is often a great deal of falling about. Agility and physical skills become important parts in the training of the performer, even to the point that the narrative may be held up while we indulge our appreciation and fear as we watch Chaplin on the edge of the precipice. The popular theatre constantly pushes its participants towards disaster, which is usually physical, but the effect of this is circumscribed, partly by our appreciation of the skill of the performers, partly by a reassuring emphasis upon conservative values. Just as we know – we remember *in extremis* – that Chaplin must survive for another day, so the satire and mockery which is an essential of the popular theatre is never entirely nihilistic. Instead, there is a celebration of what is reliable, the triumph of good, the rewards of true love, the punishment of evil. We may be tempted by the villain, who liberates our repressions, moral or sexual, but we enjoy his downfall. On the whole, the popular theatre preserves authoritative elements in society even though kings and priests may be mocked. Indeed, the popular theatre may be encouraged to allow this kind of mockery just so that it may be contained: the attitudes in the mystery cycles to Herod and the High Priests seem an outstanding example of this, and so too are the figures of law and justice, uniformed policemen especially, in English pantomime.

In spite of the emphasis upon the visual in the popular drama, there are two points to be made about words. On the one hand there may be a concern for verbal ingenuity which is in itself a

virtuoso performance. In pantomime particularly, there are frequent attempts to exploit popular idioms, catchphrases and patters.
Pantomime offers a harbour for the comedian who is identifiable
by his own verbal style – Frankie Howerd springs to mind here,
since he forces the audience to wait for his key phrases and his
unnecessary apologies, and he groans along with the audience at his
own puns and innuendoes. In a slightly different context it has been
noted that Henry Livings, who uses the mode of popular theatre,
keeps in close touch with the audience through verbal devices,
particularly the range and register of his vocabulary.[7] Beyond this,
the dramatic action may consist to a large extent of monologues,
jokes, proverbs, narratives, the stock-in-trade of the entertainer
who impresses his audience by his virtuosity and the wealth of his
resources.

But, secondly, this exploitation of words is essentially ephemeral
in a form which is itself created only for the moment in the theatre
and not for posterity. Popular theatre, being non-literary in
essence, takes little account of transmission outside the theatre
except in the persistence of the conventions it embodies. It is often
the work of an anonymous author or authors who work to a
deadline and then rework the material for the next performance.
Hence the conventions have benefit, since they can be relied upon
as basic structures. Words are the servants of this process. One
writer learns from another by imitation and plagiarism, and this
method is close to the traditional handing on from master to
apprentice. The ephemerality of the popular theatre is furthered by
its unpredictability. Popularity comes in fashions, and the success
of one style of popular entertainment may depend upon the
formula of construction, or simply the *persona* of the leading
character or performer, perhaps working the visual techniques or
the verbal elaborations I have mentioned. In many ways details of
this kind may be closely related to contemporary ideas and
expectations.

The popular theatre of the sixteenth century undoubtedly had
links with the folk rituals. The origins of these rituals are obscure,
but it seems clear that they were not created for the people so much
as by them. J. S. R. Goodlad, writing from a sociological point of
view, has tentatively suggested that such rituals contained a
cognitive function which informed individuals about the social
structure, and at the same time expressed conflict within it and

offered a means of controlling the conflict that arose.[8] Although English society was changing rapidly in this period, there seems little doubt that at the common level these processes were very much part of the theatrical experience. It seems clear, too, that the morality plays and interludes which took over the Vice may have been seeking to counter the influence of the folk drama, sometimes incorporating its material in a didactic structure.[9]

In this brief account of the popular theatre, a number of examples have been referred to: Brecht, the post-Brechtian political theatre, Joan Littlewood's Theatre Workshop, Chaplin's films, the Punch and Judy Show, the mystery cycles, the folk plays, the traditional English Christmas pantomime, the plays of Henry Livings, and the *commedia dell' arte*. It is a disparate group, and if we add to it Edwardian melodrama, Buffalo Bill, Westerns, the Harlequinade, the James Bond films, it is clear that there is little cultural unity in the popular theatre. Indeed, the imprecision of the word 'popular' remains a handicap to this investigation.[10] Nevertheless, all these items appeal to a very wide audience indeed and their methods of presentation offer striking parallels in the relationship of the performer to his audience.

II

Though the history of the Vice, his origins and development, have been much discussed, it is necessary to determine here the limits within which my comments are intended to apply. Cushman distinguished the Vice from the Devil; Withington explored his folk origins; Mares offered an important argument about when he acquired his name; and Spivack explored the moral metaphor of the Vice in its theatrical context.[11] I take him to be the heir of the folk-play fool and the presenter, the court clown, the cheeky servant, the impertinent messenger, the mystery-play Devil, all roles which are not characters so much as embodiments of dramatic forces directing the action and controlling the response of the audience. It took a long while for him to develop, and he owes his eventual popularity chiefly to the small groups of professional players of interludes which became successful from about 1550. Indeed, he contributed very largely to that success, for the relationship reciprocated.

In deciding upon who the true Vices really were, we must bear in mind the possibility that important instances may have disappeared through the accidents of history. Nevertheless, it appears that John Heywood's Merry Report and Neither-Loving-Nor-Loved were not quite Vices because they lacked moral dimension. Bale's Sedition and Infidelity came much nearer to the convention. They were conceived in about 1538 when Bale led the Lord Privy Seal's (i.e. Cromwell's) Men into the drama of Protestant propaganda, but Bale did not, unlike Heywood, call his characters 'the Vice'. Perhaps the breakthrough, the critical moment of invention, came a little later, about 1547, with Envy in *Impatient Poverty*. From then on the Vice was virtually indispensable to the writer of moral interludes for itinerant companies. His usefulness was also appreciated by those writing for court drama performed by boys. The author of *Respublica* named Avarice 'the vice of the plaie', perhaps in recognition of what had come to pass by 1553. I give here a list of the Vices relevant to this discussion, and distinguish popular plays (P: 14) from boys' plays (B: 6).[12]

P	1547	Envy, *Impatient Poverty*
P	1550	Hypocrisy, *Lusty Juventus* (R. Wever)
B	1553	Avarice, *Respublica*
P	1558	Infidelity, *The Life and Repentance of Mary Magdalene* (L. Wager)
B	1559	Politic Persuasion, *Pacient and Meeke Grissill* (J. Phillip)
P		Idleness, *The Longer Thou Livest the More Fool Thou Art* (W. Wager)
P	1560	Covetousness, *Enough is as Good as a Feast* (W. Wager)
P	1561	Ambidexter, *Cambises* (T. Preston)
B	1564	Haphazard, *Apius and Virginia* (R.B.)
P	1565	Iniquity, *King Darius*
P	1567	Revenge, *Horestes* (J. Pickering)
P		Inclination, *The Trial of Treasure* (W. Wager)
B		Vanity, *Liberality and Prodigality*
P	1568	Nichol Newfangle, *Like Will to Like* (U. Fulwell)
B		Will, *The Marriage of Wit and Science*
B	1569	Ill Report, *Virtuous and Godly Susanna* (T. Garter)
P	1571	Perverse Doctrine, *New Custom*
P	1576	Courage, *The Tide Tarrieth No Man* (G. Wapull)
P	1577	Sin, *All for Money* (T. Lupton)
P	1579	Idleness, *A Marriage between Wit and Wisdom* (F. Merbury)

If we consider the popular plays in this list, there is little doubt
that the criteria for popular theatre are present. The plays are
written to a conventional outline which involves the mockery and
destruction of the hero by the Vice. Often the hero is vindicated
and there are variations in the ways the Vice is punished or escapes.
The Vice is instantly recognizable by his noises, his language, and
probably his peculiar clothing (though he has no uniform like the
Fool's). He shows every sign of physical agility: fighting, brandish-
ing his dagger, running away nimbly. There are times when he
holds up the action with a flood of words tending to nonsense.[13] He
keeps the audience alert to his comings and goings, and tells them
about his movements and his plans. His association with the
criminal fraternity, expressed in a series of motifs concerning
hanging, thieving, drabbing and gambling offer the audience
licence from virtue, and yet there is always the sense that his
activities are circumscribed. This may be intensified at times by his
relationship with the Devil, whom he mocks and yet who has
power over him. There is a persistent custom of bursting into song
on entry or departure, especially when evil plans are consummated.

The contribution of the boys' plays needs some consideration.
There are a few differences in that the singing appears to be more
frequent, there is less emphasis upon doubling (for *Grissill*, a bogus
doubling scheme is provided), and a greater number of women's
parts. Nevertheless, the Vice was undoubtedly played by boys,
whose pertness and nimbleness shows in the texts. Avarice, in his
traditional guise of an old man, is in this respect untypical, but with
Politic Persuasion, Haphazard, and Ill Report we have examples so
complete that there is no doubt that some writers of élite plays were
thoroughly conversant with the popular mode and found it useful
to adopt it. It is likely that plays from these auspices contributed to
the development of the convention.

Since we are concerned with the way stage performance may
indicate a context in the popular theatre for the Vice, it may be
useful to consider the evidence of the stage directions in these plays.
For the popular plays one may assume that printing them was a
device to obtain extra income and that the sale may have been
aimed at other actors. This can be justified by the doubling schemes
on the title-pages and the frequency with which they were 'offered
for acting'. If these are acting editions, the stage directions would
be written with performers in mind, or they may have accumulated

in the prompt copy as a record of entrances, exits and movements. They are, of course, by no means complete schemes for each play, but they do provide insights into what the actor was expected to do at certain times. I have counted seventy-three items dealing with the Vice in these plays and I will consider a representative sample of forty-two under three heads: identifying features, skills, and improvisation.

The Vice's entry would have been a moment of theatrical importance, as he quickly set up a relationship with the audience. It seems that he was often used to change the mood or bring in new information, and it was felt necessary to give him a peculiar impact, especially in respect of costume and properties:

1 *Enter Vanitie solus, all in feathers.*   (*Liberality*, 1. 2)
2 *Enter the Vice with an olde capcase on his hed, an olde pail about his hips for hames, a scummer and a potlid by his side, and a rake on his shoulder.*   (*Cambises*, 1. 125)

There are instances where a change of costume by the Vice indicates a change of mood:

3 *Here they go out and the Vice entreth and sayeth in my best peticote &c, with a bell in his hande.*   (*Susanna*, ll. 904–5)

or possibly some deception in the plot:

4 *Put on a gowne and a cap.*   (*Mary Magdalene*, 1. 404)
5 *Put of[f] the beggares cote and all thy thynges.*
                                                                        (*Horestes*, 1. 1251)

The information or change involved may equally be indicated by properties which emphasize the trickery of the Vice:

6 *Vyce entrith with a staffe and a bottell or dyshe and wallet.*
                                                                        (*Horestes*, 1. 1233)
7. *Enter Idleness like a priest.*
                                    (*Marriage between Wit and Wisdom*, 1. 681)

The recognition extends to his use of his dagger, though no stage direction refers precisely to the '*dagger of lath*' in *Twelfth Night*, IV. ii. 125–32.

8 *He fighteth them both with his dagger.*   (*Enough*, 1. 440)
9 *Out quickly with his dagger.*   (*Tide*, A4)
10 *They strive, he draweth his dagger and fyghteth.*   (*Tide*, G4)

The Vice's weeping is an identifying feature. His grief is always insincere, since it was meant to be part of his showmanship. Comic weeping is still part of the repertoire of the modern comedian, as with Stan Laurel, Jerry Lewis, Norman Wisdom, and many a circus clown.

11 *Enter Ambidexter weping.* (*Cambises*, l. 1125)

12 *Enter Corage weeping.* (*Tide*, G3)

13 *Let the Vice weep and howl and make great lamentation to the Worldly Man.* (*Enough*, l. 706)

In *Horestes* there appears to be quite a feature of close interplay between the actor playing Horestes and the Vice:

14 *Wepe but let Horestes ryse and bid him pease.* (l. 895)

It is tempting to suppose that the impatience of Horestes would be matched by persistence from the Vice.

Though I accept Cushman's separation of the Devil and the Vice, I note that the interludes show a close acting partnership between them. This is reflected particularly in two plays where the stage directions indicate business:

15 *Here the Devill sitteth downe in a chayre and calleth for Ill Reporte who entreth in.* (*Susanna*, ll. 51–2)

16 *Here they have him to hanging, the Devill entreth saying oh, oh, oh.* (*Susanna*, ll. 1382–3)

17 *He kneleth downe.*
(*Like*, l. 204: i.e. the Vice kneels before the Devil to receive blessing.)

18 *He rideth away on the Devils back.* (*Like*, l. 1212)

The skills employed by the Vice ought to be seen in the light of what little we know about Tudor acting. It is generally assumed that acting styles were very formal, and in the serious parts of the plays gave scope for carefully contrived effects using stylized gesture and incantatory rhetoric.[14] The essence of these was that the material required decorum, and this was supported by the long-held assumption that religious plays required a sufficiently impressive style of performance. But the Vice derives from clowns, fools, and cheeky messengers, and inherits from the Devil a desire to humble all men. As professional entertainer, the actor – who was usually the principal in the troupe – would have inherited a tradition of singing, dancing, and acrobatics.[15] His homiletic function, which was to bring evil in all its realistic detail to every man, led him to comic extravagance. The actor would be tempted to abandon the formal style and to cultivate instead one which was conspicuously undignified, and one which invited the audience to perceive that he was crossing the boundary separating the permitted from the forbidden. As with Harlequin in the *commedia dell' arte*, the Vice convention exploits the actor's ability to separate himself from the other characters by special kinds of movement. These are hinted at in the stage directions about running and vigorous action:

19 *Here they fyght and runne all out of the place.*

(Impatient Poverty, l. 861)

20 *Here cometh Envye runnynge in laughyng and sayth to Conscyence . . .*   (Impatient Poverty, l. 412)

21 *Infidelitie runneth away. Mary falleth flat downe. Cry all thus without the doore and roare terribly.* (Mary Magdalene, l. 1302)

22 *Run his way out while she is down.*   (Cambises, l. 838)

23 *Here Idleness having brought him to the den of Irksomness shall leap away.*   (Marriage between Wit and Wisdom, l. 414)

24 *The Vyce running out is stayde by Sensualitie who sayeth . . .*

(Susanna, l. 486)

The word 'run' in these directions is presumably a simple instruction for a wide variety of business, for it is not difficult to make running look ridiculous, especially when there is an element of challenge or pursuit. Perhaps, like Harlequin, who wore tight trousers, the Vice's costume was specially adapted for running, but in any case rapid movement was clearly an essential at critical moments. If, as some have thought, he wore a long coat, he could tuck it up or fall over it as he felt inclined.

There is little doubt that skill in fight routines would be required of the Vice and his associates. It looks as though this was a frequent occurrence: in addition to 8, 9, 10, and 19 above, there are also:

25 *Here let hym fight.*   (Apius, l. 251)

26, 27, 28 *He fighteth. . . . He fighteth againe. . . . He fighteth againe.*   (Like, ll. 335–45)

More interesting than these simple instructions, however, are those where the Vice is given an outline as to what is to happen in the fight. Ambidexter is required to be particularly skilful:

29 *Heer let them fight with their staves, not come neer an other by three or foure yardes, the Vice set them on as hard as he can; one of their wives come out and all to beat the Vice, he run away.*

(*Cambises*, l. 812)

30 *Heer let her swinge him in her brome, she gets him down and he her down, thus one on top of an other make pastime.*

(*Cambises*, l. 833)

Revenge must also be alert for good timing in striking and running:

31 *Up with thy staf and be readye to smyte, but Hodg smit first and let the Vise thwacke them both and run out.*

(*Horestes*, l. 175)

Though few stage directions are as clear as these, it is fair to assume that expectations about the Vice were high and specific in this respect. The audience must have anticipated the actions and, being physically as close as they were, they would have appreciated the speed and effectiveness if done properly. These short episodes which are substantially comic diversions are reminiscent of the *lazzi* in the *commedia dell' arte*; though it should be remembered that the effect of the *commedia* was not felt until fairly late in the century.[16]

The Vice's singing is a characteristic in both the popular and the boys' plays. In the latter the musicianship may be more elaborate, but the popular plays require the Vice to sing regularly.

32 *Iniquytie cometh in syngyng.* (*Darius*, D4v)
33 *Enter the Vyce synginge this song to the tune of the Paynter.*
34 *Enter the Vyce singing this songe.* (*Horestes*, ll. 777, 1018)

In *Like*, the Vice is particularly active and the stage directions are explicit about his musical activities. He must be able to sing, play an instrument and dance:

35 *Nichol Newfangle must have a gittern or some other Instrument, if he may, but if they have none they must daunce about the place all three, and sing this song that followeth which must be doon though they have an instrument.* (*Like*, l. 176)

We may note that there are hints of skill with playing cards in two plays:

36 *Have a pair of cards ready.*   (*Longer*, l. 769)

37 *Heer entreth Nichol Newfangle, the Vice, laughing, and hath a knave of clubs in his hand which as soon as he speaketh he offreth unto one of the men or boyes standing by.*   (*Like*, l. 36)

More demanding may have been an ability to play with fire:

38 *Here sombody must cast fyre to Iniquytie.*   (*Darius*, F4)

This is a sign that his last moment has come, and he goes off to hell. There is perhaps a precedent in the fireworks used by Belyal in *Castle of Perseverance* (diagram on fo. 191ᵛ) and the Vice in Heywood's *Play of Love* (l. 1293).[17]

All the skills we have been discussing are performing ones: an actor might well learn them, and in the exercise of them divert the audience and hold its attention for some minutes. But perhaps the greatest skill of all is the ability to improvise and to know how to fit improvisation into the wider context of the play: a skill highly developed by the performers in the *commedia dell' arte*. It demands an awareness of how much an audience will take, and an ability to detect and play up to an audience's response. The actors playing the Vice were undoubtedly expected to do this, and stage directions give indications of open-ended business. Examples 29 and 30 from *Cambises* are typical, and Nichol Newfangle's card-trick (37) might go on for some time. Later he is given even more scope:

39 *Heere entreth Nichole Newfangle and bringeth in with him a bagge, a staffe, a bottle, and two halters, going about the place shewing it to the audience, and singing this –*

   Trim marchandise, trim, trim, trim marchandise, trim, trim.

   He may sing this as oft as he thinketh good.   (*Like*, l. 894)

Sin is required to improvise verbally:

40 *Here the Vyce shal turne the proclamation to some contrarie sence at everie time All for Money hath read it.*   (*Money*, D1)

Perhaps the most striking example of improvisation is the desperate instruction to Courage:

41 *And fighteth to prolong the time while Wantonnesse maketh her ready.*   (*Tide*, E3)

Wantonness is caught in a very quick costume change, and the Vice must use his skill in fighting to keep the audience quiet. The incident recalls the payments made at Bungay in 1566 at an unspecified entertainment:

> 42 To Kelsaye, the vyce, for his pastyme before the plaie, and after the playe, both daies . . . ijs.[18]

Pastyme is the same word as in example 30 above (*OED*, *n.* 1: recreation, diversion, amusement, sport) and suggests a 'turn' involving a skill worth paying for. Whether it was acrobatics, music or jokes, it must have been possible to prolong it at will. The occurrence of improvisation in stage directions like this suggests that the Vice's ability must have been expected by author, 'director' and audience.

The stage directions give important clues as to the way in which the Vice's part was played and the techniques which were used to control the response of the audience. To them we may add a brief consideration of two soliloquies, so that the voice of the Vice may be heard:

> Have ye no dout but all shalbe wel:
> Mary Sir, as you say, this geer dooth excel.
> All things is in redynes when they come hether
> The kings grace and the Queen bothe togither.
> I beseech ye my maisters tel me, is it not best
> That I be so bolde as to bid a gest?
> He is as honest a man as ever spurd cow:
> My Cosin Cutpurse, I meane, I beseech ye judge you.
> Beleeve me Cosin if to be the Kings gest, ye could be taken
> I trust that offer would not be forsaken.
> (Cambises, ll. 994–1003)

These lines illustrate the Vice's adeptness in managing another character – Preparation – and the audience. Line 995 is especially typical of the Vice, in the appearance of one of his commonest words, *geer*, which he uses for 'business' or 'plotting'; and he probably addresses one of the audience individually (l. 995). He speaks to the audience as a whole ('my maisters') and having introduced Cousin Cutpurse – a familiar figure among his disreputable companions – he speaks directly to him (l. 1001). Cutpurse rarely appears in the plays: the game is that he is somewhere in the audience plying his trade, and the Vice from his fellow-feeling offers conspiratorial advice. The effect of this comic motif is partly to make the Vice ridiculous, and at the same time to develop the idea of his wicked scheming. Comedy in this context reduces his stature and helps to isolate him from other characters in the play. Yet the manner of the playing involves a familiar routine joke, and probably invited much gesture and movement as contact was established. These familiar devices and the close concentration on rapport with the audience are typical of the popular theatre.

In the second example the Vice is in another mood:

> La, soule, soule, fa, my, re, re.
> I misse a note I dare well say.
> I shuld have byn low when I was so hie;
> I shall have it ryght anone verely.
> How now, mayster, how fare you now?
> How do you synce I was laste with you?
> Where are these knaves: they come not away.
> I believe I see them comyng theyr way.   (*Darius*, D4v)

The joke of singing scales badly is obvious enough, particularly as the Vice is so frequently played by a singer. The two repetitions in line 1 suggest he needs two tries to hit the note, and so does line 4. He asks someone in the audience, conversationally, how he is, and the phrase 'synce I was laste with you' makes certain that he is properly identified. After these motifs he introduces 'these knaves' (Importunity and Partiality). Thus he is here a link between episodes, but as such he works by conventional jokes in deliberately threadbare language. What he says is virtually a patter which is a formula for changing the mood and introducing new characters. The speech is in fact preceded by an episode featuring King Darius and followed by low conspiracy – perhaps the mention of 'low' and 'hie' refers punningly to this. Throughout, the speech is full of moral implications which in these conventional circumstances the audience would be sure to pick up.

III

If we look, then, at common details of the Vice role, there are strong indications that the mode is a popular one. These are matters of stage technique which form part of his general function as tempter and destroyer. Though Vices who offer no temptation are extant, the main development of the role in the morality play is undoubtedly from the stage realization of the medieval Church's configurations of the World, the Flesh, and the Devil, and of the Seven Deadly Sins. We have seen that many of the stage elements are comic, and the presence of these helps us to determine the nature of the Vice's relationship with his victim and with the audience.

On the one hand he engages the audience by his sheer outrageousness, which is always familiar. But the attention is directed not to a character but to a performer. In the real world of the audience, the Vice is a successful performer who exercises great virtuosity. He moves in and out of the personification of evil, and switches the emotional tone by violent contrasts. He is amazingly honest with the audience about himself and his purposes, and is constantly asking for the audience's understanding and admiration of his skilful plotting.[19] His comedy is full of false notes and crude deceptions, and its function, which both disarms the audience and involves him in self-ridicule, is to bring about the downfall of the hero in such a way that we cannot but perceive the workings of justice. The comedy is a means of bringing the audience together through laughter. Once they are together, the demonstration of the cunning and speciously attractive nature of evil can run its course. By being attractive – because of his skill and his apparent success – the Vice images the power of evil. But always the audience is reminded by him that what is going on is a corruption. In the end there is a shock: the Vice's power disintegrates and the comedy – apart from a few conventional parting shots from the Vice – is seen to dissolve into the grim reality of the judgement of vice and virtue. The joke is finally on the Vice and not upon the victim. The Vice, working through popular means of entertainment, shows a performance which is designed to comment upon the struggle between good and evil.[20]

But equally he is part of the play-world which the audience looks into. His function is to blend into the circumstances as though he were part of them.[21] He uses disguises, aliases, and an ability to change his demeanour and style of speech according to the people he meets. He must work his way into the confidence of the hero-victim, and whilst he cannot be regarded as naturalistic, the process by which he does this must be credible. This need accounts for the very close playing with his associate villains. Bevington is no doubt right in his account of the process by which the villain-group appears separately and exclusively from the virtuous characters.[22] But, once this was established, the villains had to develop a characteristic aura of evil which condemned them and helped to make the process of seduction more credible. Like the players in the *commedia dell' arte*, the Vice is credible but never quite real. He is never a character but an arrangement of conventional elements which give him impetus in the world of the play.[23]

A third important feature is his expository function. He acts for the dramatist, fulfils the cultural role of explaining the moral doctrine of the play. This may be explicit in soliloquy or implicit in that mode of bragging over-confidence and shabby success which is characteristic of the Vice. A good deal of his stage time is given up to exposition, and the audience presumably adapted themselves to a learning role. As we have seen, the popular theatre is much concerned with didactic experience, working through satire, ridicule, and an assumption of agreed values. Four hundred years after his heyday, the Vice's exploitation of audience response can only be guessed at: yet the texts and the stage directions imply that such a response was forthcoming. One must not overlook also the frequency of the convention, further evidence that a taste for the Vice was created and used on the popular stage. Later, by the time of *Twelfth Night* or *Old Fortunatus* or *The Staple of News*, he had gone out of fashion, and this, too, is the fate of the popular theatre in general. The ephemerality is not only a matter of the author's limited literary objectives: it derives from the way in which the popular theatre employs the accessible conventions of its day, and reflects the common assumptions and attitudes of its audience.

NOTES

1 D. M. Bevington, *From 'Mankind' to Marlowe* (Cambridge, Mass., 1962), 26–67.

2 R. Hayman, *British Theatre Since 1955* (Oxford, 1979), giving a number of possible origins for *Oh What a Lovely War*, mentions that 'Gerry Raffles . . . conceived the idea after hearing a Black and White Minstrel Show devoted to songs of the First World War' (p. 135).

3 See W. B. Yeats, *A People's Theatre* (Dublin, 1919); Romain

Rolland, *The People's Theatre*, trans. B. H. Clark (New York, 1918); Erwin Piscator, *The Theatre Can Belong to Our Century*, trans. J. Gassner (New York, 1941). All in substantial extracts in Eric Bentley (ed.), *The Theory of the Modern Stage* (Harmondsworth, 1968), 327–38, 455–70, 471–3.

4 D. Mayer, 'Towards a Definition of Popular Theatre', in D. Mayer and K. Richards (eds), *Western Popular Theatre* (London, 1977), 257–77, and J. S. R. Goodlad, *A Sociology of Popular Drama* (London, 1971).

5 Robert Redfield, *Peasant Society and Culture* (Chicago, 1956), 70–1.

6 As yet unpublished papers presented to the International Colloquium on Medieval Drama, Dublin, 1980: J. M. Wasson, 'Folk Drama in Devon' and A. F. Johnston, 'Folk Drama in Berkshire'.

7 Peter Thomson, 'Henry Livings and the Accessible Theatre', in Mayer and Richards, 196.

8 I acknowledge a considerable debt to Goodlad's analysis; see especially p. 189 which offers the conclusions upon which my argument partly rests.

9 For an illustration of this in John Bale see Richard Axton, 'Folk play in Tudor interludes', in Marie Axton and Raymond Williams (eds), *English Drama: Forms and Development* (Cambridge, 1977), 22–3.

10 K. Schoell in his paper 'Sur la notion de théâtre populaire appliquée au moyen-âge', presented to the Dublin Colloquium, echoes my concern over this. Interestingly, however, he develops his ideas in this field by consideration of medieval popular entertainment in the form of spectacle (including Carnaval), *Les Mystères*, and morality, *sottie* and farce in the French tradition.

11 L. W. Cushman, *The Devil and the Vice in the English Dramatic Literature before Shakespeare* (Halle, 1900), especially 52–3; Robert Withington, 'The "Vice": Ancestry, Development', in *Excursions in English Drama* (New York and London, 1937), 42–90; Francis Hugh Mares, 'The Origin of the Figure called "the Vice" in Tudor Drama', *Huntington Library Quarterly*, 22 (1958–9), 11–29; Bernard Spivack, *Shakespeare and the Allegory of Evil* (New York, 1958).

12 For a fuller list of examples of the Vice, his antecedents and

successors, see Peter Happé, 'The Vice: A Checklist and An Annotated Bibliography', *Research Opportunities in Renaissance Drama*, 22 (1979), 17–35. The editions used here are:

Impatient Poverty, ed. R. B. Mckerrow, 1911; *Lusty Juventus*, MSR 1971; *Respublica*, EETS, O.S. 226, 1952; *Mary Magdalene*, ed. F. I. Carpenter, 1904; *Grissill*, MSR 1909; *Longer* and *Enough,* ed. R. Mark Benbow (London, 1968); *Cambises*, ed. R. C. Johnson (Salzburg, 1975); *Apius* and *Like*, in Peter Happé, *Tudor Interludes* (Harmondsworth, 1972); *Darius*, TFT 1909; *Horestes*, MSR 1962; *Trial*, Dodsley 3; *Liberality*, MSR 1913; *Marriage of Wit and Science*, MSR 1961; *Susanna*, MSR 1937; *New Custom*, Dodsley 3; *Tide*, TFT 1910; *Money*, TFT 1910; *Marriage between Wit and Wisdom*, ed. G. Wickham, *English Moral Interludes* (London 1976).

13 The nonsense of the Vice was probably related to the topsy-turvy world of Carnival; cf. P. Burke, *Popular Culture in Early Modern Europe* (London, 1978), 185–91.

14 For discussion see A. Harbage, 'Elizabethan Acting', *PMLA*, 54 (1939), 685–708.

15 For some consideration of the theatrical skills of actors see A. S. Downer, 'The Tudor Actor: A Taste of His Quality', *Theatre Notebook*, 5 (1951), 76–81.

16 For the virtuosity of stage business see Virginia P. Scott, 'The *Jeu* and the *Rôle*: Analysis of the Appeals of the Italian Comedy in France in the Time of Arlequin-Dominique', in Mayer and Richards, 11–12. *Lazzi* were used when a scene dragged or eloquence gave out. They might consist of throwing cherry-stones, catching an imaginary fly and eating it, somersaults, walking on hands, doing the splits, climbing on boxes; cf. P. L. Duchartre, *The Italian Comedy*, trans. R. T. Weaver (New York, 1966), 36–7. Dates of earliest references in England: 1546–7, 1573, 1575, 1576; K. M. Lea, *Italian Popular Comedy* (Oxford, 1934), 352–5.

17 Fireworks were used at carnival time in France and Italy, Burke, 195.

18 E. K. Chambers, *The Medieval Stage* (Oxford, 1903), II, 343.

19 J. A. B. Somerset, '"Fair is foul and foul is fair": Vice-Comedy's Development and Theatrical Effects', in G. R. Hibbard (ed.), *The Elizabethan Theatre* v (Waterloo, Ont., 1975), 68–9.

20 For parallels between the Vice convention and a popular modern musical see Ina Rae Hark, 'Stop the World – I Want to Get Off: the Vice as Everyman', Comparative Drama, 12 (1978), 99–112; for corruption see 109–11.

21 Ann Wierum, '"Actors" and "Play-Acting" in the Morality Tradition', Renaissance Drama, n.s. 3 (1970), 190–3.

22 Bevington, 152 ff.

23 'The role [in commedia dell' arte] is not dramatic character but a form. It consists of a set of behaviours demonstrating fixed responses to stimulae [sic]', Virginia P. Scott, in Mayer and Richards, 18.

3

'THE VERY TEMPLE OF DELIGHT'

THE TWIN PLOTS OF
'MUCH ADO ABOUT NOTHING'

David Cook

Much Ado About Nothing is a compound of lovers' comedy and potentially tragic drama. However, the love-story of Beatrice and Benedick is not handled in the formally stylized mode of Belmont; nor does the more sombre part of the play approach as near to tragedy as in *The Merchant of Venice*, since the mood and the dramatic design point unequivocally to a happy conclusion throughout. Delays in the truth coming to light leave time for the repudiation of Hero, but are not so long as to lead to such irreversible consequences as in *Romeo and Juliet*, though a fatal outcome is threatened in the imminent duel between Benedick and Claudio. In *Much Ado* it is the solemn plot which is highly stylized and derived from an idyllic, courtly conception of love – the frame of reference is similar for Hero and Bassanio – while the day-to-day battle between the sexes is directly related to experience in the real world. The bringing together of different kinds of reality is one of the major features of Shakespearean comedy.

It seems, nevertheless, that *Much Ado About Nothing* is in danger of breaking out of the nicely balanced dramatic bounds which are to be clearly perceived in the structural design. The problem is that Beatrice and Benedick monopolize a greater share of the play than the underlying pattern seems to warrant. Since they are extremely attractive characters, we begrudge none of the time that we are allowed to spend with them. But the room left for the other major group of *personae* is barely enough for them to create the impression upon us that is required. Moreover, the freer style of the wit-contests, as it swells in proportion, is liable in less sensitive productions to make the manner of the other characters appear stiff and mechanical.

John Russell Brown, among others, finds *Much Ado About Nothing* to be 'intellectually articulated' to a high degree and dismisses any analysis which seeks to divide the play against itself, since it 'will not betray its secret to . . . piecemeal criticism'.[1] In essence I agree. I find the two major schools of thought about the play to be each in its way extreme. One group in effect discounts the formalized plot: 'The main Claudio-Hero-Don John intrigue is also not to be taken too seriously'; 'we are no longer fully involved. First, because the identities of Hero and Claudio have been kept to an irreducible minimum . . . they have not the core of being – or of dramatic being'; 'It is untrue to say that Beatrice and Benedick steal the limelight from them because Claudio and Hero never hold it.'[2] On the other hand, we have critics who refuse to admit that there is any issue here which needs resolving, and who say or imply that the generations who have been ill-at-ease with Claudio's presentation have no case at all: 'Claudio obtains insight into his own shortcomings and becomes, what previously he was not, a fit husband for Hero'; 'In reality, Claudio is exonerated, chiefly by the facts that Don John (as villain) draws all censure on himself and that Don Pedro (hitherto the norm, the reasonable man) is also deceived.'[3]

I believe that both views carry some force and are reconcilable in their less extreme forms. Surely it is not easy from the printed page to sympathize with Claudio, this 'absurdly solemn victim of love's young egoism'.[4] Yet I agree again with John Russell Brown that: 'The details of Claudio's denunciation – the fearful hesitancy with which he begins, and the remembrance and honour for Hero's outward beauty with which he continues and concludes – are surely meant by Shakespeare to be signs of his great inward compulsion and of his sorrow'.[5] Robert Grams Hunter argues: 'Clearly Shakespeare did not intend that we should blame [Claudio] for believing in the tableau presented for his benefit by Don John', and aptly concludes that 'Shakespeare meant us to' enter into the way 'Claudio is unreservedly forgiven' by the other characters.[6] David Horowitz's derogatory analysis of Claudio is very convincing: 'his original bond with Hero was a surface bond, not a faith . . . though he may have fancied Hero, he has never really loved her'.[7] But I came to the same conclusion as Hunter before seeing his comment: '*We* must pardon the offenders. If we cannot, the play does not, for us, end happily, and we are denied the comic experience.'[8] He strikes an honest final balance, while reserving his own position: 'Within the play, Claudio is unreservedly forgiven . . . . Whether or not the audience joins whole-heartedly in this charity is definitely less certain.'

So within the well-conceived dramatic pattern of ideas in *Much Ado About Nothing* we find a 'credibility gap'. Hero and Claudio are left somewhat shadowy. Yet if we simply condemn Claudio without sympathizing with his dilemma, this radically weakens the whole Hero/Claudio plot and hence the entire balance of the play. It is the function both of criticism and of stage production – two complementary aspects of interpretation – to decrease this imbalance: to close the gap. A good beginning is to ask questions about the dramatic intentions of the play as a whole and how far these are borne out in detail by our received text.

The problem does not lie in the conception. Nevertheless Shakespeare has clearly set himself a difficult task in combining these two modes, since the vigour of the wit-contest would have questioned the vitality of the formalistic strain even without the former appropriating more than its proper share of stage time. The Hero/Claudio plot is in constant danger of appearing stilted. Moreover, the Beatrice and Benedick plot is carefully articulated. We see them before either is deceived; when only one has been tricked; while both are absorbing the lessons of their new experience; and then emerging into love and their new selves beyond the furthest imaginings of the tricksters. This plot insists on dramatic elbow-room: it occupies no time arbitrarily.

In the stylized plot, Shakespeare outfaces his problem by making a daring experiment in presenting his antagonist. His changing situation is expressed in a series of cameos; we perceive his emotional progression in intense glimpses at different moments in the sequence, like close-up shots in a film with implied time-lapses between. We are to penetrate successive frames of mind as significant points in a passionate history and make the necessary imaginative leaps for ourselves to link them together. We see Claudio successively as infatuated lover; jealous of a rival; enraptured at success; in doubt of his innamorata's purity; as the betrayed lover. He denounces his fiancée publicly, plays the injured innocent. He repents; he mourns; he seeks to expiate his crime – and finds himself amidst a joyful happy ending. All these glimpses are brief, some almost instantaneous. The elimination of the intermediate processes can be seen as a judicious experiment in dramatic economy. Once we have realized this, it becomes clear why Shakespeare felt no need to stage the deception scene.

This method of concentration is intensified by other forms of shorthand, familiar alike in drama and society: ritual and symbol. It requires the symbolic death of Hero to purge Claudio and Pedro's offence, even if theirs is largely innocent guilt, like Oedipus's. It is plain that there is an offence to be purged, or the rituals of the last act would not be necessary. One of the main points of ritual cleansing is that it redeems offenders once and for all; Claudio has been purified before he regains Hero. There is formal aptness in Claudio's acceptance of the veiled bride. It is not an indication that he is willing to take any heiress blindfold. The cleansing must be a chosen act; in penitence he accepts the forfeiture of any right to question reparations imposed by Hero's family. He has blindly rejected Hero without recognizing her essential innocence and purity; he must now receive her again without knowing what he is acquiring, unconditionally. The pattern of the play demands that the tomb scene and the reunion with Hero be played as solemn, preordained rites. Claudio and Pedro descend into Hero's tomb and return from it. Modern society is distanced from the traditional awareness, present in all undegenerate societies, that grief, penitence, self-reproach can best be expressed publicly with utmost formality, which actually transforms the situation and the relationships within it, so that there is a cooperative purging of evil and the alienated individuals can return to the group completely untainted. Thus a ritualistic interpretation is the opposite of a remote or bookish reaction to the play. In many societies it is through ritual that drama impinges most directly on everyday life. Without some grasp of these effects, no production of *Much Ado About Nothing* can take proper advantage of the concentration it achieves through incantation and ritual forms.

Were the whole play similarly stylized, it would be obvious that Shakespeare deliberately withholds verbal chapter and verse in dramatizing Claudio's psyche. Against the brilliantly detailed presentation of Beatrice and Benedick, however, we are liable to shy at the jumps demanded by the other plot and complain that Claudio appears over-ready to entertain ungallant conclusions about Hero; and consequently we may support a vote of no confidence in him as a responsible human being. Given the purpose I have outlined, Beatrice and Benedick may seem to monopolize too much of our attention to allow sufficient dramatization of Claudio's development for us to see the situation from his viewpoint. In stage presentation it is not surprising if spectators often find him callow and uninteresting: actor and producer have a hard task to restore the portrait that seems to be intended. But, if the attempt is made, one avoids the error of thinking that the play must be rescued by emphasizing its most immediately attractive features at the expense of the rest – this is theatrical abdication. Nor shall we be blind to the challenging problem of restoring the dramatic idea inherent in the dramatic design.

Such a project seems particularly valuable in the case of a play which is so heavily dependent on dramatic patterning as opposed to the linear development of a story. Action is minimal in the first act of *Much Ado*, yet, because of the opposition and balance of forces, it is far from static.

The opening lines are solid, monumental; this is not a play to be launched in the vein of light comedy. Beatrice is present but silent for the first thirty lines. Shakespeare's professional skill is particularly evident in his openings. Here, having established a formal tone, the first movement proper is then handed over to Beatrice and Benedick. Even when Hero is discussed, it is the speakers themselves who hold our attention as the taunting vein of their intercourse is asserted.

Beatrice is the new woman of every age: 'Would it not grieve a woman to be over-mastered with a piece of valiant dust?' (ii.i.55–6).[9] But she can direct her wry humour at herself as well as at Benedick: 'I am sun-burnt. I may sit in a corner and cry "heigh-ho for a husband"' (ii.i.298–9). And she can show her nails: 'Scratching could not make it worse, an 'twere such a face as yours were' (i.i.130–1). She is both diffident and proud, eager and self-contained, contemptuous and generous, witty yet half sad. Her uncle thinks her compounded all of gaiety, but this is an over-simplification. She knows what positive effort is needed to keep her heart 'on the windy side of care' (ii.i.294), an effort which Claudio does not make.

Claudio's primness – 'Is she not a modest young lady?' (I.i.158) –
throws Benedick's self-conscious sophistication into relief: 'would
you have me speak after my custom, as being a professed tyrant to
their sex?' (I.i.160–2) (for all Shakespeare's nice ambiguity in the
word 'professed'). Claudio is more than a foil to Benedick – each
plays a part in the other's character-portrayal: 'In mine eye, she is
the sweetest lady that ever I looked on' (I.i.178–9). Benedick is a
sceptic in matters of the heart, Claudio a shy yet fiery young novice
who completes the conventional cycle which Benedick has passed
through vicariously, and abjures.

While John Palmer reminds us that '"Much Ado About
Nothing" . . . is Shakespeare's nearest approach to the comedy of
manners',[10] there are significant differences. Wits in Restoration
drama contemn marriage, not women; there is no parallel to *Love's
Labour's Lost* in the later comedy. Benedick's dismissal of
matrimony – 'Shall I never see a bachelor of threescore again?'
(I.i.189) – is part and parcel of his rejection of the whole sex: 'I
neither feel how she should be loved, nor how she should be
worthy' (I.i.218–9). He may look pale 'With anger, with sickness,
or with hunger . . . not with love' (I.i.234–5):

> I do much wonder, that one man seeing how much another man
> is a fool when he dedicates his behaviours to love, will after he
> hath laughed at such shallow follies in others, become the
> argument of his own scorn by falling in love: . . .
>
> (II.iii.7–12)

Beatrice too, while praying to God not to send her a husband – 'for
the which blessing I am at him upon my knees every morning and
evening' (II.i.25–7) – deprecates all over-mastery by 'a piece of
valiant dust'. Not, perhaps, till D. H. Lawrence are the nice
distinctions between masculine and feminine feelings again so
subtly analysed, interlocking with the individual's dual needs to
assert absolute independence and be at one with another human
being. But the outcome in Shakespeare is clearer cut: 'wisdom and
blood combating in so tender a body, we have ten proofs to one that
blood hath the victory' (II.iii.164–6).

Beatrice is closer kin to the Princess of *Love's Labour's Lost* and
the Portia of the early casket scenes than to Katherine the shrew, for
all her pointed tongue. Benedick characterizes her as a virago, but
we do not accept either's assessment of the other at face value. She

will remain her own mistress by raillery and any other weapons to hand, but her cadences are elegantly witty and deliberately fashioned rather than shrewish. Otherwise her imaginative, self-questioning response to Benedick's supposedly love-lorn plight would not be credible. And Benedick's soldierliness is emphasized; he is no mere fop. His talking (however pointedly) slightly too much betrays him, for all his bravado, as on the defensive sexually and emotionally, in much the same key as John Tanner in Shaw's *Man and Superman*, with whom he has much in common. Shaw was consciously following Shakespeare in dramatizing women's control of the battle of the sexes.

Other characters speak with ceremonious artificiality: 'Never came trouble to my house in the likeness of your grace. For trouble being gone, comfort should remain: but when you depart from me, sorrow abides and happiness takes his leave' (I.i.94–7). The contrast marks the naturalness of Beatrice and Benedick, even though their sparring matches observe strict conventions:

> *Beatrice* I wonder that you will still be talking, Signior Benedick – nobody marks you.
> *Benedick* What, my dear Lady Disdain! are you yet living?
>
> (I.i.111–14)

How intensely they are aware of each other! Their wit plays above a complex of controlled feelings and restraints. Later Benedick has no need to jest a twelve-month in an hospital like Berowne to establish his credentials as a committed individual. The seriousness of the relationship beneath the surface flippancy becomes progressively clearer.

Benedick's conscious shift of attitude – 'I must not seem proud. Happy are they that hear their detractions, and can put them to mending' (II.iii.223–5) – is matched by Beatrice's foreshadowing of Millamant's phrasing:[11] 'Contempt, farewell! and maiden pride, adieu!' (III.i.109). Indeed, Beatrice encourages Hero throughout, congratulates her on success in love, weeps for her broken heart. Though they would not declare themselves by proxy, as does Claudio, these defiant lovers can be worked upon indirectly to yield to their natural feelings. When they at length give way, it must be in 'honest plain words': 'I was not born under a rhyming planet, nor I cannot woo in festival terms' (V.ii.39–41), which reminds us of the conditions imposed by the Princess on Berowne, as also Bassanio's rejection of superficial appearance, and perhaps Henry the Fifth's blunt courtship. The two warriors for sexual independence go down fighting; yet their submission is not half-hearted. Theirs is a full capitulation, like Mirabel's and Millamant's later: 'In brief, since I do purpose to marry, I will think nothing to any purpose that the world can say against it' (v.iv. 103–5).

In the next age, Etherege was to be accused of writing 'talking plays', but already the first two hundred and sixty lines of *Much Ado* are almost pure talk, carried primarily by Beatrice and Benedick to our complete satisfaction, which is a testimony to the effectiveness of well-judged 'talk' in conveying dramatic activity and development. Thus from the start these two assume central roles, so the slightness of Claudio and Hero makes it hard for them to challenge pride of place. Happily there need be no such rivalry, since the plots are well integrated, primarily through Benedick, who is a pivotal character like Berowne or Portia. He remains the structural king-pin at the most effective climax when Beatrice dares him to 'Kill Claudio' (IV.i.288), a few moments after his first declaration to her. 'Love', as David Horowitz well says, 'is immediately the basis for decision over life itself.'[12]

Shakespeare prevents Benedick and Beatrice from displaying any excessive artificiality, which would obliterate the stylistic contrast on which the play is patterned, by allowing them the greater flexibility of prose. In the first scene, as later, we shift to blank verse for the more sober plot in the concentrated presentation of Claudio's first emotional stance.

The third component in the pattern of the first act is the Don John passage. He is not the only character nursing poisonous melancholy, but in him this is as pernicious as in Iago and its causes are as undefined as in Antonio:

> Conrade   why are you thus out of measure sad?
> Don John   There is no measure in the occasion that breeds,
>   therefore the sadness is without limit.   (I.iii. 1–4)

He is an early study in evil, a foiled rebel but ambiguously motivated: 'it must not be denied but that I am a plain-dealing villain' (I.iii. 29–30). Don John has a destructive scorn of marriage, different in kind from Beatrice and Benedick's, just as his morose-ness is different in kind from Claudio's. Round this malevolent figure flows a negative, oppressive, evil mood:

> *Conrade* Can you make no use of your discontent?
> *Don John* I make all use of it, for I use it only.   (I.iii.35–6)

The imagery which reinforces this mood is reminiscent of Webster's rather than that of *Macbeth*: 'I had rather be a canker in a hedge than a rose in his grace' (I.iii.25–6); 'Being entertained for a perfumer, as I was smoking a musty room, comes me the prince and Claudio' (I.iii.55–6). The tone is sardonic, the inferences tangential.

As a painter opposes blocks of, say, red, black and green, so Shakespeare juxtaposes brooding vindictiveness to sophisticated gaiety, and again both of these to naïve innocence. The play is painted dominantly in these three colours. Any attempt to appreciate Beatrice and Benedick in isolation from their context must obscure the force of the play as a whole. We shall not then understand fully even our favourite characters. The groups are patterned against each other and so each helps to create the other. Beatrice is posed opposite Hero; Claudio counters Benedick. And the implied comparison between these men is itself played against other contrasts between Benedick and Don John, and Benedick and Don Pedro. Individual characters and sets of relationships are nicely balanced.

It is Beatrice who first defines the opposition between Benedick and Don John: 'He were an excellent man that were made just in the mid-way between him and Benedick. The one is too like an image and says nothing, and the other too like my lady's eldest son, evermore tattling' (II.i.6–9). In Act IV, sc. i, there is the different contrast between Don John and Claudio: the former mouths his fake disgust at Hero's alleged behaviour, while Claudio really feels the horror he expresses.

The low-life characters have a different role in the structure of *Much Ado* from the one they occupy in *Love's Labour's Lost*. They are saved till late in the play when, with other groups of characters well established, they can offer an implied commentary upon them. In particular the self-importance of wit and learning is deflated: 'for your writing and reading, let that appear when there is no need of such vanity. You are thought here to be the most senseless and fit man for the constable of the watch: therefore bear you the lantern (III.iii.20–24). As is true of similar characters in other works – supremely of Bottom – they are ludicrously incongruous in alien social settings: in the magistrate's court and attempting to make their report to Leonato. But, unlike Bottom, they are also ludicrous in a setting where they should be at home as Elizabethan watch-men. And so, while they call forth some sympathy when they are legitimately out of their depth, they also provide direct topical satire on the forces of law and order. Bottom is far the more positive in that, whether he has seen the obstacles ahead or not, he blunders straight forward and willy-nilly reaches the other side. Dogberry and the Watch are also for the most part utterly unaware of the issues with which the other characters are grappling. But, when they do pick up some hint of trouble, their first instinct is to try speciously to evade it. And yet, as has often been noticed, it is the Watch's naïvety rather than the others' wit which at length by chance captures guile. In them, vanity and foolish innocence are inextricable. There is a parallel with the refined characters in that Dogberry confounds himself, while the gauche honesty of his fellows discredits all posing. As in *Measure for Measure*, verbal incongruities search into the paradoxes of morality, motivation, justice and religion:

Sexton   Which be the malefactors?
Dogberry   Marry, that am I, and my partner.

                    .   .   .

Dogberry   O villain! thou wilt be condemned into everlasting
        redemption for this.   (IV. ii. 3–4, 56–7)

Their proverbial and biblical echoes lie beyond ordinary practice or experience: 'Truly, I would not hang a dog by my will, much more a man who hath any honesty in him' (III. iii. 61–2). They underline the lesson that Benedick teaches us, that it is hard to draw firm lines between the comic and the serious.

In both I. i and II. i Claudio is on stage for sixty lines before speaking, which characterizes his rather shadowy presence, his recessive personality, his uncertainty of himself. He twice rapidly loses faith upon summary evidence, first in his friend Don Pedro and then in his beloved, Hero. He is evidently young and reckless, akin in some respects to Romeo: his youthful passion easily blows hot and cold like Romeo's for Rosaline. We are not to dismiss Claudio, but nor are we to see him as faultless: this is a many-sided Shakespearean study. We must take into account the weighty evidence presented by his deceivers – as we do in the case of

Othello – and also their social standing. But unlike Othello he makes absolutely no attempt to believe in the purity of the woman of his choice once it is thrown in doubt. As Auden justly comments: 'Had his love for Hero been all he imagined it to be, he would have laughed in Don John's face and believed Hero's assertion of her innocence, despite apparent evidence to the contrary, as immediately as her cousin does.'[13] Analogies with other Shakespearean characters tend to confirm that this is a rapid sketch of over-impulsive but not altogether unfounded disillusionment. Benedick has already been convinced of Hero's defection, even if (with a loyalty much stronger than Claudio's) he defers to Beatrice's staunch trustfulness. Earlier, when Claudio posits a division of allegiance in Don Pedro between friendship and love, he immediately yields precedence to love as proof that his companion has double-crossed him: a line of reasoning familiar from *Two Gentlemen of Verona* and *A Midsummer Night's Dream*, though with different conclusions. If the evidence we have considered is accepted, may not the apparent gap between intention and effect upon readers and spectators in the presentation of Claudio result from Shakespeare's shorthand here being too short? May the same thing not be true with Claudio's first rehabilitation of his love? 'Silence is the perfectest herald of joy – I were but little happy, if I could say how much' (II. i. 286–7). We are reminded of Antony's 'There's beggary in the love that can be reckoned.' We know from the end of *A Winter's Tale* how telling an understatement such as Claudio's can be when successfully judged. Yet here Claudio may seem to be so abrupt as to be casual unless extremely tactfully handled in production. No doubt the actor will need discreetly to infuse some intensity of emotion into the accompanying business in spite of the fact that the occasion is highly formal. But if the problem throughout this plot is once conceived to be potential over-compression, the committed Shakespearean director will surely see his way clear before him.

These arguments concerning the Claudio/Hero plot are strengthened by observing the elaborate dramatic commentary provided by the continuous counterpointing of the two actions. The plot creating a false love-relationship as a practical joke crosses with the sinister scheme to smash an already existing love-relationship. The marriage which is apparently doomed is played against the marriage-prospect which gathers momentum. Claudio is deceived out of marriage; Benedick and Beatrice are virtually deceived into marriage. If Benedick and Beatrice are at first too sure of their self-determined roles *vis-à-vis* each other, Claudio courts disaster by his unsureness. Whereas Benedick is ready to believe good news of Beatrice, Claudio over-hastily believes bad accounts of Hero. Such development as we see in Hero's character is apparent in carrying out the deception of Beatrice and Benedick. In both plots, life and love are a gamble amidst complex forces; the control of events is beyond those who are involved. The only touchstone is to accept and foster real feeling when one is fortunate enough to encounter it or find it within oneself; characters are shown to be behaving positively or negatively according to their response to this doctrine. But there is no over-simplification: Beatrice's right feelings about Hero lead her to the potentially disastrous conviction that Claudio should be killed – a response that would have forestalled any solution or reconciliation.

Claudio shows a culpable readiness to court disaster, to help shape events towards his unsubstantiated yet fateful prognostications: 'If I see any thing to-night why I should not marry her to-morrow, in the congregation, where I should wed, there will I shame her' (III. ii. 115–17). If Hero falls short of the image he has created, he will throw down his idol in the very sanctuary where his worship should have culminated. There is something here of the morbidity we find in Antonio of *The Merchant of Venice*. Claudio is shown to be a loser, anticipating the circumstances that will make him so. He is a danger to himself and to those close to him, since he is bent on casting himself on to a downward spiral heading for calamity. He seems to find his true voice only when he has cause to indulge unqualified sorrow:

> For thee I'll lock up all the gates of love,
> And on my eyelids shall conjecture hang,
> To turn all beauty into thoughts of harm,
> And never shall it more be gracious.   (IV. i. 104–7)

But the experience seems to have left little mark on him in Act V, so we feel it to be confirmed that his sorrow has been a self-indulgence reminiscent of Olivia's. Hero's melancholy forebodings chime in on a less selfish note; she appears free of self-pity and is akin to Juliet in her well-founded fears that circumstances are against her. Indeed, Claudio's eventual forgiveness by us, the audience, for his wilful and almost fatal mistrust, is earned in some significant degree by the merit of Hero and the fact that it is such a woman that he chose for his future wife in the first place.

The melancholic strain is deepened by Leonato's profound sadness beyond rational relief. This aspect of the drama is deliberately weighted. The most telling scene in this plot is that in the church in Act IV, provided actor or reader has established Claudio's sincerity. His speeches here convey the incipiently tragic tangle at the heart of the action:

> She's but the sign and semblance of her honour.
>
>   . . .
>
> O Hero! What a Hero hadst thou been,
> If half thy outward graces had been placed
> About the thoughts and counsels of thy heart!
>
> (IV. i. 32, 99–101)

This is the playwright of *Othello*. Hero's swooning impresses on us dramatically the seriousness of the events: in Elizabethan terms there could be no doubt of the absolute importance of unsullied chastity. Though Shakespeare was anything but a puritan, he well understood the symbolic power of the idea of virginity; like Spenser, he regarded chastity as humanly positive, not sterile, a virile affirmation of the significance of a real relationship. Now even Hero's father believes the evidence against her. It is the Friar – often a figure of unconventional force in Shakespeare (witness *Romeo and Juliet* and *Measure for Measure*) – who perceives innocence emanating from Hero:

> And in her eye there hath appeared a fire,
> To burn the errors that these princes hold . . .
>
> (IV. i. 161–2)

The Friar sees Hero's fate as epitomizing human perversity:

> That what we have we prize not to the worth,
> Whiles we enjoy it, but being lacked and lost,
> Why then we rack the value, then we find
> The virtue that possession would not show us . . .
>
> (IV. i. 217–20)

The wheel having turned and Hero's integrity having been vindicated, the Friar sketches for Claudio a progression of repentance and regeneration in faint anticipation of the culmination of *A*

Winter's Tale. In further anticipation of the last plays, the group around the injured party are first to seek a positive solution:

> this wedding-day
> Perhaps is but prolong'd. (IV. i. 252–3)

Leonato now shows a new conviction of Hero's innocence which needs no further substantiation though it has developed off-stage. In this there is some parallel with Claudio, whose own willingness to admit that he has been wrong is as sudden as his earlier reversals. This abruptness must be seen as part of Shakespeare's consistent stylization of his role. The dramatic method remains constant. Claudio is still tongue-tied, as he has been throughout most of the play: in nine lines he confesses that he has erred and agrees to marry the woman of Leonato's choice. Dramatic tact demands imperatively that due ritual significance now be given to the dirge before Hero's monument, which recalls the lament over Juliet before she has in fact died.

The two plots have already been fully integrated in Act IV with the scene in which Beatrice spurs Benedick into challenging Claudio. This scene is a kaleidoscope of seriousness, romance and witty banter, bringing together not only all the main threads of the subject matter but also the varying moods of the play. While Beatrice's fury channels the audience's own anger against those who have trammelled the innocent Hero, it also rallies our sympathies for Claudio. While in a confused sense he is partly culpable, he no more merits death than Hero, and so they both become subjects of our pity and concern, as also Benedick, who gallantly jeopardizes himself. Thus the two elaborate patterns have merged into one, the various parts of which are played off against each other in formal and ritual terms in Act V till each is resolved in a consortium of reconciliation.

In the rediscovery of Hero, there is again a faint foreshadowing of the finale of *A Winter's Tale*, but this forward glance must not distract us from the beautifully patterned achievement of *Much Ado About Nothing* itself. It is an ambitious work, interrelating a complex of ideas, in large part through harmonizing contrasting styles. It is unhelpful to gloss over the strain the play places upon its interpreters, on and off the stage, but the more clearly we comprehend its aspirations, the more willing we shall be to forgive internal stresses, and the better shall we be placed to restore in reading or performance the greatest possible measure of the play's intentions, which are clearly enough to be perceived in our received text.

NOTES

1 John Russell Brown, *Shakespeare and His Comedies* (London, 1957; references are to the paperback edn, 1968), 121.

2 Francis Fergusson, *The Human Image in Dramatic Literature* (New York, 1957), 152; Graham Storey, 'The Success of *Much Ado About Nothing*', in John Garrett (ed.), *More Talking of Shakespeare* (London, 1959), 140; John Crick, 'Much Ado About Nothing', *The Use of English*, XVII, 3 (spring 1966), 225.

3 W. H. Auden, 'The Fallen City: Some Reflections on Shakespeare's "Henry IV"', *Encounter*, XIII, 5 (November 1959), 30–1; T. W. Craik, '*Much Ado About Nothing*', *Scrutiny*, 19 (October 1953), 314.

4 Fergusson, 150.

5 Brown, 116–17.

6 Robert Grams Hunter, *Shakespeare and the Comedy of Forgiveness*, (New York, 1965), 98, 104–5.

7 David Horowitz, *Shakespeare: An Existential View*, (London, 1965), 28.

8 Hunter, 103.

9 Quotations from *Much Ado About Nothing* are from the New Cambridge edition by Sir Arthur Quiller-Couch and John Dover Wilson (Cambridge, 1953).

10 John Palmer, *Comic Characters of Shakespeare* (London, 1946), 117.

11 *The Way of the World*, IV.i.185–9. Herbert Davis (ed.), *The Complete Plays of William Congreve* (Chicago, 1967).

12 David Horowitz, 32.

13 W. H. Auden, *The Dyer's Hand and other essays* (London, 1963), 518.

4

TORCH, CAULDRON AND TAPER

LIGHT AND DARKNESS IN 'MACBETH'

William A. Armstrong

In *Shakespeare's Imagery and What it Tells us*, Caroline Spurgeon states that 'one of the chief symbolic ideas' in *Macbeth* is that 'light stands for life, virtue, goodness; and darkness for evil and death'.[1] This symbolic idea had a wide currency in Shakespeare's time and can be illustrated by the following passage in Roger Ascham's *Toxophilus* (1545):

> For on the nighte time & in corners, Spirites and theves, rattes and mice, toades and oules, nyghtcrowes and poulcattes, foxes and foumerdes, with all other vermine, and noysome beastes, use mooste styrringe, when the daye lyght, and in open places, whiche be ordeyned of God for honeste thynges, they darre not ones come, whiche thinge Euripides noted verye wel sayenge.
>
> Il thinges the night, good thinges the daye doth haunt & use.[2]

Spirits, mice, toads, owls and crows are likewise invoked in *Macbeth* to implement a contrast between the powers of night and day. But Shakespeare's contrast is not always the simple antithesis expounded by Ascham and Caroline Spurgeon. It is complicated by ambiguities, paradoxes and seeming contradictions which strengthen and diversify the texture of the play like knots in the grain of wood.

This complexity of Shakespeare's treatment of light and darkness becomes manifest in the first two scenes of the play. The conventional association of evil with darkness and nauseating obscurity is suggested by the 'fog and filthy air' (I. i. 12)[3] which envelop the witches at the close of the first scene. In performance, these words may have been reinforced by burning resin to create smoke to swirl around the witches as they disappeared down the big central trap at the Globe. But the direct connection of the witches with darkness has been qualified a line earlier by their paradox, 'Fair is foul, and foul is fair', which Professor Kenneth Muir and other editors of the play have aptly related to Thomas Nashe's remark in *The Terrors of the Night* (1594) that 'every thing must bee interpreted backward as Witches say their Pater-noster, good being the character of bad, and bad of good'.[4] In the following scene, a kindred paradox informs the imagery of light which the bleeding Sergeant applies to Macbeth when he says:

> As whence the sun 'gins his reflection
> Shipwrecking storms and direful thunders break,
> So from that spring, whence comfort seem'd to come,
> Discomfort breaks.   (I. ii. 25–8)

G. L. Kittredge explains these somewhat puzzling lines as follows: 'As from the east, whence comes the sunrise, storms often break forth, so from the seeming source of comfort (the victory over Macdonwald) a disadvantage came to the Scottish army – for the King of Norway attacked them with fresh troops in the disarray of victory'.[5] It is part of the calculated doubleness of the passage, however, to associate Macbeth with 'the sun' and 'that source, whence comfort seem'd to flow'. The east, corresponding to Macbeth, is represented as the origin of storms, thunder and shipwreck. Adverse phenomena of the same kind are associated with the witches in the first and third scenes of Act I. Unconsciously but potently the Sergeant's words prefigure the disasters which Macbeth's Lucifer-like ambition brings on Scotland. There is an obvious connection between the Sergeant's simile and Malcolm's paradox:

> Angels are bright still, though the brightest fell . . .
>   (IV. iii. 22)

which involves Lucifer, Macbeth, destructive ambition, and light.

Darkness is twice invoked during the hours before Duncan's murder. In these invocations the contexts suggest an awareness on the part first of Macbeth, then of Lady Macbeth, of the turpitude of what they plan to do by night. The moral implications of Macbeth's words just before he leaves Duncan in the fourth scene of the play:

> Stars, hide your fires!
> Let not light see my black and deep desires . . .
>
> (I. iv. 50–1)

are sharpened by the significance given to the light of the stars by Duncan's words a few seconds earlier:

> signs of nobleness, like stars, shall shine
> On all deservers . . .   (I. iv. 41–2)

as well as by the blackness that Macbeth attributes to his desires. Lady Macbeth's invocation is more violent; it sets heaven and hell in opposition, and declares her allegiance to the powers of darkness:

> Come, thick Night,
> And pall thee in the dunnest smoke of Hell,
> That my keen knife see not the wound it makes,
> Nor Heaven peep through the blanket of the dark,
> To cry, 'Hold, hold!'   (I. v. 50–4)

'Peep', in Elizabethan usage, means 'gaze steadily'. Taken in conjunction, the two invocations carry the suggestion that the stars are like the eyes of heaven staring through the dark. The underside of the roof which covered the rear half of the stage of the Globe was decorated with stars and the signs of the zodiac.[6] Situated in shadow, these painted stars gave visual support to the ideas at work in the imagery of the invocations.

Torches are used in the three scenes (I. vi., I. vii., II. i.) immediately before the murder of Duncan. In accordance with customary Elizabethan stage practice, they indicate the approach or descent of night, but in each case they have other implications. Shakespeare fuses the conventional with the original. In Act I, sc. vi, as the opening stage direction indicates, Duncan's entry with his noblemen is preceded by hautboys and torches.[7] The musicians and torch-bearers have a ceremonial function: they do honour to the King as they lead him to Macbeth's castle. Irony underlies this appearance of fealty, however, for the conspiracy to kill Duncan began in the preceding scene; the torches are lighting his way to dusty death. They also signify gathering sunset, with enough light shining on the battlements to make visible the nest of the 'temple-haunting martlet', symbol of life and procreation (I. vi. 4). Duncan and his followers pause to enjoy its beauty and the purity of the air surrounding its habitation (I. vi. 10). For the spectator there is an ironical and ominous contrast between this twilight moment of contemplation and Lady Macbeth's harsh conjuration of 'thick Night' and 'the dunnest smoke of Hell' a minute or so earlier.

The next scene begins with another ceremonial entry: '*Hautboys and torches. Enter and pass over the stage, a Sewer and divers Servants with dishes and service.*' The music and the torches signify the festivity and hospitality about to be enjoyed by Duncan and his nobility. Perhaps we are intended to think that the torches will be placed in sconces in the off-stage banqueting-hall. The hierarchical relationships between Duncan and his nobles is paralleled by that between the Sewer, the chief servant, and his subordinates. So the torches have a double function: they indicate that it is night-time and are also part of a spectacle which symbolizes the ideals of hospitality and loyalty that Macbeth is about to violate. These ideas are reinforced by the ensuing soliloquy in which Macbeth acknowledges his duties as Duncan's subject and his host (I. vii. 13–15), but by the end of the scene the plot to kill the King has been completed.

The following scene occurs in a courtyard of the castle, and its first ten lines emphasize in various ways the intense darkness of the night. At the outset we have the direction '*Enter* BANQUO *and* FLEANCE, *with a torch before him*'. Nine lines later, another direction – '*Enter* MACBETH, *and a Servant with a torch*' – shows a torch again being used as a conventional indication that it is night. The opening dialogue reveals that the moon is down, that it is after midnight, and that the 'candles' of heaven (i.e. the stars) are blacked out. The last detail is an ominous fulfilment of Macbeth's demand that the stars hide their fires. A further indication of deep darkness comes from the fact that the light of the torches is not sufficient to enable Banquo to recognize Macbeth when he enters, for he is obliged to ask, 'Who's there?' Fleance illustrates ideals of filial duty and hierarchical order by acting as his father's torch-bearer and carrying his sword for him (l. 4). Another function of his torch is to prefigure his destiny as the life-bearer who will found a line of kings.

In the final speech of Act II, sc. i, there is a prefigurement of another kind, prompted this time by images of darkness and its associations. After Macbeth has described how night has taken possession of the hemisphere – 'o'er the one half-world nature seems dead' (ll. 49–50) – he broods over night as a time when

> wither'd Murther,
> Alarum'd by his sentinel, the wolf,
> Whose howl's his watch, thus with his stealthy pace
> With Tarquin's ravishing strides, towards his design
> Moves like a ghost.   (II. i. 51–6)

These sinister associations of night combine prophecy with self-condemnation, for 'wither'd Murther' corresponds to Macbeth; the wolf, to Lady Macbeth; his howl, to the bell she strikes as a signal to Macbeth; Tarquin's ravishing strides to Macbeth's outrage against hospitality: the movement of the ghost, to Macbeth's silent steps as he goes to Duncan's bedchamber.

Night is again associated with a creature of ill omen and prefigurements of disaster in the following two scenes, II. ii and iii. Soon after she has sent her husband on his murderous mission by striking the bell off-stage, Lady Macbeth enters, hears the screech of an owl, and comments,

> It was the owl that shriek'd, the fatal bellman,
> Which gives the stern'st good night.   (II. ii. 3–4)

The phrase 'fatal bellman' connects the owl with herself and her recent signal to Macbeth, as well as with the officer who at the time of the play's earliest performances went to Newgate gaol to ring a handbell at midnight before an execution. The ill repute of the screech-owl as the harbinger of a public calamity goes back to Roman times, and Pliny's comments on it were well known to many Elizabethans. Describing it as 'the very monster of night', he declares that 'the Scritch Owle . . . is most execrable and accursed, and namely, in the presages of publick affaires'.[8] The idea of the owl as a nocturnal presager of public disaster is taken up again in the following scene, when Lennox tells Macbeth that 'the obscure bird' (i.e. the bird of darkness, the owl) clamoured 'the livelong night', prophesying 'dire combustion and confused events' (ll. 59–61). The ominous happenings of the unruly night include the blowing down of chimneys, lamentings, 'strange screams of death', and rumours of earthquakes (II. iii. 55–62). As editors of the play often note, such portents were believed to accompany the death of kings. They fulfil the owl's message. Macbeth's terse rejoinder, ''Twas a rough night', is loaded with irony.

A similar irony invests the scenes concerned with Banquo's murder and its aftermath (III. i., ii., iii.). The first hint of his peril springs from his image personifying night:

> go not my horse the better,
> I must become a borrower of the night,
> For a dark hour or twain.   (III. i. 25-7)

This leads to the ironies of Macbeth's injunction, 'Fail not our feast', and Banquo's reply, 'I will not' (III. i. 28), and of Macbeth's echoing of Banquo's words when he tells the murderers that Fleance as well as his father 'must embrace the fate / Of that dark hour' (III. i. 135-6). Other ironies develop from the fact that, whereas Macbeth regards night as his ally, she is already abetting his punishment. Noting that painful and evil thoughts were 'supposed to be put into men's minds by dreams during the helplessness of the will in slumber', G. L. Kittredge cites Bishop Patrick's prayer for Wednesday night, 'Defend us from all the powers of darkness'.[9] In III. ii., Macbeth describes to his wife 'these terrible dreams / That shake us nightly' (ll. 18-19) and his subsequent references to steel, poison, 'Malice domestic, foreign levy' show that he dreams of being murdered.

But Macbeth's faith in night as his accomplice continues and prompts his second great invocation of her:

> Come, seeling night,
> Scarf up the tender eye of pitiful Day,
> And with thy bloody and invisible hand
> Cancel and tear to pieces, that great bond
> Which keeps me pale!   (III. ii. 46-50)

Night's hand is 'invisible' because of the absence of light, 'bloody' because of her severing her victims' bond with life; 'tear to pieces' adds a beastlike quality to the personification. Macbeth's next words illustrate the 'seeling', darkening activity of night, inducing twilight and robbing good men of vitality and vigilance – 'Light thickens . . . / Good things of Day begin to droop and drowse' (III. ii. 50-2). Contrasting with this menace is the beauty of the twilight described by the First Murderer a few seconds later:

The west yet glimmers with some streaks of day;
Now spurs the lated traveller apace
To gain the timely inn . . .   (III. iii. 5–7)

though the image of the 'lated traveller' creates suspense by
reminding us of Banquo and making us wonder whether he will
reach the safety of the castle.

Shakespeare is at pains to indicate that the twilight gives way to
darkness quickly; off-stage Banquo demands, 'Give us a light there,
ho!' (III. iii. 9), and a few seconds later we have the direction, '*Enter
BANQUO, and FLEANCE, with a torch*'. As before, Fleance illustrates
ideals of duty and order by serving his father as a torch-bearer.
Rapidly deepening darkness is suggested by the implication that a
light is now necessary to make it possible for the Third Murderer to
see Banquo:

2 Mur.   A light, a light!
3 Mur.   'Tis he.   (III. iii. 14)

This suggestion is augmented by Banquo's comment, 'It will rain
tonight' (l. 15), which implies that the sky is thick with clouds.
Consequently, when the First Murderer extinguishes the torch, the
darkness is so great that Fleance is able to make good his escape.
Stage business involving the knocking of the torch to the ground
and stamping out its flame may have served to distract the
murderers' attention from Fleance. This is a great turning-point in
the play. Macbeth has received his first set-back and his fortunes
decline from this time onwards. Night has betrayed him; paradoxically, she has supported good against evil, preserving the great
bond of life represented by Fleance.

In *Macbeth*, torches are the most frequently used of the physical
conventions designed to indicate darkness on Shakespeare's stage.
Two other physical devices are employed in the play: the cauldron
and the taper. The cauldron is frequently used as an emblem of Hell
in medieval and Renaissance art. Most editors of *Macbeth* give the
location of the cauldron scene (IV. i.) as 'a cavern', though neither
the dialogue nor the directions of the play describe it as such. In
III. v., Hecate speaks of 'the pit of Acheron' (l. 15) as the place to
which Macbeth will come to learn his destiny. In Shakespeare's
time, 'Acheron' was usually taken to mean 'hell', and the central
position of the cauldron in the scene shows that he intended it to

create an aura of supernatural evil. It is reasonable to assume that the cauldron of hell-broth was placed just in front of the 'grave' trap in the platform of the Globe, so that the apparitions could rise behind the cauldron, and so that stage-hands could withdraw and lower it below stage at the appropriate moment. It may have been mounted on a large tray, and there may have been a fire under it, as the words 'Fire, burn' suggest (IV.i.35). The cauldron may have contained burning resin or some other smouldering substance. Hence the gory '*armed head*' and the '*bloody child*' may have loomed through smoke arising from the fire and/or the cauldron in tableaux accordant with the verbal images of blood and darkness which pervade the play.

Whether or not we think of the setting as pit or cavern, the cauldron scene is envisaged as a place of darkness. Macbeth greets the witches as 'black, and midnight hags' (IV.i.48) and some of the ingredients that the witches throw into the cauldron recall creatures already associated with the malevolent powers of darkness, such as the 'howlet's wing' (l. 17) and the 'tooth of wolf' (l. 21). Other ingredients are poisonous plants which have been made more potent by having been gathered by night, when their evil and destructive properties were supposed to be increased, such as 'Root of hemlock, digg'd i' th' dark' (l.25) and 'slips of yew / Sliver'd in the moon's eclipse' (ll. 27–8). As Dover Wilson and other editors have remarked, an eclipse of the moon was regarded as a time of almost complete darkness.[10]

In the first line of the sleep-walking scene (V.i.), the Doctor tells the Gentlewoman, 'I have two nights watched with you', so indicating that the present occasion is by night, but the principal means of establishing that it is night is the taper carried by Lady Macbeth in accordance with the First Folio direction, '*Enter Lady, with a Taper*'. Besides this conventional purpose, it has distinctive symbolic functions. A taper was a small candle, one of the smallest forms of artificial illumination available on Shakespeare's stage. It could effectively symbolize the frailty and brevity of life, as it does in Macbeth's exclamation, 'Out, out, brief candle' (V. v. 23), and Job's declaration, 'How oft is the candle of the wicked put out' (21:17). Lady Macbeth's awareness of being one of the wicked gives her taper another symbolic meaning. For her, it has a talismanic power which wards off the evil forces of darkness. When the Doctor asks, 'How came she by that light?', the Gentlewoman reveals that 'she has light by her continually; 'tis her command' (v. i. 22–3). Lady Macbeth's only direct expression of fear – 'Hell is murky' (l. 35) – shows that it is dread of damnation that makes her so dependent on the frail taper. Her revulsion from the darkness of hell is a pathetic and ironic contrast to the confidence of her earlier invocation of 'the dunnest smoke of Hell' as Night's fitting garb (II. iv. 50–1).

Dread of damnation has an important bearing on the stage business of this scene. One of Mrs Siddons's chief innovations as Lady Macbeth was to put the candle on a table so as to free both her hands for the business of trying to rub off the imaginary blood-stains and going through the motions of dipping her hands in water at times. Richard Brinsley Sheridan, manager of the Covent Garden Theatre, where Mrs Siddons planned to make these innovations, urged her not to put down the candle, telling her that her new stage business would be regarded as presumptuous, and reminding her that Mrs Pritchard, famed for playing Lady Macbeth in Garrick's production of the play, had kept the candle in her hand throughout the scene.[11] Drawing on hearsay, John Wilson tells us: 'I have been told that the great Mrs. Pritchard used to touch the palm with the tips of her fingers, for the washing, keeping candle in hand; – that Siddons first set down her candle, that she might come forwards and wash her hands in earnest, one over the other, as if she was at her wash-hand basin'.[12] An engraving published in *The Universal Magazine* in April 1768 shows that Mrs Pritchard held the candle in her left hand on a level with her shoulder at the outset of the sleep-walking scene.[13]

There is evidence that Mrs Yates, one of Mrs Pritchard's successors in the role of Lady Macbeth, followed her practice of not putting the candle down. A humorous tale, first published in 1777, describes how a young lady became stage-struck after seeing Mrs Yates as Lady Macbeth. On being given a candle after she got home, she 'shut her eyes, held the light at arm's length, and began to rub her hand Lady Macbeth-like'.[14] As the pre-Siddons tradition did not require the putting down of the candle, and as there is no demand in Shakespeare's text that it should be relinquished, there is a distinct possibility that the tradition went back to the Globe and derived from the instructions that Shakespeare gave to the boy who first played Lady Macbeth. Our knowledge of the stage business employed by Mrs Pritchard and Mrs Yates is limited, but it is sufficient to show that their interpretation was delicate and symbolic compared to Mrs Siddons's vigorous and naturalistic method. The extension of the arm and the rubbing of the palm of the hand that held the candle suggest a ritual cleansing, symbolizing fear of damnation and desire of purgation. The candle is not put down because it represents a safeguard against demonic powers in the surrounding darkness. *Pace* Mrs Siddons, Mrs Pritchard's method accords well with the physical frailty and nervous hallucinations of Lady Macbeth in this scene.

Shakespeare invented the sleep-walking scene. The most important passage about light and darkness in his source materials occurs in Raphael Holinshed's *The Chronicles of England, Scotlande, and Ireland*, where we are told that after Donwald murdered King Duff, 'For the space of six moneths together, after this heinous murder thus committed, there appeered no sunne by day, nor moone by night in anie part of the realme, but still was the skie covered with continuall clouds, and sometimes suche contagious windes arose, with lightenings and tempests, that the people were in great feare of present destruction', and that 'Monstrous sights' were seen in Scotland that year, including the strangling of a sparrowhawk by an owl. As soon as the body of King Duff was exhumed, 'the aire began to cleare up, and the sunne broke foorth, shining more brighter than it had beene seene aforetime'.[15]

Some passages in II. iii and iv of *Macbeth* are clearly indebted to Holinshed. In II. iii, Lenox's account of the ominous events of the 'unruly' night of Duncan's murder illustrate the 'great destruction' and the 'outragious windes' described by Holinshed: 'Our chimneys were blown down. . . . some say, the earth was feverous and did quake' (ll. 56, 61, 62). The debt to Holinshed is greater in II. iv, where Ross's comment:

> Thou seest the heavens, as troubled with man's act,
> Threatens his bloody stage: by th' clock 'tis day,
> And yet dark night strangles the travelling lamp . . .
>
> (ll. 5–7)

elaborates Holinshed's statement, 'there appeered no sunne by day'. Ross's metaphorical description of the earth as man's 'bloody stage' may have been given additional force in performance by having Ross and the Old Man position themselves well to the rear of the Globe platform, where they would be shadowed by the stage cover. The sun, 'the travelling lamp', painted on the ceiling of the cover, would likewise be in shadow.

Holinshed's reference to an owl's having killed a sparrowhawk is significantly modified by Shakespeare in the Old Man's comment:

> On Tuesday last,
> A falcon, towering in her pride of place,
> Was by a mousing owl hawk'd at and kill'd.
>
> (II. iv. 11–13)

The falcon is a superior species to the sparrowhawk, and serves man when it 'towers' to reach its highest point in flight before swooping on the prey that he requires. Shakespeare's application of the denigrating term 'mousing' to the owl emphasizes its low status in the hierarchy of birds. Even more significant is the implication that the owl was seen to kill the falcon 'on Tuesday last': paradoxically, the bird of night operated in daylight – one of the 'good things of day' was brought low by a creature of darkness. A moral barrier seems to be broken: the supremacy of creatures of light is questioned. It is likewise significant that Ross's commentary on the moral import of the darkness of the morning hours culminates in a question which contrasts with Holinshed's certitude:

> Is't night's predominance, or the day's shame,
> That darkness does the face of earth entomb,
> When living light should kiss it?   (ll. 8–10)

The Old Man cannot decide whether the darkness is due to the powers of light or darkness; all he can say is that:

> 'Tis unnatural,
> Even like the deed that's done.   (ll. 8–9)

The issue is left ambiguous, its foulness or fairness unresolved.

What this survey reveals is that Shakespeare's treatment of light and darkness in *Macbeth* is most sustained and varied in the scenes which precede and follow the murders of Duncan and Banquo. Both murders take place at night. Both are heralded by tremendous invocations in which the personification of night is accompanied by references to creatures and spirits of ill omen, especially the owl. In both sequences, the onset of night is preceded by a moment of twilight whose charm contrasts potently with the violence that follows it. In both instances, Shakespeare makes a finely calculated use of the Elizabethan stage convention whereby torches indicate that night is close or has descended, and augments their effect by associating their light with ideals that are outraged by the murders. Closely associated with the latter is the feasting by night, which in both instances symbolizes the hospitality, loyalties and decencies violated by the killings. It is particularly significant that the murder of Banquo is given almost as much emphasis in terms of light and darkness as the murder of Duncan. Regicide was one of the worst of crimes by Elizabethan standards, and Shakespeare treats it as such. But he treats Banquo as much more than a nobleman. He is the predestined founder of a line of kings, of which the House of Stuart is the latest dynasty.

NOTES

1 Caroline F. E. Spurgeon, *Shakespeare's Imagery and What it Tells us* (Cambridge, 1935), 329.

2 W. A. Wright (ed.), *Roger Ascham: English Works* (Cambridge, 1904), 24.

3 Kenneth Muir (ed.), *Macbeth*, New Arden (London, 1955). Later citations are from this edition.

4 R. B. McKerrow (ed.), *The Works of Thomas Nashe*, rev. F. P. Wilson (Oxford, 1958) I, 361.

5 *Sixteen Plays of Shakespeare* (Boston, 1941), 893.

6 For discussion see J. C. Adams, *The Globe Playhouse* (New York, 1961), 376–8.

7 In Elizabethan and Jacobean masques it is a common practice for eminent personages to be accompanied by torch-bearers. Some of the earliest spectators of *Macbeth* would be well acquainted with this practice.

8 Quoted by Kenneth Muir, ed. cit., 65, from Philemon Holland (trs.), *Natural History* (1634), XII, 276.

9 Kittredge, 912.

10 See his edition of *Hamlet* (Cambridge, 1941), notes to I. i. 125 on p. 147.

11 A. C. Sprague, *Shakespeare and the Actors* (Cambridge, Mass., 1948), 270.

12 H. H. Furness, *A New Variorum Edition of Shakespeare: Macbeth* (New York, 1963) 303–4, n. 20, quoting from 'Dies Boreales', *Blackwood's Magazine* (November 1849), 643.

13 See Anthony Vaughan, *Born to Please: Hannah Pritchard, Actress, 1711–1768* (London, 1979), pl. 7.

14 A. C. Sprague, 269.

15 G. Bullough (ed.), *Narrative and Dramatic Sources of Shakespeare* (London, 1973), VII, 483–5.

5

THE POLITICS OF PAGEANTRY

SOCIAL IMPLICATIONS IN JACOBEAN LONDON

M. C. Bradbrook

The Roman reward for a conqueror, his Triumph, became the term of the London livery companies for the procession that on St Simon and St Jude's Day, 29 October, marked – as it still marks – the installation of the Lord Mayor. The themes for celebration were the greatness of the City and its history; the worthiness of the Lord Mayor's company; the praise and exhortation due to himself from his fellows. Reciprocity of gifts and favours was demonstrated by the Yeomen or Bachelors of the company in supplying the pageant its devices or accompanying speeches, whilst the Lord Mayor and Sheriffs provided the feast at Guildhall, which as early as 1575 cost £600.

The Mayor, chosen from among the governing élite of the Twelve Great Companies, was elected after a sermon had warned all of their duties. Next day the brethren of his livery waited to escort the Lord Mayor to Guildhall for installation, after which they embarked at the Three Cranes in the Vintry for the state voyage to Westminster, where he took his oath before the Barons of the Exchequer. Returning, he landed below St Paul's, where he was met by the full procession, including the pageant, ready in the yard of the Bell Inn. By way of St Paul's churchyard and Cheapside, all set forward for the Guildhall feast, returning for evening service at St Paul's, and ending with an escort and final speeches before the Lord Mayor's residence. Largess and loyalty combined in a ceremony half carnival, half consecration.

The route was cleared by fencers and 'wildmen' with fireworks; workmen were liberally paid to take down signs or even remove a shop; attendants who were maimed had to be compensated. The almsmen of the livery company paraded in new blue gowns, their schoolboys received breakfast and partook of the feast in return for their speeches; in addition to their pay, the porters who bore the pageant were liberally supplied with drink. The livery had new gowns, half the Bachelors being furred with marten (or 'foynes') and half with lambskin (or 'budge').

Sugar loaves, spices, or, in the case of the Fishmongers, live fish were thrown from the pageant 'ship' to the crowd. The senior company, the Mercers, allowed the fortunate girl who represented the Mercers' Maid, always carried in pageant by their Bachelors, to keep the rich garments and jewels she wore. She had presumably once represented the Virgin Mary. With the clamour of all the bells from London's fifty-seven churches, the royal trumpeters blowing, the gunners of the Tower shooting off their ordnance, the fireworks, the crowd's cheering and impromptu witticisms, any speeches made to the Lord Mayor must have been largely inaudible even to him. As the procession grew in stateliness, he was encountered at different points by different pageants which wheeled into position before him and joined the procession; in the late sixteenth and early seventeenth century, the dramatists from the public playhouses were used to supply the 'devices', which, although agreed with the livery company beforehand, were then printed by the author and offered to the liverymen. Thus definition crystallized the power of the City as it was celebrated; such a manifesto could define attitudes or even initiate policy.

The dramatic growth of London in late Elizabethan and Jacobean times led to increased splendour; and among the Twelve Great Companies, the Drapers, Haberdashers, Mercers, and above all, the very rich Merchant Taylors developed pageantry for the great expansion of the cloth trade, England's chief export. Seven-eighths of England's overseas trade went through the Port of London, of which three-quarters was in wool and cloth. Neptune as presiding deity rivalled Londinium herself. Since the leading citizens were now capitalists and merchant-venturers rather than craftsmen, it is noted in the records of the Merchant Taylors for 1602[1] that a mayor and a sheriff from their company both being merchants, the ship pageant is very properly used; in 1605, the present style of the company is noted as having being given by King Henry VII[2] since:

>   . . . they traded, as no men did more
> With forren Realmes by clothes and Merchandize,
> Returning hither other Countries store,
> Of what might best be our commodities.[3]

From the first quarter of the seventeenth century, three of the five Triumphs given for the Merchant Taylors have survived, which show a continuous development of political significance. These are Munday's, Dekker's and Webster's for 1605, 1612 and 1624.

A notice of this company as early as 1553, when Sir Thomas White, founder of St John's College, Oxford, was installed, includes a pageant of their patron saint, St John the Baptist.[4] The Lord Mayor was translated into the stream of mythology and the history of his own company: thus Sir Thomas was to be revived as a benefactor whose memory lived as late as 1624. Any Lord Mayor whose name would bear it was graced with emblematic devices; in 1568, such mighty figures as David, Arion and Amphion harped in the Triumph of Sir Thomas Harper; in 1561, Sir John Roe received a sermon from St John (written by Richard Mulcaster, High Master of the scholars) which was followed by a song, 'Behold the Roe so swift in chace, yet tarrieth still to hear . . .'. This equated him with the Lion and Camel of the company's arms, or the Holy Lamb of their crest, which was liable to turn into the Golden Fleece. Sir John Lemon's lemon tree might be stored for future pageants with these emblematic objects; any mayor with a name as pliable as Webb, Campbell or even Bennett might receive the sort of heraldic greeting that the town of Linlithgow once extended to King James VI, by the use of the Scottish coat of arms, the lion rampant:

> Thrice royal Sir, here I do you beseech,
> Who art a lion, to hear a lion's speech.
> A miracle, for since the days of Aesop,
> No lion till these times his voice dared raise up
> To such a Majesty; then, King of men,
> The King of beasts speaks to thee from his den;
> Who, though he now enclosed be in plaster,
> When he was free, was Lithgow's wise schoolmaster.[5]

A voice from the depths of a plaster lion was evidently a joke, but in late Elizabethan Triumphs the metamorphosis of the Lord Mayor was accompanied by something like the descent of a goddess. The frequent use of the metaphor that the Lord Mayor was married to the City not only echoed the royal image of the monarch being married to the kingdom – Elizabeth spoke of her coronation ring as her wedding-ring – it also implied that, like Peleus or Anchises, he had married an immortal.

Two of the Triumphs by George Peele survive in print from the sixteenth century; he succeeded his father, James Peele, clerk of Christ's Hospital, but was also a pageant writer for the Court and contributed to the cult of Elizabeth as Astraea.[6] In his pageant for Sir Wolstan Dixie in 1585, London is seated at the apex of the pageant, under the arms of her royal mistress, and surrounded by contributory trades and arts. In *Descensus Astraea*, 1591, he used Elizabeth's title, especially favoured by the lawyers; but in the City the goddess-shepherdess carried a sheep-hook, and further mercantile interpretation was given to the pastoral convention by a child who sat spinning at the rear of the pageant – the Lord Mayor being named Webb.

The last mayoral triumph of Elizabeth's reign was devised by Anthony Munday for the Merchant Taylors, with a speech for one of the boys from their school written by their Master. John Webster, father of the dramatist and a member of the company, was paid thirty shillings for the hire of the chariot that drew the children.[7]

Next year, the peaceful accession of James I relieved the suppressed anxieties of a decade. The grand entry for the monarch was still London's celebration, however; James himself was an unknown quantity, though greeted with high hopes as a Protestant monarch who could provide an heir apparent and seemed to guarantee peace by uniting the crowns of England and Scotland. The Lord Mayor became the greatest officer in England at the demise of the Crown, all royal offices being vacated until reconfirmed; he closed Ludgate until he received promise that the Lord Treasurer meant to proclaim the King of Scots. Cecil sent in his Garter insignia as pledge. James's entry had been planned for his Coronation, as had Elizabeth's in 1559; but it was postponed by plague and, when it took place on the Ides of March, 1604, it was, ominously, for the opening of his first Parliament.

Dekker, who took the leading part within the City group, mentions how everyone had joined in the work of measuring and building the seven great triumphal arches, from Fenchurch in the east, where James entered from the Tower, to Temple Bar in the west. 'Such a fire of love and joy was kindled in every brest' that even children would have helped;[8] the rivals Dekker and Jonson, who had just been engaged in theatrical war, combined with young Thomas Middleton, who wrote one speech for Zeal, and Mulcaster, now High Master of St Paul's School, who wrote another, recommending his scholars to James's charity and himself to favour. Jonson published his two contributions separately, adding a panegyric on the opening of Parliament which consisted largely of warnings and admonitions to the King.

All subsequent Triumphs were to derive from this grand entry, London's own exorcism of the gnawing fear of civil strife at a disputed succession, London's own relief, when, like an older medieval city, great and small combined for their pageantry. The livery companies who lined the route from Mark Lane to the conduit in Fleet Street were on this occasion part of the city audience and not on parade; all were unified as in one family. It was as if the disappearance of the Elizabethan legend had released for London a new sense of her own identity. Camden described London as the epitome of the kingdom and, in a speech where the Genius Loci was to have encountered St George and St Andrew on horseback, Dekker borrowed from the works of his fellow Shakespeare, who on this occasion was part of the procession, clad in his royal livery as one of the King's players. Dekker substituted London for Shakespeare's 'royal throne of kings':

> This little world of men; this precious Stone,
> That sets out *Europe* . . .
> This Jewell of the Land; Englands right Eye:
> Altar of Love; and Spheare of Majestie.[9]

This speech was discarded in favour of Jonson's at the great arch of Fenchurch, surmounted by a cut-out representation of the entire city. Dekker had shown London as a woman, traditionally; Jonson, more classically, made the Genius masculine, and the part was taken by Edward Alleyn, in dialogue with the Thames. Jonson's, too, was the final triumphal arch in the form of entrance to a temple; beyond, in the Strand, Westminster presented the tableau of a rainbow and the King was given a speech of apotheosis from the starry Pleiades. Within the City itself, Dekker's relatively unstructured Elizabethan lavishness was held together; at the conduit in Cheapside a device adapted from *Descensus Astraea* showed a miniature drama. Here Britannia-Arabia was transported from mourning to joy by the King's approach, various evil characters seated in the arch were destroyed, and a fountain suddenly ran with wine. The maximum number of spectators in the broad thoroughfare could enjoy this tranformation in Nova Felix Arabia.

Significantly however, the overt religious appeals to which Elizabeth at her coronation had responded with such dramatic skill – clasping the Bible presented to her to her breast – were here largely confined to the arch erected by the United Provinces of the Netherlands. Seventeen figures representing the states were presented by Dutch merchants, and they delivered exhortations about the purity of the reformed faith with the good example set by Elizabeth. The Italian merchants, though but few, expressed their loyalty in another arch, tactfully praising the King as philosopher and poet. The reformed faith was established; future problems were to be constitutional.

Only at the end did Dekker reveal that many of the speeches went unspoken: the King had asked for their omission. Many citizens must have known that James had most reluctantly consented to this entry, on the understanding that he would never be called upon to repeat it. Nowhere did he respond as Elizabeth had done, reciprocating the welcome; in a few months, Shakespeare was to put the royal disclaimer into the mouth of his wise Duke:

> I'll privily away. I love the people,
> But do not like to stage me to their eyes:
> Though it do well, I do not relish well
> Their loud applause and *Aves* vehement . . .[10]

Dekker declared that, as the King left the City, she was '(like an Actor on a Stage) stript out of her borrowed Maiestie' for the royal presence had made the 'Citie appeare great as a Kingdome'. But at a time when Parliament was itself less an institution than an occasional event, the regular, permanent city government really represented the country, especially in resisting royal encroachment, driving hard bargains in return for financial favours; it often appeared, indeed, that the Crown was more dependent on the City than the City on the Crown. Even at this time, one song caused some resentment and Dekker had to explain that 'Troynovant is now no more a city' did not really mean that London was giving up her privileges in becoming for the day a summer arbour, or an eagle's nest or a bridal chamber. It may have been that the boys of Mulcaster's school could lift only the words of the refrain audibly above the roar of the crowd and the din of bells.

Dekker had a fling at the learning of Ben Jonson about his male Genius of the City;[11] and in future London persisted in being depicted as a female, often crowned with towers, as she had been in the play that had been written by Robert Wilson for the Armada triumph of 1588, *The Three Lords and Three Ladies of London* (1588–90).

Anthony Munday, citizen and draper, remained the usual writer for the mayoral Triumphs, in spite of being caricatured by John Marston as Posthaste (in *Histrio-mastix*) and by Jonson as Antonio Balladino (in *The Case is Altered*). This 'Pageant Poet to the City of Millaine' asserts: 'I supply the place sir: when a worse cannot be had, sir!' He favours the use of traditional properties: 'I do use as much stale stuffe, though I say it my selfe, as any man does in that kind, I am sure.' His defence is that he keeps the 'old *Decorum*' and writes plainly for the common people, not to please the gentlemen.[12] The wickerwork City giants and the ship pageant were stale for Jonson, but scholarship was 'stale' for Dekker; the audience did not relish academic commonplaces. If, on a later occasion, Munday showed Robin Hood as son-in-law to Henry Fitz-Alwin, the first Lord Mayor, he joined the ancient figure of woodland freedom, defiance of the law, with an ancient emblem of civic power and legal authority; their conjunction is something better than mere ignorance.

Munday's device for the Merchant Taylor, Sir Leonard Halliday, in 1605 – *The Triumphes of re-united Britania* – gave a heroic role to James, but Elizabeth had already been hailed as 'beauteous Queen of Second Troy' and the City was much more firmly united than the tenuously unified kingdoms. Munday prefixed a summary of British history from the time of Noah, through the period of Albion and the giants, sons of Neptune – two giants drew Britannia's chariot – to civilization by the Trojan Brute, founder of Troynovant, who at one point was revived from his tomb, with his three sons.[13] Troynovant and Thames, with tributary rivers, sing paeans as the three sons deliver up their divided crowns. Britannia, with the three kingdoms attendant, sat on the Mount, the most prominent of the pageants; but that stale piece, the company's ship, renamed the Royal Exchange, distributed its cargo of spices among the crowd, for the Lord Mayor was to be in 1611 one of the founders of the East India Company and later its Treasurer. The customary eulogies bring Halliday among the immortals, with many quibbles on Halliday and holiday. Fame named all the royal members of the company from the past, and remarked that one place is yet unfilled. Neptune and his Queen, parents of the Giant Albion, in their epilogue from the backs of the Lion and the Camel, assuming their modern form, 'wish all good to Leonard Halliday'.

The name of Britannia had furnished the answer to the riddle Jonson had propounded to the Court in his Twelfth Night *Masque of Blackness*, which had brought the twelve Daughters of the Niger to James's revels; this may have carried some overtones of the wealth rolling up the Thames to the Port of London, in a less fanciful and exotic, a more mundane symbolism, than is commonly allowed.

The vacant place in the ranks of royal Merchant Taylors was filled in 1607 at their great feast by the election of the heir apparent, Prince Henry; and a lost Triumph by Munday of the year 1610 presented, for the Merchant Taylors, Merlin in the rock, which reproduced the theme of Prince Henry's Barriers of that same year, where the Prince appeared as an Arthurian knight, and both Merlin and King Arthur were represented.

The next Triumph for the Merchant Taylors, in 1612, was prepared with great care at a cost of £900; for as well as Prince Henry, the Elector Palatine, bridegroom of Princess Elizabeth, was to attend the feast inaugurating the year of Sir John Swinnerton – himself much interested in the press and the theatres.

By its very title, Dekker's *Troia-Nova Triumphans* asserted once more that 'the heap of our sovereign kingdoms are drawn in little and are to be found in this city', but Swinnerton received no less than three separate warnings of the hazards of office. If the problems of rulers had been set forth on the stage, the Lord Mayor was recognized to be as exposed as any prince by the position he filled. These warnings, it should be remembered, were agreed with the company; the dramatist was certainly not hazarding a personal opinion. The first warning came from Neptune, who rode in a sea-chariot with many smaller ships dancing round it, escorting the company's ship pageant, distributing wine. Virtue gave the second warning; attended by the Seven Liberal Arts (mothers of trades and professions) and escorted by armed representatives of the Twelve Great Companies, she alerts the Lord Mayor to Envy, who was inhabiting a 'forlorn castle' near to the Little Conduit in Cheapside. Envy's attack on Virtue is repelled by the bright shield the goddess raises, but on the return journey from Guildhall the attack is renewed, when Envy and her castle are destroyed by the twelve knightly companions discharging their pistols – hardly a knightly weapon. Finally Fame, from her House which enshrines the royal members of the company, dead and living, invites Swinnerton to join her band of immortals, but once more warns him of danger.

Identity is created by Fame; we are in truth what others make of us. Envy, the second of the Seven Deadly Sins, is secularized, and shown as poverty-stricken, lean and malignant. In 1604 the political resentment of the have-nots had been shown in religious terms as 'sedition, a friar' at the Fountain of Virtue – which, like the Castle of Envy, had been in Cheapside. London was the only city in Britain with an underworld, a criminal quarter where the Lord Mayor's power did not extend. Envy had been used by Jonson in *Every Man out of his Humour* (1600), witches had appeared to give this threat in *The Masque of Queens* (1609), and Envy reappeared as Prologue to his *Catiline* this same year, 1612. Henceforth, she often menaced Triumphs.

The risks of office were real enough; a week after taking his place, Sir Leonard Halliday had to deal with the situation arising from the Gunpowder Plot, and now, even as Swinnerton was greeted with the final song: '*Honor . . . / Waken with my Song . . . / So shall* Swinnerton *nere dye, / But his vertues upward flye . . . / He is living, living ever*',[14] the Prince of Wales was already very sick. On 6 November, just over a week later, he died; and with him were buried many of the City's hopes for a strong Protestant regime. The times were out of joint.

Although Dekker had praised the moderation of the Triumph – compared presumably with the cost of court masques – yet it ruined the poet, who for failing all the obligations he had incurred was cast into a debtor's prison, where he stayed for six years. Among other creditors, John Webster the elder claimed from Dekker £40 for chariots.

The next year's Triumph went to Thomas Middleton, who for

his namesake, Sir Thomas Myddelton, a grocer of strong Puritan convictions, devised the most expensive of all such events, *The Triumphs of Truth*, at a cost of £1300. Based even more firmly on the model of the Moral play, and directed personally to the Lord Mayor, it portrays the conflict of Error and Zeal. This highly religious Triumph was indeed to win support for Middleton, who succeeded the 60-year-old Munday as the regular purveyor; but little of it can have been audible to the bystanders, and it is unique in its address being to the Lord Mayor himself. On his first landing, Error appears accompanied by Envy 'eating of a human heart, mounted on a rhinoceros, attired in red silk, suitable to the bloodiness of her manners, her left pap bare, where a snake fastens . . .'. Truth, her opponent, is copied in the greatest detail from that Truth whom Jonson had depicted in the Barriers for the marriage of the Earl of Essex, prefixed to *Hymenaei* (1606). Truth's Angel and Zeal defend the Mayor; a ship, steered from afar by Truth, contains a baptized king of the Moors – a notable defeat for Error. Even before his embarkation, London had delivered a sermon to the Lord Mayor; now, placed on a Mount in Cheapside, she is from time to time by Error shrouded in mist. At the very threshold of the Lord Mayor's dwelling, Error is finally destroyed by fire darted from the head of Zeal.

This pageant, by one of the most strongly Puritan of the companies, was succeeded by two by Anthony Munday for the Drapers, which are concerned with the City's struggle against a particular menace. The Cockayne Project, launched in 1614 with royal support, endeavoured to ensure for England a monopoly of finishing the country's cloth before it was exported to the Low Countries. The King's Merchant Venturers, a new company, were given sole rights to export, the rights of the old Merchant Venturers in unfinished cloth being withdrawn. The result was disastrous. The Dutch promptly banned all imports of English cloth, finished or unfinished, and, as they controlled the carrying trade, which England had neither the ships nor the organization to take over, the country towns producing cloth for the London market, and the weaving and spinning areas, were faced with unemployment whilst the London merchants were ruined. After bankruptcies and riots on a wide scale, the King admitted defeat, the policy of the 'new Draperies' was rescinded and the Merchant Venturers regained their old privileges. *Himatia-Poleos. The*

Triumphs of olde Draperie, or the rich Cloathing of England (1614) presents several English wool-producing cities grouped round London; among the figures who repel adversaries are Councell and Discreet Zeale, defending Old Drapery herself, who sits on a high Mount supported by figures engaged in the industry. The next year, *Metropolis Coronata: The Triumphes of Ancient Drapery: or Rich Cloathing of England* celebrated the election of another member of the Drapers' Company as Lord Mayor, doubtless to meet the growing trade crisis. This was largely a water show (it was the exports that had been hit) and the main theme, Jason's search for the Golden Fleece; Neptune, Fame, Time and various Lord Mayors of olden days are travelling in a boat shaped like a whale. On land, the pageant ship is named for the Lord Mayor, the *Jewel*, 'appearing to bee lately returned, from trafficking Wool and Cloth with other remote Countries' (B2 v). London sits crowned and surrounded by the Twelve Great Companies, but the final song is entrusted to Robin Hood, that lawless provincial. One of the chief opponents of the Cockayne Project was the former Lord Mayor, Sir Thomas Myddelton, whose family spoke bitterly in Parliament against it. Eventually however, Cockayne was himself to become Lord Mayor.

In 1614, in the preface and dedication of his *Odyssey*, George Chapman had sneered at 'popular vapours' like the Lord Mayor's Show; but the game of 'vapours', as Ben Jonson that same year was to demonstrate in *Bartholomew Fair*, consisted in contradicting the last speakers. Here, the City defied the Crown.

Old Anthony Munday, who had been attacked by Middleton, although he had had some share in the Triumph of 1613, came back a last time for the Fishmongers' Triumph of 1615, showing how William Walworth, Lord Mayor, had suppressed revolt in the time of Richard II. This, too, was a topical gesture, for the unemployed weavers were beginning to riot. In the pageant of 1617, Middleton introduced a comic Spaniard, who spoke in Spanish, and two ugly Spanish women. This was the first note of an increasingly anti-Spanish mood that prevailed in the City, derived as much from trade rivalry as from religious zeal, and leading to new differences with the Crown.

In 1618, the execution of Sir Walter Ralegh, James's sacrifice to the Spaniards, was deliberately fixed for the day of the Lord Mayor's Triumph, so that popular interest might be distracted. In

1620, the Puritan company of the Haberdashers very surprisingly resurrected their patron saint, Catherine of Alexandria, while in 1623 the Drapers' Triumph for Sir Martin Lumley celebrated openly the City's rejoicing at the return of the Prince of Wales from Spain without the Spanish bride he had gone to woo. Their traditional canopy of three crowns and a cloud pierced by a sunbeam is interpreted as the mist of heresy pierced by a gospel ray:

> More to assure it to succeeding men,
> We have the crown of Britain's hope agen,
> Illustrious Charles our prince . . .[15]

Such was the popular rejoicing that Ben Jonson, who had written a court masque on the same theme, *Neptune's Triumph for the Return of Albion*, found that Spanish protests had prevented its performance.

This Lord Mayor's *The Triumphs of Integrity* implicitly criticized the Crown by complimenting Lumley on having risen from humble origins, as superior to those who:

> stand fix'd,
> As if 'twere competent virtue for whole life
> To be begot a lord; 'tis virtuous strife
> That makes the complete Christian . . .[16]

This was reinforced by the figures of Tamburlaine and Pertinax – who overthrew monarchs.

By 1624 unofficial hostilities against Spain had started, especially from the armed merchantmen of the Port of London. Middleton's audacious comedy, *A Game at Chess*, in August that year, drove him into hiding, but it is quite likely that the allegory against Spain was supported by highly placed persons at Court.[17] His temporary disappearance, however, gave the last Lord Mayor's Triumph of King James's reign to John Webster, the tragic poet, Merchant Taylor, who devised his *Monuments of Honour* for the installation of Sir John Gore (a relative of the Davenant family, stepfather to the actor Nicholas Tooley).[18] This Triumph introduces several motifs from recent celebrations, but adds also to the union of the living past with the present in a strong note of protest. Like his predecessors, Webster, in publishing his piece, which he proclaims is 'invented and written' by himself, associates with it 'the great care and alacrity of the right Worshipful the Master and Wardens' and their committees 'both for the curious and judging election of the Subject' and for providing the setting 'answerable to the Invention'. (Gerard Christmas, who for years had provided the carpentry and the sea Triumphs, was official painter to the Navy.)

The sea Triumph opens with the usual rhetorical enquiries from Thetis to Oceanus:

> *What brave Sea-Musicke bids us Welcome, harke!*
> *Sure this is* Venice, *and the day Saint* Marke
> *In which the* Duke *and Senats their course hold*
> *To wed our* Empire *with a Ring of Gold.*[19]

By this comparison with the Republic, London is invested with sovereign power. The second sea pageant presents a fair globe encircled by seven English navigators, including Drake, Frobisher, Hawkins and Humphrey Gilbert, for the London merchants were the heirs of the West Country privateers; by 1624 many merchants who had never been to sea were engaged in this profitable business. The company's venerable ship pageant brings, hanging in her shrouds, the Golden Fleece. Troynovant is seated in the Temple of Honour in Paul's Churchyard, attended by five other cities, including Venice; in the lower level of the Temple sit five eminent poets and scholars, all associated with London, and including Sir Thomas More and Sir Philip Sidney.[20] Troynovant presents the '*worthy men, / Who do eternize brave acts by their pen*':

> *These beyond death a fame to Monarckes give,*
> *And these make Cities and Societies live.*[21]

A knight in armour, wearing the company's colours, identifies himself as Sir John Hawkswood, who gained fame in the Italian wars, but who firmly proclaims his humble origin. He is followed by Queen Anne of Bohemia, consort of Richard II, riding alone. She had been admitted to the company; but her ensign would suggest to the crowd the contemporary Queen of Bohemia, their beloved Princess Elizabeth, symbol of the Protestant cause in Europe, and a centre in the City for anti-Spanish feeling, since the Spaniards had overrun her territory. Two knights of St John who had defended Malta and Rhodes against the Turk follow her.

The patron of the company was St John the Baptist, and Webster had carefully sought out connexions with the old Priory of St John in Clerkenwell, as well as finding Hawkswood. Repeating from last year's triumph that virtue may ennoble humble men, he used the company's motto, *Concordia parvae res crescunt*, recited in chorus by the English kings who were free of the Merchant Taylors, and who are now seated in the Chariot of Fame. These include King Richard III, previously omitted, but restored by Webster as 'a bad man but a good king'.[22] The resurrected figure of Sir Thomas White, in the Monument of Charity and Learning, revives a Lord Mayor who held his Triumph seventy-one years earlier. The Lord Mayor, holding office for one year only, could not be deified as the monarch was deified in the court masque, but he became part of a historical continuum, a succession; in the living union of past and present he acquired his immortality. Hence the 'monuments' – a word restricted to those erected for the dead – culminated in the Monument of Honour, the Mount, which always made the grandest display. If Sir Thomas represented historically, as the patron of learning, the Seven Liberal Arts, a rock of jewels represented the City's opposition to Spain. For on it, raised on a pedestal of pure gold, stood the figure of Henry, Prince of Wales, dead twelve years since – Henry, the Protestant champion, reincarnation of the chivalry of Sir Philip Sidney and steadfast opponent of the Spanish alliance proposed for himself. He had indeed been a member of the company; but the silent rebuke of this figure, especially when coupled with Anne of Bohemia, was emphasized when he was distinguished in the final speech to the Lord Mayor as:

> *Worthy Prince* Henry, fame's best president,
> Cald to a higher Court of Parliament . . .[23]

For City and Parliament were drawing together in opposition to the Crown. He is immortal; as dusk fell, the Prince of Wales's feathers on the four pyramids that marked Henry's earthly decease were lit up, and his jewels glowed. The poet who had written his funeral elegy, where 'Sorrow' masked in 'pleasure['s] garment'[24] was using the celebration both for mourning and for assertion of living values. *Non norunt haec monumenta mori* ('These monuments do not know how to die') appeared as motto on his title-page.

The way forward could be found in such tentative combinations of powerful images, for these did not involve the difficulty of putting new political statements into direct words. Tentative, uncommitted, they made their silent appeal to the common people and gave a united affirmation to ideas that as yet 'dodged conception' – the unfocused lines of those politics to be hammered out by lawyers and Parliament men in the coming decades. As early as 1604, the fragility of affirmations made in the Triumphs had been noted by Dekker: 'Behold how glorious a flower happiness is, and how fading. The minutes that lackey at the heels of Time run not faster than do our joys.' Webster echoed those sentiments in the verses he also offered in 1604 for the triumphal arches that marked James's entry.[25] Yet, he had added, by printing these devices, they had been given 'new life when they were dead'. So, too, were historic figures from the past.

Webster's own tragic structures, where he had renounced the classic Messenger and Chorus, were a precedent for his now renouncing the 'tediousness' of quoting classical precedents from Rome, which might weary the Lord Mayor and would assuredly 'puzzle the understanding of the Common people'. Dekker, not Jonson, provided him with a model.

Webster himself, in wishing prosperity to the Lord Mayor, ironically enough introduced another year of disaster. The plague broke out with greater virulence than at any time since 1603; the Lord Mayor's house was itself infected and for a time his deputy discharged his functions. This catastrophe coincided with the death in March 1625 of King James; Charles I was thus enabled to forgo any coronation entry. The citizens who had begun to erect triumphal arches took them down. The new monarch never entered Troynovant in state.

If he were not acting in Webster's pageant, a 16-year-old youth, now in the highest form at St Paul's, would certainly be marching. He was the future author of *The Tenure of Kings and Magistrates*, John Milton.

NOTES

1 *Malone Society Collections*, III, 58–9. A full list of all recorded and all surviving Triumphs is given here, xliv–xlvi.

2 Formerly they had been known as Taylors and Linen Armourers – providing padded harness for knights and their steeds. See following note.

3 A. Munday, *The Triumphes of re-united Britania*, C2r. Later in the stanza he writes: 'Henry the seventh . . . To Merchant Taylors did exchange their name'.

4 J. G. Nichols (ed.), *The Diary of Henry Machyn* (London, 1848), 47.

5 Quoted by D. Harris Willson in his *King James VI and I*, (London, 1956), 392–3.

6 See 'Queen Elizabeth as Astraea' in Frances A. Yates, *Astraea* (London and Boston, 1975), 29–87, for a full discussion of the political and imperial implications of this title.

7 *Malone Society Collections*, III, 60.

8 Fredson Bowers (ed.), *The Dramatic Works of Thomas Dekker*, II (Cambridge, 1955), 258.

9 Bowers, II, 256.

10 J. W. Lever (ed.), *Measure for Measure*, New Arden (London, 1965), I. i. 67–70.

11 'To make a false florish here with the borrowed weapons of all the old Maisters of the noble Science of Poesie . . . were to play the Executioner and lay our Cities household God on the rack . . . . Such feates of Activitie are stale, and common among Schollers before whome it is protested we come not now (in a Pageant) to Play a Maisters prize for *Nunc ego ventosæ Plebis suffragia venor*', Bowers, II, 254–5.

12 C. H. Herford, Percy and Evelyn M. Simpson (eds), *Ben Jonson*, III (Oxford, 1925), I. i. 29, 30–1, 48–50.

13 Compare the awakening of Bohun from his tomb in Robert Greene's *The Scottish History of James the Fourth*, ed. Norman Sanders (London, 1970), 4–10.

14 Bowers, III, 243–5, ll. 461, 495, 501–2, 506.

15 A. H. Bullen (ed.), *The Works of Thomas Middleton*, III (London, 1886), 387.

16 ibid.

17 See ch. 10 of Margot Heinemann's *Puritanism and Theatre* (Cambridge, 1980).

18 Information from Mary Edmond.

19 F. L. Lucas (ed.), *The Complete Works of John Webster*, III, (London, 1927), 318.

20 See M. C. Bradbrook, *John Webster, Citizen and Dramatist* (London, 1980), 180–2.

21 Lucas, III, 320.

22 See Bradbrook, 178, for similar sentiments elsewhere.

23 Lucas, III, 326–7.

24 Lucas, III, 279.

25 Lucas, III, 259.

6

THE ROLE OF LIVIA IN 'WOMEN BEWARE WOMEN'

Kenneth Muir

Since T. S. Eliot wrote on Middleton, critics have generally concurred with his opinion that *The Changeling*, though a work of collaboration, and despite the admission that 'it is long-winded and tiresome', was his greatest play. Eliot said nothing about the underplot, which everyone agrees is inferior to the Beatrice plot. As a whole, surely, *Women Beware Women* is the better play. Eliot's account of it concentrates on the decline and fall of Bianca, which can be compared with that of Beatrice; but he does not discuss the equally interesting fall of Isabella, and, more oddly, he omits all mention of the central character, Livia.

It is Livia who unites the two main plots, unites them so well that they cannot be discussed apart. It is she who provides the title of the play, for she brings about the ruin of Bianca in one plot and of Isabella in the other. Her motives are comparatively simple in one case and complex in the other. She hopes for advancement from the Duke by putting Bianca in his power. Yet even here there is a suggestion that she enjoys manipulating other people – an enjoyment symbolized by the game of chess – and of dragging them down to her level. She conveniently, if honestly, believes that she is doing Bianca a good turn, and that her initial unwillingness to be the Duke's mistress is caused by a foolish scruple that she will soon outgrow.

Her other success is to persuade Isabella to return Hippolito's love by pretending that they are not really related, her mother having been seduced by a Spanish nobleman. Here Livia's motives are disputed, and they are certainly complex and ambivalent. She is

corrupt herself and delights in corrupting others. Isabella, like
Bianca, is innocent at the beginning of the play. Like Iago, Livia
enjoys making other people her puppets. She has a sisterly fondness
for her brother and will do anything to promote his 'happiness';
but, beyond all this, she harbours a suppressed incestuous passion
for him, a passion which obtains a vicarious satisfaction from his
relationship with her niece.[1]

Livia's first reaction to Hippolito's confession is a conventional
one. To love one's kindred sexually is 'unkindly', that is, un-
natural. Moreover, to love within such a confined circle is wasteful:
the world is full of beautiful women, so why choose one's niece?

> So he Heaven's bounty seems to scorn and mock,
> That spares free means, and spends of his own stock.
>
> (II. i. 15–16)

After this moralizing, Livia suddenly changes course. The reason
she gives is her love for her brother:

> Nay, I love you so,
> That I shall venture much to keep a change from you
> So fearful as this grief will bring upon you –
> 'Faith, it even kills me, when I see you faint
> Under a reprehension –   (II. i. 18–22)

such as the reproof she has given him. But her next words suggest
that the very difficulty of obtaining Isabella's conversion is a
challenge to her powers of persuasion and to her ingenuity. 'It is
apparently impossible', she seems to be thinking, 'and therefore I'll
do it':

> 'tis but a hazarding
> Of grace and virtue, and I can bring forth
> As pleasant fruits as sensuality wishes
> In all her teeming longings. This I can do.   (II. i. 29–32)

She boasts in her next speech:

> Sir, I could give as shrewd a lift to chastity
> As any she that wears a tongue in Florence:
> Sh'ad need be a good horsewoman and sit fast
> Whom my strong argument could not fling at last.
>
> (II. i. 36–9)

In fact she is exaggerating her powers of persuasion. It is not by argument that she brings about the falls of Isabella and Bianca. Isabella is convinced by a lie; and Bianca is lured into a trap where she can be seduced, or raped, by the Duke.

She does not name the sin she is snaring Isabella to commit: she remarks that to name it would not be 'handsome'; and she sends Hippolito off, promising to 'minister all cordials' to him:

> a strange cure . . .
> As e'er was wrought on a disease so mortal
> And near akin to shame.   (II. i. 50–2)

The arrival of Isabella is announced by a servant who speaks of her significantly, if unrealistically, as the 'virtuous Isabella': but, just before her entrance, Livia reaffirms in soliloquy her original motive – love for Hippolito. This love is genuine enough. In the second scene of the play she has told him:

> My best and dearest brother, I could dwell here;
> There is not such another seat on earth
> Where all good parts better express themselves.   (I. ii. 146–8)

But she knows and admits, despite her frequent euphemisms, that what she is doing is evil. In this respect she is more clear-sighted than Middleton's other female sinners:

> Beshrew you, would I loved you not so well!
> I'll go to bed, and leave this deed undone;
> I am the fondest where I once affect,
> The carefull'st of their healths, and of their ease, forsooth,
> That I look still but slenderly to mine own.
> I take a course to pity him so much now,
> That I have none left for modesty and myself.
> This 'tis to grow so liberal – y'have few sisters
> That love their brother's ease 'bove their own honesties:
> But if you question my affections,
> That will be found my fault.   (II. i. 63–73)

There is no reason to doubt that she believes what she says. She has grown 'liberal' – tolerant and permissive – by her fondness for her brother. She is willing to sacrifice her moral standards, or at least the taboo against incest, for the sake of doing him a kindness. It is

possible to speak of her, as Margot Heinemann does, as 'the good-
natured Court procuress'.[2] But her character and motivation are
really more complex. In some ways she resembles the Marquise de
Merteuil in Laclos's great novel.

Livia's other success, the procuring of Bianca, is more straight-
forward. Here she has no moral scruples: she believes that to be a
Duke's mistress is obviously better than to be the wife of an
impoverished factor. Any regrets expressed by the girl, she ascribes
to the inexperience of youth:

> Are you so bitter? 'Tis but want of use;
> Her tender modesty is sea-sick a little,
> Being not accustomed to the breaking billow
> Of woman's wavering faith, blown with temptations.
> 'Tis but a qualm of honour, 'twill away;
> A little bitter for the time, but lasts not.
> Sin tastes at the first draught like wormwood water,
> But drunk again, 'tis nectar ever after.   (II. ii. 471–8)

Livia's own downfall, which, with uncharacteristic blindness,
she ascribes to ambition – 'My own ambition pulls me down to
ruin' – is due rather to her purchase of Leantio's favours and the
violence of her attachment to him, which makes her the enemy of
the brother she has loved. When Hippolito tries to explain that he
killed Leantio to avenge their family honour, Livia cries out the
truth of his relations with Isabella:

> The reason! that's a jest hell falls a-laughing at!
> Is there a reason found for the destruction
> Of our more lawful loves? and was there none
> To kill the black lust 'twixt thy niece and thee
> That has kept close so long?   (IV. ii. 63–7)

This revelation is the charge which explodes in the last act, for it
causes a whole chain of hatreds. Livia hates Hippolito for killing
her lover; Hippolito hates Livia for revealing his incestuous
relationship; Isabella hates Livia for causing her to commit incest;
Guardiano and his Ward hate both Isabella and Hippolito. The
reciprocal hatreds make them plot to destroy each other in the
masque designed to celebrate the Duke's wedding. Some of the
deaths are accidental. Guardiano falls into the trap he had prepared
for Hippolito, and the Duke is poisoned by the cup intended for the

Cardinal, his brother. But such accidents convey a sense of providential justice more effectively than deliberate killings:

> as if the plagues of sin
> Had been agreed to meet here altogether.   (v. ii. 156-7)

We need not greatly concern ourselves with the details of the masque. We know that Livia and Guardiano are plotting against Isabella and Hippolito for making the Ward a cuckold. Isabella is plotting against Livia. In the scene of feigned reconciliation in which they all agree to take part in the masque, Livia is to play her old part of Juno, the goddess of marriage; Isabella is to play the Nymph who offers sacrifice to appease her wrath. This does not quite fit the plot of the masque, in which Juno is not wrathful; but it applies, of course, to Livia's wrath and the sacrifice of Isabella she is planning. Livia remarks:

> Methinks 'twould show the more state in her deity
> To be incensed.   (IV. ii. 219-20)

By a nice quibble this looks forward to her death by the poisoned incense, and Isabella has an aside in which she proposes to 'teach a sinful bawd to play a goddess' (IV. ii. 221).

The poisoned incense could symbolize the corrupted atmosphere of treachery and lust which emanates from Livia; the shower of fire with which Livia kills Isabella could likewise symbolize the unwitting incest, and the witting adultery, committed by the victim. Juno in her first lines says that the affections of the three suitors:

> Seem all as dark to our illustrious brightness
> As night's inheritance, hell . . .   (v. ii. 103-4)

The cupids – Livia's pages – shoot Hippolito with their poisoned arrows, symbolizing his incestuous love. Guardiano, the pander, falls into the trap prepared for Hippolito, the accident presumably being due to his foolish ward.

It is given to Hippolito to point the moral:

> Lust and forgetfulness has been amongst us,
> And we are brought to nothing.
>
>   .   .   .
>
>   Leantio's death
> Has brought all this upon us – now I taste it –

And made us lay plots to confound each other:
The event so proves it; and man's understanding
Is riper at his fall than all his lifetime.
She, in a madness for her lover's death,
Revealed a fearful lust in our near bloods,
For which I am punished dreadfully and unlooked for;
Proved her own ruin too: vengeance met vengeance
Like a set match.

⋅ ⋅ ⋅

But how her fawning partner fell, I reach not,
Unless caught by some springe of his own setting –
For on my pain, he never dreamed of dying;
The plot was all his own, and he had cunning
Enough to save himself: but 'tis the property
Of guilty deeds to draw your wise men downward.
Therefore the wonder ceases.

(v. ii. 144–5, 147–56, 158–64)

Not every member of the audience is likely to follow every detail of this last scene, but everyone will obtain a general impression of what is happening. If one listens to the words one is told plainly that Isabella, as she confesses, has poisoned Livia; Isabella's death is explained by Hippolito; Hippolito knows he has been wounded by poisoned arrows; and Bianca confesses that the Duke has drunk the poison intended for the Cardinal. At the last production at Stratford-upon-Avon, however, the action was not made clear, largely because the director was anxious to draw a thematic parallel between the chess game of Act II and the masque of Act v.[3]

G. R. Hibbard has severely criticized Middleton for the way he kills off all his main characters without bothering about motivation;[4] and other critics have regarded Hippolito's sudden concern for family honour a mere theatrical device to precipitate the final catastrophe. This concern surprises, but it is not implausible. A more serious flaw is the motivation of the Cardinal, the spokesman for morality in the second half of the play. In the first scene of Act IV he warns the Duke that he will certainly be damned if he continues to keep a mistress:

> and fall into
> A torment that knows neither end nor bottom
> For beauty but the deepness of a skin . . .   (ll. 243–5)

The Duke, who has just incited Hippolito to kill Leantio, professes to be repentant and swears that he will never more keep a woman unlawfully. The Cardinal is delighted, not knowing that the Duke was proposing to have Leantio murdered so that he could marry Bianca. On his next appearance, the Cardinal tries to prevent the marriage because it was being used as a cloak for lust – 'lust's offerings . . . on wedlock's sacred altar'. The Duke protests that he has kept to the letter of his vow, and Bianca complains of the Cardinal's lack of charity. Middleton, I believe, was never the detached observer of Eliot's imagination, and a spokesman for orthodox morality is desirable at this point in the play. What is less satisfactory is that Middleton makes no attempt to explain how the Cardinal has become reconciled to the marriage he has passionately denounced; and he gives only a perfunctory explanation of Bianca's motives in attempting to murder him. But the Cardinal's presence in the last scene enables Middleton to dispose of the two principal sinners not involved in the masque; and, as the only important surviving character – and as almost the only virtuous cardinal in the whole of Jacobean drama – the Cardinal can pronounce with authority of the Church the final judgement on the characters of the play and on the destruction which has overtaken them:

> Sin, what thou art, these ruins show too piteously!
> Two kings on one throne cannot sit together
> But one must needs down, for his title's wrong:
> So where lust reigns, that prince cannot reign long.
>
> (V. ii. 220–3)

Livia is dangerous to other women for the reasons we have outlined. She is clear-sighted, she knows what she wants, and she is without scruples. Above all, she is a good psychologist and knows how to turn the weaknesses of others to good account. But it is important to recognise that her two chief victims, although they come to commit adultery and murder, are initially innocent. They are not, like Beatrice, moral morons.

Bianca, who elopes with Leantio, is prepared to accept a much lower standard of living than the one to which she is accustomed. She marries for love; and, if some difficulties of adjustment may be expected, her love is genuine and involves sacrifice of worldly standards. As she is almost as young as Juliet, she can hardly be expected to realize the defects of character hidden beneath Leantio's

handsome exterior. However much Leantio is enamoured of his
wife's beauty, there is something egotistical and possessive about
his love. The language he uses about her is all in terms of treasure
that he owns.[5] She is an invaluable purchase, a treasure, a beauty
able to content a conqueror, a noble theft; her beauty is her dowry,
her virtues are jewels locked up in cabinets. He urges his mother
not to teach her to rebel by suggesting that he is unable to support
her in the way to which she is accustomed. It would, of course, be
wrong to suggest that his love is not genuine, but the imagery
implies that he regards her as a possession which he is proud of
acquiring. Moreover, it suits his commercial occupation. Bianca's
own expression of love is less open to criticism. She tells her
mother-in-law:

> Kind mother, there is nothing can be wanting
> To her that does enjoy all her desires.
> Heaven send a quiet peace with this man's love,
> And I am as rich, as virtue can be poor . . .   (1. i. 125–8)

At the end of the scene Leantio decides to ask his mother to ensure
that his jewel is not seen by others when he is away on business:

>   O fair-eyed Florence!
> Didst thou but know what a most matchless jewel
> Thou now art mistress of—
>
>   .   .   .
>
>   But 'tis great policy
> To keep choice treasures in obscurest places:
> Should we show thieves our wealth, 'twould make 'em
>   bolder.
>
>   .   .   .
>
> The jewel is cased up from all men's eyes:
> Who could imagine now a gem were kept,
> Of that great value, under this plain roof?
>   (1. i. 161–3, 165–8, 170–2)

In the next scene in which Leantio appears, he is torn between
feelings of uxoriousness and his business. Game in a new-married
couple, he says, spoils all thrift. Bianca begs him to stay for one
more night, and he reads her a lesson:

> love that's wanton must be ruled awhile
> By that that's careful, or all goes to ruin.
> As fitting is a government in love
> As in a kingdom; where 'tis all mere lust
> 'Tis like an insurrection in the people
> That, raised in self-will, wars against all reason:
> But love that is respective for increase
> Is like a good king, that keeps all in peace.   (I. iii. 41–8)

We can see here the beginnings of a clash between bourgeois principles and the claims of love.

When the Duke's messenger arrives, Bianca is commanded to hide: she is 'a gem no stranger's eye must see'; but when she insists on going to the banquet, Leantio declares that wedlock is 'the ripe time of man's misery' and he applies the jewel imagery to celibacy:

> What a peace
> Has he that never marries! if he knew
> The benefit he enjoyed, or had the fortune
> To come and speak with me, he should know then
> The infinite wealth he had, and discern rightly
> The greatness of his treasure by my loss.   (III. i. 280–5)

At the banquet he speaks of himself as 'the poor thief that stole the treasure' and he imagines he is being punished for the pain he has caused Bianca's relatives. He is very conscious of the fact that he is her social inferior.

The chess scene is one of Middleton's greatest triumphs, not least because the class difference between Livia and Leantio's mother is brilliantly suggested. They are neighbours and the old woman is invited, out of charity, to Sunday dinner and Thursday supper. Lamb regarded the scene as a faithful transcript from life. Livia, he said, 'is as real a creature as one of Chaucer's characters. She is such another jolly housewife as the Wife of Bath.' This remark shows how 'Specimens' can be misleading. Livia is pretending to be more neighbourly than she really is, and, unlike the Wife of Bath, she is a wealthy aristocrat. The class difference between the two women is brought out by the deference paid by the mother to her hostess. Bianca, after her seduction by the Duke, contrasts the poverty of Leantio's home with the standard of living she had formerly enjoyed: she regards as necessities what her mother-in-law regards as unobtainable luxuries. Later in the play the Duke knows that Hippolito will be horrified at the news that Livia is having an affair with a mere factor; and Leantio behaves with vulgar ostentation as a middle-aged woman's gigolo.

Bianca is trapped by Livia and Guardiano, and she puts up more than a token resistance to the Duke. We should remember that she still loves her husband at this point in the play and her first exclamation when she encounters the Duke is: 'Oh treachery to honour!' (II.ii.321). She struggles in his grasp, and her struggles merely increase his lust. She tells him that, if adultery is not a sin, 'there's no religion' (l. 349). She calls 'for strength to virtue' (l. 359). The Duke makes it clear that, whatever she does, she is not going to escape him. He prefers 'A passionate pleading 'bove an easy yielding' (l. 361). But he warns her that he:

> never pitied any: they deserve none
> That will not pity me. I can command:
> Think upon that.   (II.ii.362–4)

He speaks, finally, of the advantages of being loved by him: freedom from poverty, vain regrets that she has married a man who cannot give her the luxuries her beauty deserves, and 'glory' which he urges her to seize. Bianca doesn't reply and we can assume that she has been cowed into submission more than tempted by what the Duke offers. After her seduction she curses the two who engineered it. Guardiano congratulates himself on his achievement:

> Never were finer snares for women's honesties
> Than are devised in these days . . .   (II.ii.398–9)

but Bianca tells him:

> sin and I'm acquainted,
> No couple greater; and I'm like that great one
> Who, making politic use of a base villain,
> 'He likes the treason well, but hates the traitor';
> So I hate thee, slave.   (II.ii.441–5)

Her quotation from Machiavelli reveals her ambivalent attitude to her adultery and it is a prelude to her moral deterioration in the rest of the play. But Eliot, I believe, is wrong to state that her fall is due to vanity. It is due rather to the temptation of wealth, made the more powerful by the contrast between the life-style of her family and that of Leantio, and also to a realization that her adultery, however unwilling, cannot be undone.

The deterioration is apparent already in Act III. Her continual complaints to her mother-in-law contrast with her contentedness in the first scene of the play; her refusal of a kiss from Leantio contrasts with her former demand for kisses; and the apparent absence of moral qualms in her insistence on going to the banquet are indications that she hopes now for the things the Duke has promised her. In the banquet scene, she makes disparaging remarks about marriage and cuckolds, knowing that Leantio will overhear. In Act IV she and Leantio have a sordid slanging-match, and immediately afterwards she acquiesces in his murder. She cannot forgive the Cardinal's condemnation of her adultery and plots to have him poisoned. The innocent girl has developed into a ruthless killer.

She does not entirely forfeit the sympathy of the audience. Her relationship with the Duke, after her unwilling seduction, has changed from acquiescence to ambition, and, as the final scene shows, to love. She is given no conventional speeches of repentance, although she feels she is being justly punished for her adultery. She kisses the lips of the dead Duke in the hope of absorbing some of the poison. Some of it, indeed, burns her lips and face, and, as she says, 'A blemished face best fits a leprous soul' (v. ii. 203). This line, as Roma Gill suggests, reminds the audience of Bianca's first reactions after her seduction:[6]

> Yet since mine honour's leprous, why should I
> Preserve that fair that caused the leprosy?
> Come, poison all at once!   (II. ii. 425–7)

As she dies, she is completely isolated; the mistress, even the wife, of a dead duke, who is a self-confessed murderess, has no tolerable future:

> What make I here? these are all strangers to me,
> Not known but by their malice, now th'art gone,
> Nor do I seek their pities.   (v. ii. 204–6)

Middleton makes her remind us that the original fall was involuntary, and remind us too of the title of the play:

> Oh the deadly snares
> That women set for women – without pity
> Either to soul or honour! Learn by me
> To know your foes. In this belief I die:
> Like our own sex, we have no enemy.   (v. ii. 209–13)

She tastes the same death as the Duke in a cup of love, and the hated
Cardinal is left to rule Florence.

Livia's other victim, Isabella, is depicted with still more initial
sympathy. She has been created merely to be 'a saleable product'.[7]
She is about to be married, against her wishes, to the Ward. Her
father is sacrificing his daughter's happiness for sordid mercenary
reasons, so that Livia is moved to protest:

> I . . . call't injustice
> To force her love to one she never saw.
> Maids should both see and like . . .   (i. ii. 30–2)

The Ward, moreover, is half-witted, coarse and vulgar, and
Middleton plainly agrees with Isabella's plaint:

> Marry a fool!
> Can there be greater misery to a woman
> That means to keep her days true to her husband,
> And know no other man, so virtue wills it!
> Why, how can I obey and honour him,
> But I must needs commit idolatry?
> A fool is but the image of a man,
> And that but ill made neither.   (i. ii. 161–8)

Contrasted with this obvious misalliance is the marriage of true
minds exemplified in the close friendship of Isabella and Hippolito.
This is vouched for by Isabella's father and the Ward's uncle:

> Those two are nev'r asunder; they've been heard
> In argument at midnight, moonshine nights
> Are noondays with them; they walk out their sleeps –
> Or rather at those hours appear like those
> That walk in 'em . . .   (i. ii. 63–7)

When they approach, Guardiano, the disreputable pander, exclaims:

> Oh affinity,
> What piece of excellent workmanship art thou?

> 'Tis work clean wrought, for there's no lust, but love in't,
> And that abundantly . . .   (I. ii. 69–72)

Of course, the lines prove to be ironical, although Isabella is not aware of the sexual element in her friendship with her uncle.

When Hippolito involuntarily confesses his love, Isabella is at first too innocent to understand his meaning and, when she does understand, she is horrified:

> Farewell all friendly solaces and discourses;
> I'll learn to live without ye, for your dangers
> Are greater than your comforts. What's become
> Of truth in love, if such we cannot trust.
> When blood that should be love is mixed with lust!
>
>   (I. ii. 225–9)

When Livia purports to prove that she is not related to Hippolito, Isabella immediately proposes to take him as a lover and to conceal their relationship by marrying the Ward. This is the beginning of her moral deterioration, although Holmes is surely wrong to suggest that 'The word "love" is used mockingly throughout the play', that Hippolito is satirized, and that Isabella has only been posing as a platonic lover.[8] When Livia reveals the truth, Isabella's farewell to Hippolito reveals not merely how far she has been corrupted, but also the distinction she makes between the shame and horror of incest, and what she still feels is a comparatively innocent adultery:

> 'Tis time we parted, sir, and left the sight
> Of one another; nothing can be worse
> To hurt repentance – for our very eyes
> Are far more poisonous to religion
> Than basilisks to them. If any goodness
> Rest in you, hope of comforts, fear of judgements,
> My request is, I nev'r may see you more;
> And so I turn me from you everlastingly,
> So is my hope to miss you.   (IV. ii. 133–41)

As Eliot says, 'in flashes and when the dramatic need comes', Middleton is 'a great poet, a great master of versification'.

In a less corrupt society, and in one less dominated by greed, both Bianca and Isabella might have led happy and virtuous lives;

and one cannot say of them, as Eliot said of Beatrice, that they 'become moral only by becoming damned'. Although they both become involved in mortal sin through 'the stamp of one defect', the instrument of their ruin is Livia. Middleton intends us to pity them.

NOTES

1 The point is made by Roma Gill, among others, in her New Mermaids' edition (1968), xxiii. Later citation is from this edition.

2 Margot Heinemann, *Puritanism and Theatre* (Cambridge, 1980), 183.

3 The best account of the masque is in Inga-Stina Ewbank's essay, '"These pretty devices": a Study of Masques in Plays', *A Book of Masques* (Cambridge, 1967), 405–48.

4 'The Tragedies of Thomas Middleton and the Decadence of the Drama', *Renaissance and Modern Studies*, i (1957), 35–64. Hibbard argues that Middleton was inhibited by three things: the idea that a tragedy should end in a blood-bath, that it should be overtly moral, and that it should contain comic relief. As a result, the naturalistic, psychological drama of the first three acts turns into a melodramatic revenge play, with Middleton doing violence to his characters; and the overtly religious speeches of the Cardinal are 'alien to the whole tone and significance of the earlier part of the play . . . . What begins as something that might not be unfittingly described as seventeenth-century Ibsen, ends as a kind of mongrel, the illegitimate offspring of an incongruous union between *The Revenger's Tragedy* and *A Warning for Fair Women*' (pp. 53, 54). I doubt whether the audience's expectations were quite as Hibbard suggests and, in any case, I do not think Middleton was inhibited by them, or that he suffered from a failure of nerve.

5 See C. B. Ricks's article, 'Word-Play in *Women Beware Women*', *RES*, n.s. 12 (1961), 238–50.

6 ed. cit., 111.

7 Hibbard, 46.

8 David M. Holmes, *The Art of Thomas Middleton* (Oxford, 1970), 165, 166.

7

THE RESTORATION

AGE OF FAITH, AGE OF SATIRE

Earl Miner

> Satire is a poem of a difficult nature in itself, and is not written to vulgar readers.   Dryden, *Discourse Concerning Satire*

> Now faith is the substance of things hoped for, the evidence of things not seen.   Hebrews 11:1

Although there is no immediate danger of unanimity of opinion on the subject of satire, it does seem arguable that there are large agreements among those who deal with this subject, and that the state of the art is probably in advance of that of lyric. There must be significance in the fact that American classicists turned directly to satire when they wished to show that they, too, were literary critics with the analytic skills of the vernacular critics.[1] But the real proof has come in a series of excellent books that have appeared in a period of about two decades.[2] The many studies that might be named have given us understanding of the origins of satire, of the satirist's world and method, of the literary resources drawn on, of recurrent elements, of the psychology of the satiric writer and reader, and of the values entwined in this most curious art. In what follows, I shall try to assess one of the periods of satiric writing, the Restoration, in terms that will probably do less to add to advance what is known than to subtract what I think are some errors.

Both satire and the Restoration seem to require greater attention than has been given to what people were writing about satire in the seventeenth century, and to the relationship of satire to other literary activities. Four propositions emerge from various pronouncements, and since a little anthology of relevant passages will follow, the four concepts may be set down here.

1 Satire is a kind of narrative.
2 Satire is one of a complex of interrelated kinds, others of which it often enters or exploits.
3 Satire has a range of rhetorical and cognitive features that govern its nature as knowledge and moral judgment.
4 Satire has social and political implications.

Other propositions (such as the danger of satire to satirist and satirized) could be set forth also, but the four isolated deal with more interesting and problematic matters.

The passages to be considered are not arcane, but they acquire a fresh meaning when they are brought together. The first comes from Hobbes's 'Answer' to Davenant's *Preface to Gondibert*: the setting is that of discussion of the nature of heroic poetry and the special social contributions made by poets rather than by the many other kinds of people discussed by Davenant. The date is 1650. Hobbes begins his second paragraph by comparing the division of the 'Universe' of scientists ('Philosophers') 'into three Regions, *Celestiall*, *Aëriall*, and *Terrestiall*' to:

> Poets (whose worke it is, by imitating humane life in delightful and measur'd lines, to avert men from vice and incline them to vertuous and honorable actions) have lodg'd themselves in the three Regions of mankinde, *Court*, *City*, and *Country*, correspondent in some proportion to those three Regions of the World [distinguished by scientists] . . . .
>
> From hence have proceeded three sorts of Poesy, *Heroique*, *Scommatique*, and *Pastorall*. Every one of these is distinguished again in the manner of *Representation*, which sometimes is *Narrative* . . . and sometimes *Dramatique* . . . . There is therefore neither more nor less than six sorts of Poesy [later dismissing lyrics and other shorter pieces as 'but Essayes and parts of an entire Poem']. For the Heroique Poem narrative, such as is yours, is called an *Epique Poem*. The Heroique Poem Dramatique is *Tragedy*. The Scommatique Narrative is *Satyre*, Dramatique is *Comedy*. The Pastorall narrative is called simply *Pastorall*, anciently *Bucolique*; the same dramatique, *Pastorall Comedy*.[3]

Poetry is treated as a human science, or kind of knowledge,

comparable to that of the philosophers of nature. A hierarchy in society corresponds to a scientific topography. Satire is the narrative version of the middle sphere, the city. As a treatment of that sphere it is most nearly allied to comedy. As narrative in procedure, it is more nearly allied with the epic and pastoral. We need not agree with Hobbes, but it is important that we recognize the very great claims for poets (the context is Davenant's preface) and the particular placement of satire.

The next quotation cannot be dated certainly, since it is derived from Butler's notebooks, and like everything else from him requires intellectual ten-foot poling. According to the author of *Hudibras*, satire is 'a kinde of Knight Errant that goe's upon Adventures, to Relieve the Distressed Damsel Virtue, and Redeeme Honor out of Inchanted Castles, And opprest Truth, and Reason out of the Captivity of Gyants and Magitians'.[4] Butler no more believed in his Gyants than we do. But the proper context is *Hudibras*, a narrative poem (however steadily the narrative is diverted and spoilt), and the metaphor of the passage is derived from romance, more particularly from Cervantes. Yes, the end of satire is to assist virtue, honor, truth, and reason. This is far more important business for Butler than anything scientific or philosophical, as many poems and prose passages show. At the same time, the tone of the passage shows that any hope of success is (as Hobbes might have put it) wholly '*Romantique*'.

The next critic is Dryden, from whom much might be culled. One of the points he makes most strongly is the Hobbesian one of the relation between kinds of poetry. But where Hobbes gives the impression of anatomizing literature into six parts, no more or fewer, Dryden seems to conceive of a kind of participation by the kinds with each other. The place to begin is surely a passage from the 'Account' he prefixed to *Annus Mirabilis* in 1667:

Such descriptions or images . . . are, as I have said, the adequate delight of heroic poesy; for they beget admiration, which is its proper object; as the images of the burlesque, which is contrary to this, by the same reason beget laughter: for the one shows nature beautified, as in the picture of a fair woman, which we all admire; the other shows her deformed, as in that of a lazar, or of a fool with distorted face and antic gestures, at which we cannot forbear to laugh, because it is a deviation from nature. But though the same images serve equally for the epic poesy, and for the historic [such as *Annus Mirabilis*] and panegyric, which are branches of it, yet a several sort of sculpture is to be used in them.[5]

The examples of the beautiful woman and the deficient or ridiculous derive from Sidney's *Apology*.[6] The concern to classify everything possible in relation to heroic is Dryden's own and, if anything, grows stronger with time. Talk of the burlesque could only have meant one thing in 1667, *Hudibras*. The passage must also be understood in the context of the poem before which it appears, a poem heroic, historical and panegyric by turns. Dryden was not to be a satirist for over a decade more, so we shall have to attend to later remarks before fitting satire wholly into his scheme.

We may respect history the more by following its order, however, and so the later Dryden will have to wait. From about 1670 to about 1680, the concern best voiced involves the rhetorical techniques of satire and their relation to truth. An anonymous tract appeared in 1673, *Raillerie à la Mode Consider'd: or the Supercilious Detractor*, a witty satiric sally against wit and satire:

> One may observe a Sort of Natural Rhetorick, even among the *Common* Professors of the Art of Railing; they have their Figures, Graces, and Ornaments peculiar to their Kind of Speech, though they do not distinguish or use them Grammatically, by the Names of *Sarcasmus, Asteismus, Micterismus, Antiphrasis, Charientismus*, or *Ironia*, yet they have their Dry *Bobs*, their Broad *Flouts*, Bitter *Taunts*, their Fleering *Frumps*, and Privy *Nips* . . . accusing others by justifying themselves.[7]

The basic distinction is the one dear to the century, between a rhetoric natural and a rhetoric artistic. But it is one without a difference here, since the highfalutin 'grammatical' terms are taken from Puttenham's *Arte of English Poesie* (1589; III:xviii), as are also the lively English terms, which were devised by Puttenham, with a few slight modifications. Art and nature are at one in the rhetoric of satire.

One of the remarkable moments in Restoration literature is that of Rochester's last days, after which Gilbert Burnet published an account of Rochester's contrition and repentance – with certain reservations. Burnet records that Rochester 'often defended' satire 'by saying that there were some people that could not be kept in Order, or admonished but in this way'. Burnet shared the common fear that a satirist might be carried away into malice that would harm innocent people:

> To this he answered, A man could not write with life, unless he were heated by Revenge: For to make a *Satyre* without Resentments, upon the cold Notions of *Phylosophy*, was as if a man would in cold blood, cut mens throats who had never offended him: And he said, The lyes in these Libels come often in as Ornaments that could not be spared without spoiling the beauty of the *Poem*.[8]

Marvell said at one time that Rochester was the best satirist in English. If so, it may have had something to do with animation by 'Resentments' and a willingness to part from truth to gain effective 'Ornaments'. The truth issue will come up again. Once more, however, the centrality of rhetoric is affirmed.

By no means the brightest wit of his age, Mulgrave yet had his say on satire in his *Essay upon Poetry*. His concern lies with the moral effect, the problems of language and rhetoric, and the place of truth:

> Of all the ways that Wisest Men could find
> To mend the Age, and mortify Mankind,
> *Satyr* well writ has most successful prov'd,
> And cures because the remedy is lov'd. . . .
> Of well-chose words some take not care enough,
> And think they may be, as the Subject, rough.
> This great work must be more exactly made,
> And sharpest thoughts in smoothest words convey'd:
> Some think if sharp enough, they cannot fail,
> As if their only business was to rail;
> But 'tis mens *Foibles* nicely to unfold,
> Which makes a Satyr different from a Scold.
> Rage you must hide, and prejudice lay down:
> A Satyr's Smile is sharper than his Frown.
> So while you seem to scorn some Rival Youth,
> Malice it self may pass sometimes for Truth.[9]

The muddle in Mulgrave's mind needs no special pointing out, but he does at least raise some questions about satire's best rhetoric or language, its psychology, and its passing of 'Malice' for 'Truth' (in a love situation, it seems).

That was 1692. In 1693, Dryden published his *Satires*, including Juvenal done by himself and others, Persius done by him, and an immensely long and rambling epistle dedicatory to Dorset. This huge, overstocked warehouse of a preface (Watson, II, 72–155) begins with flattery of Dorset so excessive that, if we can see the fact plain, we must assume that neither its author nor recipient were deceived: in plain English it establishes Dorset as a noble lord to whom Dryden owed favors, and Dryden himself as a poet-critic. The next wares we come upon are those of the epic. It is only thereafter that we observe, as it were among all the heaps, the three kinds of label that enable us to sort out matters satiric. Two kinds enable Dryden to make his distinctions: historicism and comparison. The critic discriminates by a differentiating historicism, as when he says, although not by way of conclusion, 'thus I have given the history of satire' (Watson, II, 142), but much more often by relating especially the satire of Horace and Juvenal to the ages in which they lived. Comparison leads Dryden to group and discriminate Persius, Horace and Juvenal; Homer and Virgil; Cowley, Milton and Spenser; as well as other pairs and groups. The last category involves Dryden's ideas about how to write modern satire.

Dryden postulates, not altogether perspicuously, certain features that modern satirists should seek out. The most famous passage concerns 'fine raillery', 'to make a malefactor die sweetly', after the manner of his characterization of Zimri in *Absalom and Achitophel*:

> 'tis not bloody, but 'tis ridiculous enough. And he for whom it was intended was too witty to resent it as an injury. . . . I avoided the mention of great crimes [Buckingham had lived in double adultery and killed the husband of his mistress], and applied myself to the representing of blindsides, and little extravagancies. . . . It succeeded as I wished; the jest went round, and he was laughed at in his turn who began the frolic.   (Watson, II, 137)

So he says. Buckingham's six lines 'To Dryden' give a different view:

> As witches images of man invent
> To torture those they're bid to represent,

And as that true live substance does decay
Whilst that slight idol melts in flames away,
Such and no lesser witchcraft wounds my name,
So thy ill-made resemblance wastes my fame.[10]

As Lord says, this well illustrates Elliott's point about the origins and 'power of satire' (see n. 2). Dying sweetly under the axe of Jack Ketch or with the rapier of John Dryden is still death, and this 'fine raillery' may perhaps be a mask worn with the same motive that animated Persius to be obscure, 'the fear of his safety' (Watson, II, 118).

Dryden's other precepts are more general. Satire should have 'unity of design': 'The poet is bound . . . to give his reader some one precept of moral virtue, and to caution him against some one particular vice or folly' (Watson, II, 145, 146). This may be one kind, perhaps the best kind, of satire. Clearly it constitutes a reason why Dryden prefers Juvenal's 'tragical satire' to Horace's 'comical' (ibid., 140). As this shows, we share the great defect of most of our accounts of satire with Dryden, although the terms may be different: we postulate Juvenal as the norm and scarcely know what to do with Horace, unless it be to dismiss him as 'comical'.[11] To the extent that satire is to be considered a kind of narrative, Horace's slight plots provide extended situations with diverse elements unlike Juvenal's unity by subject and absence of anything like as much plot development. Yet Dryden's stated preference appears to describe not *Hudibras*, *Mac Flecknoe*, or the 'painter poems' by Marvell (perhaps) and others, but the satires of Rochester and his own poem, *The Medall*. No one would read *Mac Flecknoe*, *Absalom and Achitophel*, or *The Hind and the Panther* as well developed plots; nor would one so read Horace on being detained by a bore in the Via Sacra (I. ix – the great favorite of the century from Donne to Marvell and Oldham). But such poems do have some manner of plot, of a kind we associate with Horatian mini-plots more readily than we do the powerful invective of Juvenal.[12] In this respect, Dryden's practice belies his precept, as in fact did most of the satire of the age, from Butler forth.

Dryden posits another feature for modern satire that relates it to his own practice far more closely. He prefers 'the English heroic' prosody rather than Hudibrastics as the verse medium (Watson, II, 147) and extols those schemes of syntactic and cognitive

repetition that he calls 'turns': 'Had I time, I could enlarge on the
beautiful turns of words and thoughts; which are as requisite in this
[satire], as in heroic poetry itself, of which the satire is undoubtedly
a species.'[13] This pronouncement takes us back to Davenant and
Hobbes, with whom this catalogue of the satiric ships began, or to
Dryden's remarks prefatory to *Annus Mirabilis*. That is, Dryden
postulates not the way satire must be in order to be satire, but the
way he and his contemporaries wished the best satire to be:
elevated, heroic. The remark also takes us to Dryden's most
theoretical discussion of the nature of literature and, within it, of
the kinds he practiced.

Two years after putting together his warehouse, Dryden undertook the different task of writing *A Parallel Betwixt Poetry and
Painting* (1695), most of which need not concern us. But in one
section of it he turned his thoughts to the crucial fourth chapter of
Aristotle's *Poetics*, correcting his master and giving a final summary
of his views of the relations between the kinds of literature, the
rhetorical scope they possess, and the terms on which they achieve
morality and knowledge:

> The imitation of nature is therefore justly constituted as the
> general, and indeed the only, rule of pleasing, both in poetry and
> painting. Aristotle tells us that imitation pleases, because it
> affords matter for a reasoner to inquire into the truth or false-
> hood of imitation, by comparing its likeness, or unlikeness, with
> the original. But by this rule, every speculation in nature whose
> truth falls under the inquiry of a philosopher [scientist], must
> produce the same delight, which is not true. I should rather
> assign another reason. Truth is the object of our understanding,
> as good is of our will; and the understanding can no more be
> delighted with a lie than the will can choose an apparent [glaring]
> evil.[14] As truth is the end of all our speculations, so the discovery
> of it is the pleasure of them; and since a true knowledge of nature
> gives us pleasure, a lively imitation of it, either in poetry or
> painting, must of necessity produce a much greater. For both
> these arts, as I said before, are not only true imitations of nature,
> but of the best nature, of that which is wrought up to a nobler
> pitch.   (Watson, II, 193–4)

This is obviously a normative rather than a purely descriptive
statement: 'true . . . the best nature . . . a nobler pitch'. Within such

terms, and given the presumptions of mimesis, Dryden's argument stands. A little later he deals clearly and momentously with a number of matters that hitherto we have seen but darkly and by the way:

> In the character of an hero, as well as in an inferior figure, there is a better or worse likeness to be taken: the better is a panegyric, if it be not false, and the worse is a libel [satire, the obverse of panegyric]. Sophocles, says Aristotle, always drew men as they ought to be, that is, better than they were; another whose name I have forgotten, drew them worse than naturally they were. Euripides altered nothing in the character, but made them such as they were represented by history, epic poetry, or tradition.[15]

Like tragedy, satire or panegyric may be true even if the poet alters something 'in the character', taking a better or worse likeness within the bounds of truth.

This characteristic and crucial passage raises as many problems as it solves.[16] But it will make clear that, from Hobbes to Dryden, we discover a concept of literary art as a cognitive and moral science of human life parallel to, or even better than, the speculations of the natural philosophers. A number of rhetorical and cognitive means assist to that end, and the poet may be more or less deeply involved in – or detached from – the social and political events of the time. Finally, to the extent that 'satire is undoubtedly a species' of the epic, it and its obverse (panegyric) participate in a common literary enterprise by which better or worse likenesses serve the ends of truth and goodness; to the extent that it involves history, its mimesis is doubly real.

I do not argue that all this is necessarily true of literature, or that satire must be of the kind Dryden proposes. But the evidence is clear enough from Hobbes's three regions of mankind to Dryden's likenesses within the sphere of truth: critics and poets during the Restoration held to a concept of literature that was dignified, grand, and perhaps even exorbitant in claims for our subject, satire. Above all, they held that satire is not dirty work. It is concerned with the reality of human life, 'nature', just like any other mimetic art. It is narrative, powerful, like the epic. It is at once rhetorical in depicting the moral character of instances and subjects, as also cognitive in possessing a status beyond the imaginative or inventive, because it can claim to truth. These large claims on behalf of

Virtue, Honor, Truth and Reason led Butler to despair, Milton to what everybody must consider epic triumph, and Dryden to a career as poet in which the abstractions just named are as deeply interfused as they are in our lives.

All this, no less, is the claim entered by Restoration non-dramatic literature (and dramatic also, but that is another story). Given these claims, either they or some of the usual presumptions about the Restoration must give way. The readiest way to test the claims historically is to set them in the context of religion, asking with some sharpness how satire can be accommodated to the claims of faith.

Just what years we choose to include in a concept of the 'Restoration' may be open to question. In the strictest sense, the period runs from the return of Charles II in 1660 to his death in 1685. My own taste prefers a view of this period that is longer and integral to the seventeenth century – 1640 to the death of Dryden in 1700 is not too long for me. Others prefer to think of a double entity, the Restoration and eighteenth century. As long as we say what we mean and abide by rules of evidence within the saying, various formulations seem just enough. So also does the usual view of the Restoration seem accurate if we leave it as a partial description. It was an age of licentiousness, some free-thinking inconsistent with faith, of no little folly, of worse perfidy, and, worst of all, sheer human waste. I part from the usual attitude because of an incurable skepticism: the description fits with nearly every age in history. In any event, the greatest non-dramatic writers of this age seem to be, beyond question, Butler, Rochester, Milton, Bunyan and Dryden. It is to an age distinguished by these and other worthies that we must now address questions of faith that will allow us to consider satire.

Many people surely think that satire does not sort with such grand things as faith and heroic imagination. Perhaps among those who do think such consorting possible, there remain a large number who think that the Restoration was too frivolous, or contrariwise, too much part of a new age of reason, to allow for faith as well as satire. What can be given as persuasive evidence when fixed notions, received wisdom, and truisms of old histories all constitute the evidence to prove themselves true? Perhaps a little raillery, a little urging to attend to what happened in the Restoration and earlier will prove more efficacious than syllogisms and enthymemes (the latter of which I never truly remember, any-how) or statistics (which are said to prove anything).[17]

Did not the Merry Monarch preside over the revels during a time of increasing secularization? No doubt he, his spaniels, and his mistresses did, but the process of secularization appears to have begun even earlier than that other old acquaintance of ours, the rise of the middle classes, since secularization began with the Fall. (This is not wholly banter – read *Paradise Lost*, IX–X, and wait to see what Dryden will say.) When Charles died from uremic poisoning, he went to his Maker with many sins on his head, although how many more or less than Henry IV, Henry V, Henry VII, Henry VIII, Elizabeth I and her two successors I shall leave to 'an higher' tribunal. But Charles died sacramentally, having taken, as he wished to, the last rites of the popish persuasion. What he did in secret, James did openly – espouse that Good Old Cause that predated the later, 'puritan' one of the seventeenth century. James's steadfast, principled, and honest pigheadedness, aided by a Prot-estant wind, put an end to a regime, only to cause a constitutional and ecclesiastical upheaval when many of the bishops and clergy would not 'jure', or swear allegiance to William and Mary.

Among those who chose to lose their sees rather than swear to princes while their *de jure* monarch was alive, there was Thomas Ken, Bishop of Bath and Wells. He had opposed James's reading of the Declaration of Indulgence (toleration for Catholics and Dis-senters) vigorously enough to have been sent to the Tower. When he was dismissed from his see, it was discovered that he had almost no money, having given it out as charity in his diocese. It is thought that Dryden pictures him in 'The Character of A Good Parson', a Chaucerian imitation toward the end of *Fables*. His poem is certainly at once a panegyric on the rare good shepherd and a satire on the majority 'of our corrupted Clergy then in their height', as Milton puts it in a striking passage in *Lycidas* (1637, 1645, Trinity MS. for various versions). Milton's anti-prelatical tracts ought, however, to be consulted for genuinely swingeing satire of the clergy. Ken himself was a poet, although he will probably be longer remembered as a good man; at least I recall of his sacred epics little more than that I do not wish to read them again.

It does seem to be true that from 1660 to 1700 people were taking religion seriously. From what is observable during all times, it would be astonishing if during those years religion did not get entangled in politics, financial matters and preferment to honors. But the rebellion by the miserable Fifth Monarchy Men (1662), the Popish Plot, the Rye House Plot, and the Glorious Revolution were in fact more religious in motive than were most of the rebellions against Elizabeth I, James I's peace policy, Charles I's Ship Money or Cromwell's assuming the Protectorship. On the other hand, the second and third Dutch wars were obviously as commercially inspired as was the first under Cromwell. Throughout the century, as always, the things that mattered most were never from people's minds, and the things tended to blend with each other. Religion could not fail to matter in the age of Milton, Bunyan and Dryden. In addition to the nature of the second half of the *Leviathan*, which few people have heard of, there is this from Samuel Butler:

> When *civil* Fury first grew high,
> And men fell out they knew not why;
> When hard words, *Jealousies* and *Fears*,
> Set Folks together by the ears,
> And made them fight, like mad or drunk,
> For Dame *Religion* as for Punk . . .

So *Hudibras* opens, with Butler trying to make the two decades from 1641 seem meaningless: 'men fell out they knew not why' in *civil* strife. Four lines later, however, we learn a prime motive, that good and divisive dame, religion. There are more paradoxes in this poem than are necessary. The greatest is no doubt that this attack on irrational, rebellious, self-serving religion was written by one of the more tolerant men of the age and yet does not mention either God or the King. But the efforts of Zachary Grey and other Anglican divines in the next century show that they were trying to make up for the neglect of Butler touched on by Dryden's sharp-tongued Hind:

> Unpitty'd *Hudibrass*, your Champion friend,
> Has shown how far your charities extend.
> This lasting verse shall on his tomb be read,
> *He sham'd you living, and upbraids you dead.*[18]

Clearly 'men' knew why they had been falling out, discovering as the race has ceaselessly that, when religion matters, it may be as divisive as anything else of central human importance.

From later satire the impression has grown that satirists deal with secular matters, and that they are as it were scavengers on the dead body of epic: once there was Milton, and then there was satire. But there was satire a long time before Milton. The Bible itself has satire, particularly in the books of the prophets and in Proverbs. Or, as Dryden says, in his essay on satire:

> If we take satire in the general signification of the word, as it is used in all modern languages, for an invective, 'tis certain that it is almost as old as verse; and tho' hymns, which are praises of God, may be allowed to have been before it, yet the defamation of others was not long after it. After God had cursed Adam and Eve in Paradise, the husband and wife excused themselves by laying the blame on one another; and gave a beginning to those conjugal dialogues in prose which the poets have perfected in verse. The third chapter of Job is one of the first instances of this poem in holy Scripture [poetic satire, earlier instances being in prose]; unless we take it higher, from the latter end of the second, where his wife advises him to curse his Maker.
>
> （Watson, II, 97）

We are not to be surprised at that, 'since *all* [my stress] poetry had its original from religion' (ibid., 100) and, in particular, 'the poetry of the Romans, and that of the Grecians, had the same beginning at feasts and thanksgiving . . . and the Old Comedy of the Greeks, which was invective, and the satire of the Romans . . . were begun on the very same occasion' (ibid., 101). For that matter, Dryden found 'a kind of satire' from 'Homer himself in his *Margites*' (ibid., 110).

Poor Dryden, unable to get his mind off satire? Here is another critic, Aristotle:

> Poetry, however, soon broke up into two kinds according to the differences of character in the individual poets; for the graver among them would represent noble actions, and those of noble persons; and the meaner sort those of the ignoble. The latter class produced invectives at first, just as others did hymns and panegyrics. We know of no such poem by any of the pre-Homeric poets, though there were probably many such writers among them; instances, however, may be found from Homer downwards, e.g., his *Margites*, and the similar poems of others.

In this poetry of invective its natural fitness brought an iambic metre into use; hence our present term, 'iambic', because it was the metre of their 'iambs' or invectives against one another. The result was that the old poets became some of them writers of heroic and others of iambic verse.[19]

If Dryden errs, he errs on as good authority as he could have chosen. And given what Robert Elliott has shown (n. 2), it is astonishing what nonsense has been said about satire in connection with the heroic.

If Dryden had chosen to follow back his native tradition a century, he would have come on the claim of Joseph Hall:

> I First adventure, with fool-hardie might
> To tred the steps of perilous despight:
> I first adventure: follow me who list,
> And be the second English Satyrist.[20]

From Hall it would have been easy passage to his enemy Marston, and thence to John Donne. Of this group of early modern satirists, only the Dean of St Paul's seems to have been familiar to Dryden, who thought his satires too much like Horace's, and in particular too harsh in style (Watson, II, 144). That is mostly to say that what was still known as 'satyr' to a Hall or Donne entailed a different decorum. For that matter, the lyricism of Donne, Jonson and their followers is shaded with satiric hues.[21] Given usual truisms about religion, it is striking how little religious satire there is in Donne's time (in spite of his wonderful third satire). No doubt something must be attributed to the heavy censorship and the other violently repressive features of late Elizabethan times. When, in June 1599, a book dedicated to Essex appeared, the Bishop of London came down on the booksellers, burning satires and naughty Ovidian poems along with those deemed seditious. Donne wisely kept his satires restricted to as small a group as possible, and Jonson found it expedient to alternate laudatory epigrams to people named by real names with satiric epigrams addressed to types. But in that time of rising Calvinism, one would think that there might have been more religious satires. By the fourth decade of the century there is no lack – also by the fourth decade there is once more a narrative practice.

The Restoration was no doubt a more tolerant age: one could say things at Court about the King that would have met with execution

under Elizabeth and James. And although the religious lyrics of
Vaughan and Traherne certainly do not measure up to those of
Donne and Herbert, the Restoration includes theirs in a great age
for religious literature. Everyone must be glad, not only that
Milton escaped execution, but also that his busy left hand was at
last tied up and he could get on with his proper business as a poet.
Nobody knows when, or over exactly what period, his three
greatest poems were written. But we know when they were
published and read, and we know also that there could have been
no obstacle to their being published earlier if they had been written.
There are also Dryden's two religious poems, partly narrative,
partly confessional, partly ecclesiastical and partly much else, but in
any event the sole two poetic declarations of religious belief to
come from any single major writer in the century. There is also that
greatest prose narration of the century, the product of a jailed
Baptist tinker, Bunyan's masterpiece. I would like to suggest that it
would be impossible to frame a definition of satire that would
include passages in *The Hind and the Panther* labelled satiric and
exclude the Apollyon or Vanity Fair sections of *The Pilgrim's
Progress*, or indeed a definition including them and excluding such
passages in *Paradise Lose* as the exchanges after the Fall between
Adam and Eve already mentioned; the sarcasm of Satan and Belial
on inventing and using gunpowder; or God's smiling remarks,
such as this:

> Neerly it now concernes us to be sure
> Of our Omnipotence, and with what Arms
> We mean to hold what anciently we claim
> Of Deitie or Empire, such a foe
> Is rising, who intends to erect his Throne
> Equal to ours, throughout the spacious North;
> Nor so content, hath in his thought to trie
> In battel, what our Power is, or our right.
> Let us advise, and to this hazard draw
> With speed what force is left, and all imploy
> In our defence, lest unawares we lose
> This our high place, our Sanctuarie, our Hill.

God's gentle ironies earn a reply:

> To whom the Son with calm aspect and cleer
> Light'ning Divine, ineffable, serene,

Made answer. Mightie Father, thou thy foes
Justly hast in derision, and secure
Laugh'st at thir vain designes and tumults vain . . .
(v. 721–37)

This is of a piece with God's later remarks on Satan's designs,
concluding that he assumes he will be able to manage, 'and in a
moment will create / Another World' (VII. 154–5). So much for
Satan's waging war in Heaven. Even the narrator's first extended
mention of Satan (I. 33–49) is shot through with satire, ending as it
begins with a 'Who' line – 'Who durst defie th' Omnipotent to
Arms'. It would be no less difficult to frame a definition of satire
including those passages so labelled in *The Hind and the Panther* that
excluded exchanges between Satan and Jesus in *Paradise Regained*,
most notably Our Saviour's characterization of Greek learning,
including that of the style of the Greek authors, 'As varnish on a
Harlots cheek' (IV. 344); or for that matter the exchanges between
Samson and Dalila, or Manoa's dry bob to his Samson, 'I cannot
praise thy Marriage choises, Son' (l. 420).

Clearly Dryden was on to what the literary genius of his age was
typically about. Satire was regarded as a kind of narrative participating in the heroic, enabling narrative poets (and prose writers)
to take a worse likeness as well as the better of panegyric. Dryden
wrote simple truth in his poem to Sir Godfrey Kneller, when he said
that 'Satire will have room, where e're I write' (l. 94), and the truth
is applicable to his greatest contemporaries as well, just as we must
add that panegyric also had its room, and that the rooms were
rented in the spacious if sometimes cluttered halls of poetic and
prose narrative modelled on the grand designs of the heroic.

Of course there are differences between the poets. Butler wrote
little except satire. None of Milton's mature poems can be termed a
proper satire, although all draw on it. Dryden has two poems that
are proper satires, *Mac Flecknoe* and *The Medall* (about 540 lines all
told). There are also other differences. Milton, Bunyan and Dryden
wrote their works as narratives in which the stance taken is one of
superiority, of control, of power. Marvell on the Dutch, on the
anniversary of Cromwell's power, on Tom May (if that poem be
by him), and on Flecknoe also assumes a position of power, but his
stance in the Painter poems (if by him) and *The Rehearsal Transpros'd*
is far more ambiguous. Butler assumes power to dismiss but not to

make the dismissal work. For all his great satiric power, Rochester is the victim of his own sense of self as much as of the world. If we drop to lesser writers, Cotton's popular burlesques, or parodies in hudibrastics, bang along confidently enough, and most of Oldham's satires till his last year or so seem to explode bogeymen with more gunpowder and smoke than anyone since has thought necessary. Later on, the likes of Flatman, Durfey, Norris, Radcliffe and Gould continued to explore the satiric mines in their various ways, but for lack of poetic power or ability to define urgent issues they do not much accelerate one's pulse. And they do not much alter Dryden's scheme. Perhaps Butler best identified the issue in one of his lighter poems, *The Elephant in the Moon*:

> And, therefore, with great Prudence does,
> The World still strive to keep [Truth] close;
> For if all secret Truths were known,
> Who would not be once more undone?
> For Truth has always Danger in't.   (ll. 423–7)

This glance at the Fall in Eden shows that satire (panegyric, history and the capacious heroic of the time) required something more than merely the desire to take a worse likeness. As always for literature, the issues had to matter, and the writers had to have the gifts to make them matter to readers.

The affective power, the ability to make matter, were the grounds of Dryden's preference of Juvenal over Horace and Persius. That preference seems to have guided us all in our attempts to frame definitions of satire that include seventeenth-century writing. But to the extent that we can agree with that age that satire is a narrative art, we must connect a Homer with the *Margites*, and we must find room for the genius of the first Roman satirist we really know, Horace. Moreover, since so much of the satire in the best work by Butler, Milton, Bunyan and Dryden comes in dialogue, we shall have to study Lucian more thoroughly than we have. Dryden did not forget him, of course.[22] In such study, we shall be wise to heed the lesson implicit in Butler's lines on the risks of truth, positing as a first and always dangerous truth for the Restoration the hazards and the benefits that religion gave to an age of faith, an age of satire – both of them, in Dryden's phrase, species of 'heroic poetry itself'.

NOTES

1 See J. P. Sullivan (ed.), *Satire: Critical Essays on Roman Literature* (London, 1963).

2 See, if only for rich example, Alvin B. Kernan, *The Cankered Muse: Satire of the English Renaissance* and *The Plot of Satire* (New Haven, Conn., 1959 and 1965); Robert C. Elliott, *The Power of Satire: Magic, Ritual, Art* (Princeton, N.J., 1960), and *The Shape of Utopia: Studies in a Literary Genre* (Chicago, 1970); Edward Rosenheim, *Swift and the Satirist's Art* (Chicago, 1963); Ronald Paulson, *The Fictions of Satire* (Baltimore, Md, 1967); and Michael Seidel, *Satiric Inheritance, Rabelais to Sterne* (Princeton, N.J., 1979), which, in a manner suiting its title, has a very useful bibliography. Besides these and other fine books, there are of course numerous helpful articles, of which the most famous is that by Mary Claire Randolph, 'The Structural Design of Formal Verse Satire', *Philological Quarterly*, 21 (1942), 368–84, which I have found of use for a minority of verse satirists, chiefly Rochester.

3 Quoted from J. E. Spingarn (ed.), *Critical Essays of the Seventeenth Century*, 3 vols (Oxford, 1908), II, 54–5.

4 Hugh de Quehen (ed.), *Prose Observations* (Oxford, 1979), 215.

5 George Watson (ed.), *Of Dramatic Poesy and Other Critical Essays*, 2 vols (London, 1962), I, 101; hereafter mostly cited in the text by volume and page number.

6 *An Apology for Poetry*, in G. G. Smith (ed.), *Elizabethan Critical Essays*, 2 vols (Oxford, 1904), I, 199–200.

7 Quoted from Ruth Nevo, *The Dial of Virtue* (Princeton, N.J., 1963), 210. Much else in this fine book tells us how seventeenth-century writers viewed satire.

8 Burnet, *Some Passages of the Life and Death of the Right Honourable John Earl of Rochester* (London, 1680), 25, 26.

9 From Spingarn, II, 290.

10 Printed by George deF. Lord (ed.), *Poems on Affairs of State*, I (New Haven, Conn., 1963), liii.

11 To blame no others, I shall say that my own attempt to incorporate Horace into a view of satire seems inadequate: 'In Satire's Falling City', in H. James Jensen and Malvin R. Zirker, Jr (eds), *The Satirist's Art* (Bloomington, Ind., 1972), 3–27.

12 On satiric plots, see Kernan (second title) and Rosenheim (n. 2).

13 Watson, II, 149. On the centrality of the heroic to Dryden's criticism, see H. T. Swedenberg, Jr, 'Dryden's Obsessive Concern with the Heroic', *Studies in Philology*, E.S. 4 (1967), 12–26, which I think not only profoundly right but also the finest Dryden essay by this now dead old friend.

14 Cf. Dryden's preface to the *Satires*: '''tis a harder thing to make a man wise than to make him honest; for the will is only to be reclaimed in the one, but the understanding is to be informed in the other', Watson, II, 128–9.

15 Watson, II, 202. In the existing text of the *Poetics*, the distinction is made a few times, once including the same threefold distinction for painters.

16 As concerned me in discussing Dryden's 'higher Mimesis' in *The Restoration Mode from Milton to Dryden* (Princeton, N.J., 1974), 343–64, where I gave a number of instances in which Dryden has been supposed to have related historical fact, although the only evidence derives solely from what he wrote. If the central problem be the adequacy of poetic invention as a criterion for historical truth, Dryden's conception of a 'better or worse likeness' within the bounds of morality and truth may seem obvious but is none the less daunting.

17 Using statistical evidence, Lawrence Stone holds that on the evidence of illegitimate births (and some other matters), the Restoration was in fact more moral than the century following. See his *Family, Sex and Marriage: England 1500–1800* (New York, 1977), 144 (seventeenth-century decline) and 629–30, 637–8 (eighteenth-century increase).

18 *The Hind and the Panther*, III, 247–50. In l. 264 (and elsewhere) Dryden refers to such passages as 'satyr'.

19 *Poetics*, ch. 4, trs. Ingram Bywater in W. Hamilton Fyfe (ed.), *Aristotle's Art of Poetry* (Oxford, 1940), 10.

20 *Virgidemiarum*, I, Prol., in Arnold Davenport (ed.), *The Poems of Joseph Hall* (Liverpool, 1969), 11, changed from italics.

21 The point will be obvious for Jonson. In her edition of Donne's *Elegies and Songs and Sonnets* (Oxford, 1969), 163, Dame Helen Gardner speaks of 'the satiric edge that [Donne] gives to even his gayest songs'. Ch. 4, 'Satire and Song', of my *Metaphysical Mode from Donne to Cowley* (Princeton, N.J., 1969) examines such interfusions.

22 See his life of Lucian, partly printed by Watson (II, 209–15), with, among much else, this characteristic passage: 'If the pleasure arising from comedy and satire be either laughter, or some nobler sort of delight which is above it, no man is so great a master of irony as our author' (p. 211).

8

OLDHAM'S VERSIONS OF
THE CLASSICS

Raman Selden

Harold Brooks's essay on the 'Imitation'[1] remains the standard account. The prominent and distinctive part played in the development of the Imitation by John Oldham is there firmly adumbrated. The absence of an authoritative edition[2] of Oldham's poetry has inhibited the fuller exploration of the poet's techniques of translation and imitation. The considerable attention given to Pope's and Johnson's imitations and to Dryden's translations has borne fruit sufficient to suggest that the work of their most important predecessor in the art should not be neglected.

Oldham's modern reputation, such as it is, centres almost exclusively on 'Satyrs upon the Jesuits' (written 1679), a pungent sequence of vituperative satires which look back to the tradition of Hall and Marston. However, Oldham's work of the period from 1680 to his death in 1683, much of which was published in *Some New Pieces* (1681) and *Poems and Translations* (1683), includes more poems of a distinctly classical turn, including many direct translations, paraphrases or imitations of classical models.

Oldham was well versed in classical Greek and Latin, and Renaissance Latin. The course of studies he must have followed at Tetbury Grammar School and St Edmund Hall gave him a sure grounding in classical literature and grammar. His poetical works contain manifest evidence of this knowledge and of its fruits. 'Satyrs upon the Jesuits' draws frequently upon Buchanan's 'Franciscanus',[3] Phineas Fletcher's *Locustae*,[4] and on occasion from Varenius's account of Japan. His versions of classical literature include some of his best work. He made versions of most major

Roman poets: Virgil, Horace, Juvenal, Ovid, Catullus and Martial. His interest in Greek literature is less marked but not inconsiderable for a writer of this period.[5] His general range of classical allusion and reference was wide.[6]

'Upon the Works of Ben. Jonson', written early in 1678 for an anticipated reprint of Jonson's works which never appeared (at least in Oldham's lifetime), is a Cowleian 'Pindarique' ode celebrating the great master of earlier English classicism. The ode claims that Jonson was the 'mighty *Founder* of our Stage' who completed the 'Design' left unfinished by others: 'All the fair Model and the workmanship was thine'. As the first section of the poem progresses, Jonson's independence from antiquity becomes more emphatic; following his example, we may now 'steer a course more unconfin'd and free, / Beyond the narrow bounds, that pent Antiquity'. The poem's second section, in a passage which heavily influenced the *Dunciad* Bk 1, describes how the theatre 'groan'd under a wretched Anarchy of wit' and was 'A rude and undigested lump . . . Like the old Chaos ere the birth of light and day':

> Till thy brave Genius like a new Creator came,
>   And undertook the mighty frame; . . .
>   And strait appear'd a beauteous new-made World of
>   Poetry.   (ll. 39–40, 54)

The manner of the poem resembles Cowley's Pindariques on Hobbes and on the Royal Society, which combine a strict common-sense rationalism of outlook and a stylistic 'enthusiasm' which draws its materials from neoplatonic idiom and, in Oldham's case, is enriched by Miltonic grandeur. Oldham's emphasis on rigour and laborious art is apparently (to the modern ear) at odds with the 'divine frenzy' of the utterance. The judiciousness of Dryden's comparison of Jonson and Shakespeare in *Of Dramatic Poesy* (1668) highlights Oldham's excessive and paradoxical claims for Jonson's natural powers, which defined *ab initio* the rules of art for succeeding generations:

> Rich in thy self, to whose unbounded store
> Exhausted Nature could vouchsafe no more:
> Thou couldst alone the Empire of the Stage maintain,
> . . . Boldly thou didst the learned World invade,

> Whilst all around thy pow'rful Genius sway'd,
> Soon vanquisht Rome and Greece were made submit,
> Both were thy humble tributaries made,
> And thou returnd'st in triumph with their captive Wit.
>
> (ll. 171–3, 183–7)

This passage evidently borrows from Dryden's 'He invades authors like a monarch, and what would be theft in other poets is only victory in him.'[7] While Dryden makes it clear that Jonson's was a victory of learning and scholarship, Oldham's hyperbolic account grants Jonson independent powers of invention. Neither view is the whole truth.

Jonson was an important model as a classicist. His view of the poet and tradition was Baconian in approach: classical literature provides the modern writer with monuments to be emulated and not merely copied. The poet must always discover nature afresh as if it had not been done before: 'For to all the observations of the *Ancients*, wee have our owne experience . . . . Truth lyes open to all; . . . *Patet omnibus veritas; nondum est occupata*'.[8] Jonson's own practice as a classicist embodies some of the contradictions inherent in this independent-mindedness. Some of his translations are accurate and at the same time idiomatic; his partial imitations ('To Celia' for example) are studiedly classical and yet contemporary in style and outlook. It has often been observed that English neo-classicism was much less servile than the French and more imbued with the vitality of the native tradition. Oldham's own view of Jonson's poetic 'garb' is equally uncompromising:

> No French commodity, which now so much do's take,
> And our own better manufacture spoil;
> Nor was it ought of foreign Soil;
> But staple all, and all of English growth and make.
>
> (ll. 104–7)

The 'Imitation' proved to be the appropriate form to contain the contradictions within such a militantly chauvinistic classicism. In Rochester, the chauvinism results in a total appropriation of the classical model; 'An Allusion to Horace' is not only a very free rendering in modern terms of Horace's satire, but does not always reflect Horace's ideas; the substitution of Dryden for Lucilius changes the poem's meaning at more than one level. Oldham, it is true, wrote poems of this kind, alluding to Boileau (in 'The Eighth Satire of M. Boileau, Imitated') and Juvenal (in 'A Satire Address'd to a Friend' and 'Spencer's Ghost'); however, in so far as Rochester's 'Allusion' parallels Horace consecutively passage for passage, it remains a model for the 'Imitation'. Evidently Oldham wanted to combine the faithfulness of translation with the topical freshness he found in the imitations of Cowley, Sprat and Rochester. Oldham's own 'Allusion to Martial' is clearly an imitation, but closer to the original than Rochester's 'Allusion'.[9]

Harold Brooks has shown that Oldham's practice of imitation was strongly influenced by Dryden's programmatic remarks in his preface to *Ovid's Epistles* (1680). Dryden's preference for the moderation of paraphrase over both the excessive servility of metaphrase and the libertinism of imitation apparently impressed Oldham at first: his 'The Passion of Byblis out of *Ovid's Metamorphoses*' appears in *Satyr upon the Jesuits* (1681) but is frankly regarded as unsuccessful in the Advertisement. Oldham soon undertook to show in practice that Dryden's rules for paraphrase were not incompatible with modernization. Oldham's taste for native wit and the flavour of the modern (so apparent in the 'Satyrs') led him to reject a path that might lead him into remoteness of reference. He argued in the Advertisement to *Some New Pieces* (1681) that his modernization of Horace's *Ars Poetica* 'would give a kind of new Air to the Poem, and render it more agreeable to the relish of the present Age' (a1ᵛ). Even when writing formal 'paraphrases', Oldham often included extensive modernization. Indeed, the more one examines his practice, the more one sees it as a positive challenge to Dryden's theory. For example, in the paraphrase of Horace's *Odes*, II. xiv., Oldham expands and modernizes freely, but preserves the general sense, while Congreve refrains from modernizing Horace but is less concerned to preserve Horace's sequence of thoughts.[10]

Oldham's first ambitious attempt to follow Dryden's lead was his 'Byblis', in which Ovid's 180 lines (*Metamorphoses*, IX. 453–632) are expanded to 350 lines but without modernization. Oldham evidently was impressed by the characterization of the Roman poet in *Ovid's Epistles*, in which Dryden considers him the master 'in the description of the passions'. In *Of Dramatic Poesy* (1668), Dryden had actually mentioned 'Byblis' as an example of Ovid's dramatic talent, revealed especially in his ability 'to show the various movements of a soul combating betwixt two different passions'.[11] Oldham's paraphrase is notable for its development of the 'passions' in the Restoration manner. 'Byblis' is influenced by the vogue of the heroic and tragic drama of the 1670s. The Bodleian MS. (Rawlinson, poet. 123), which contains drafts of Oldham's poems, included annotations from the most exuberant plays of the period, such as Settle's *The Empress of Morocco* (1673), Otway's *Don Carlos* (1676) and Lee's *The Rival Queens* (1677). In his final rhymed heroic play, *Aureng-Zebe* (1676), Dryden began to temper the display of passions by the use of wit and irony. However, his *theories* encouraged the vivid rendering of the passions; it is argued in *Of Dramatic Poesy* that 'every alteration or crossing of a design, every new-sprung passion, and turn of it, is a part of the action, and much the noblest'.[12] This un-Aristotelian emphasis, together with the singling out of Ovid's 'Byblis', no doubt gave Oldham his cue.

We must not ignore the fact that Oldham regarded 'Byblis' as a mistaken venture in paraphrase and that 'his vein' lay 'another way'. However, in certain respects the attempt enabled him to draw on some of his poetic strengths, notably in the display of intense feelings. Byblis' incestuous love is studied with great psychological insight by Ovid. Oldham heightens the Latin in several ways. Subjectivity is enhanced by the introduction and elaboration of physiological interest. Awake, Byblis represses her desire, but 'when she is relaxed in peaceful repose, she often sees what she loves'.[13] Oldham has:

> but when returning night
> With Sleep's soft gentle spell her Senses charms,
> Kind Fancy often brings him to her Arms.   (ll. 37–9)

Ovid's 'vision of the night' (*noctis imago*) becomes 'This boading form, that nightly rides my dreams'. 'Dreams' (*somnia*) become 'this too charming Vision'. Later, Byblis begs her brother, by letter, not to let 'fear' restrain them; *timor* becomes 'any gastlier fantom, fear can frame'. Oldham explores the situation in terms of thoughts, passions and general *inward* turmoil. In Ovid, 'shame' and 'defiance' mingle 'in her face'; Oldham expands this to:

> shame and hope and fear
> Wrack her tost mind, and in her looks appear.
>   (ll. 149–50)

Ovid's 'So great is the uncertainty of her mind'[14] is extended to:

> such is her unsettled mind,
> It shifts from thought to thought, like veering wind,
> Now to this point and now to that inclin'd.   (ll. 342–4)

Oldham also elaborates the outward symptoms of passion; Ovid's simple reference to Byblis' unsisterly love (l. 456) is Oldham's cue for a psycho-physical rendering of her state:

> *Caunus* she lov'd, not as a Sister ought,
> But Honour, Shame and Blood alike forgot:
> *Caunus* alone takes up her Thoughts and Eyes,
> For him alone she wishes, grieves and sighs.
>
>   (ll. 9–12)

Ovid's two lines[15] describing the vividness of Byblis' dreams are translated into a full-scale display of abandoned passion in the manner of heroic drama:

> I clap'd the Vision to my panting breast!
> With what fierce bounds I sprung to meet my bliss,
> While my rapt soul flew out in every kiss!
> Till breathless, faint and softly sunk away,
> I all dissolv'd in reeking pleasures lay!   (ll. 65–9)

Ovid's terms are purely external and physical; Oldham adds a neo-Platonic heightening to a description of sensual indulgence. Byblis wishes herself in the tomb and that her brother might kiss her (*det oscula frater*). Oldham expands the three Latin words into a tragic rendering of pity and fear:

> Let him [my kind *Murderer*], while I breath out my soul
>   in sighs,
> Or gaze't away, look on with pittying eyes:
> Let him (for sure he can't deny me this)
> Seal my cold Lips with one dear parting Kiss
>
>   (ll. 101–4)

He elaborates the scene dramatically and emotionally.

Heightening of emotion is also produced by hyperbolic and figurative means. The following passage is representative:

And yet, though rankling grief my mind distrest,
Though raging flames within burnt up my breast,
Long time I did the mighty pain endure,
Long strove to bring the fierce disease to cure:
Witness ye cruel Pow'rs, who did inspire
This strange, this fatal, this resistless fire,
Witness what pains . . .
This helpless wretch to quench't did undergo:
A thousand Racks, and Martyrdoms, and more
Than a weak Virgin can be thought, I bore.

                                        (ll. 177–86)

The metaphors of fire and disease are developed from only two
Latin phrases, *grave vulnus* and *furor igneus*. The hyperbolic
couplet (lines 175–6) has no parallel in Ovid and is in the manner of
the heroic rant so much beloved by Oldham. By these means
Oldham's Ovid approximates to Dryden's image: 'he of them [the
Ancients] who had genius most proper for the stage was Ovid; he
had a way of writing so fit to stir up a pleasing admiration and
concernment, which are the objects of a tragedy'.[16]

In 1692 John Dennis published a rival version of 'Byblis' and
presented a number of arguments against Oldham's. He emphasized
the naturalness of Ovid's exploration of passion; 'the very sound of
the verse' is 'so soft and so pathetick'. Amorous verse of this kind
should avoid far-fetched similes and conceits: 'To succeed in it,
required neither Force nor Genius, but only Tenderness of soul
(which Mr. *Oldham*'s Masculine temper disdain'd)'.[17] Dennis's
version of Ovid's lines 540–5 may be compared with Oldham's
above (ll. 177–86):

But yet tho' deep, ah deep! the flaming Dart,
Piercing my burning breast, transfix'd my heart,
Alarm'd, like wretches by nocturnal Fire,
And trembling at the terrible desire,
Long time I strove its fury to asswage,
And long time struggling Vertue stopt its rage.
This Truth, O all ye chaster Powers attest!
Ye saw the fearful conflict in my Breast,
When Honour, Piety, Remorse and Shame,
My very Vitals tore t'expel my flame.
In misery grown obstinate, I bore

What never tender Virgin did before.
When what I suffer'd other Maids but hear,
'Twill wound their gentle hearts, and force a tear.

(p. 4)

If Dennis aimed at a 'feminine' tenderness and compassion, this does not mean he was less passionate. Emotive words are piled on: 'flaming', 'piercing', 'trembling', 'terrible', 'struggling', 'fearful', 'fury', 'rage', 'tore'. Dignity of feeling is gained by the use of abstract nouns (absent in Oldham): 'Vertue', 'Truth', 'Honour, Piety, Remorse and Shame'. 'Feminine' pathos is produced by an appeal to softer emotions, especially in the last three lines ('tender' 'gentle hearts', 'tear'). Oldham's epithets are evidently more 'masculine': 'rankling', 'mighty', 'cruel Pow'rs' (Dennis has 'chaster Powers'), 'weak' (Dennis has 'tender'). Oldham's Byblis suffers 'A thousand Racks, and Martyrdoms', which one imagines would scare 'other Maids' out of their wits to hear, rather than elicit a touching tear.

Oldham was able to modernize Ovid without placing the action in the modern world. The same principles guided his imitation of Catullus VII. The poet's attempt to calculate the number of kisses that will suffice allows Oldham to indulge in his characteristic cumulative rhetoric. To Catullus' sands and stars he adds miser's gold, or drops of ocean,

> Or think how many Atoms came
> To compose this mighty Frame   (ll. 11–12)

till 'no malicious Spy can guess'

> To what vast height the Scores arise.   (l. 16)

Such is the 'height' to which Oldham raises the number of kisses that he is compelled to contradict Catullus' modest limitation of his desires: 'to kiss you with so many kisses, Lesbia, is enough and more than enough for your mad Catullus!' Oldham has:

> All these will hardly be enough
> For me stark staring mad with Love.   (ll. 19–20)

Ben Jonson, in his fine modernized imitation, unlike Oldham, allows the number of kisses to remain finite. Oldham seems to have believed that a Restoration heroic lover would not have allowed his fancy to be so meanly confined.

While Ovid and Catullus gave Oldham opportunities to explore the passions, it was Roman satire which provided him with the best vehicle for writing to 'the present Age' in specifically modern terms. Horace's satire on the bore (I. ix) was a favourite model, since Jonson's adaptation of it in the third act of *Poetaster* and Donne's in the first and fourth satires. Oldham knew of Jonson's use of the poem and also refers to Bishop Sprat's imitation in Brome's *Horace* (1666). Marvell's poem on Flecknoe and Rochester's 'Timon' also echo the satire. Juvenal's satires seem to have had a particular appeal for the Restoration writers, judging by the number of translations and imitations done in the period.[18]

In all his poetry Oldham preserves a stylistic decorum. In the Advertisement to *Some New Pieces*, he hopes that he has 'hit . . . the easie and familiar way of writing, which is peculiar to Horace in his Epistles' (in this case his *Ars Poetica*). In the same Advertisement, he defends the 'roughness of my Satyrs formerly publisht' (viz., the 'Jesuits') with the claim that 'no one that pretends to distinguish the several Colours of Poetry, would expect that Juvenal, when he is lashing of Vice, and Villany, should flow so smoothly as Ovid, or Tibullus'. The Prologue to the 'Jesuits' confirms this view of satire by borrowing directly from Juvenal's first satire:

> For who can longer hold? . . .
> Nor needs there art or genious here to use,
> Where indignation can create a muse . . .   (I. 28–9)

Oldham whips up a frenetic tone in the factitious manner of John Marston, the Elizabethan wild man of satire:

> All this urge on my rank envenom'd spleen,
> And with keen Satyr edge my stabbing Pen:
> That its each home-set thrust their blood may draw,
> Each drop of Ink like *Aquafortis* gnaw.   (ll. 57–60)

However, Oldham's view of satire seems to have mellowed after the crisis of the Popish Plot. The style adopted in the imitations of both Juvenal and Horace is less vehement.[19] When William Soames advised Oldham to 'refine' his 'rude Satyrs' by the 'Rules' of Horace,[20] he was evidently thinking of the 'Jesuits' and not the imitations, which show the chastening influence of Boileau and Dryden.[21]

Oldham's versions of the two satirists share a relatively plain style but show certain differences which correspond to the traditional distinction between Horace's 'comic' and Juvenal's 'tragic' modes. However, Oldham's conception of Juvenal's style is quite unlike Dryden's, and a comparison of their versions of the third satire of Juvenal confirms the temperamental and stylistic differences between the two writers which Dryden so gracefully and generously discussed in 'To the Memory of Mr. Oldham'. In Dryden's version of Juvenal, an epical dignity of style is preserved in conformity with his view of heroic satire as a combination of 'the majesty of the heroic' and the 'venom' of satire.[22] Oldham still retains something of the 'roughness'[23] of the 'Jesuits'.

Juvenal laments the fact that money counts for more than virtue, and refers to the example of Lucius Metellus who saved the Palladium from the flames. Dryden translates:

> Or him who bid th' unhallow'd Flames retire;
> And snatch'd the trembling Goddess from the Fire.
>
> (ll. 233–4)

The lines capture precisely Juvenal's epically phrased *vel qui / servavit trepidam flagranti ex aede Minervam*. Oldham, finding a parallel in the virtuous Noah and Lot, concludes his version with:

> Or *t'other*, who the flaming Deluge scap'd,
> When *Sodom's* Lechers Angels would have rap'd.
>
> (ll. 209–10)

The style is in the hyperbolic manner of the 'Jesuits'. The poor man's oaths are not credited, and, as Dryden has it:

> Swear by our Gods, or those the *Greeks* adore,
> Thou art as sure Forsworn, as thou art Poor.
>
> (ll. 243–4)

Again, Oldham's equivalent of the high style is derived from the 'Jesuits', this time even more directly:

> Should I upon a thousand Bibles Swear,
> And call each Saint throughout the Calendar,
> To vouch my Oath; it won't be taken here.   (ll. 219–21)

Such oaths were sworn by the Jesuits during the Popish Terror and are ridiculed thus in 'Jesuits II':

> By the Mass and blessed *Sacraments* he swears,
> This *Mary's Milk*, and t'other *Mary's Tears*,
> And the whole muster-role in *Calendars*.   (ll. 194–6)

The possibly unconscious echo of the perjured Jesuits virtually undermines Juvenal's argument; Oldham seems to have regarded hyperbole as particularly Juvenalian.

Juvenal's thirteenth satire is usually regarded as a recantation of his savage indignation.[24] The satirist reproves Calvinus for his immoderate anger with a friend who has failed to pay a debt. Juvenal sustains his stoic attitude with difficulty, and a growing undercurrent of indignant feeling makes itself felt. He describes the perjured oaths of a thief, who swears by the various attributes of the gods (Mars' lance, the arrows of Artemis, Neptune's trident, etc.), and finally by his own son's life. Oldham turns this into a fully dramatized and heightened scene in the manner of the 'Jesuits':

> The Rascal lays his hand upon the Book:
> Then with a praying Face, and lifted Eye
> Claps on his Lips, and Seals the Perjury:
> If you persist his Innocence to doubt,
> And boggle in Belief; he'l strait rap out
> Oaths by the volley, each of which would make
> Pale Atheists start, and trembling Bullies quake;
> And more than would a whole Ships crew maintain
> To the *East-Indies* hence, and back again.
> *As God shall pardon me, Sir, I am free*
> *Of what you charge me with: let me ne'er see*
> *His Face in Heaven else: may these hands rot,*
> *These eyes drop out; if I e're had a Groat*
> *Of yours, or if they ever touch'd, or saw't.*
> Thus he'l run on two hours in length, till he
> Spin out a Curse long as the Litany:
> Till Heav'n has scarce a Judgement left in store
> For him to wish, deserve, or suffer more.   (ll. 111–28)

Juvenal mocks the absurd grandiosity of the perjurer's oaths and deflates it with a puncturing final word: '"May I eat", weeping he declares, "my own offspring's head boiled, and dripping with

Egyptian vinegar"'[25] (*Pharioque madentis aceto*). Oldham steadily builds up a picture of grotesque excess culminating in his final hyperbolic couplet. A similar passage in 'Jesuits II' concludes with the perjured Jesuit who, determined to make good his 'lie', will 'Mortgage his Soul upon't, his Heaven and God'. Oldham hammers home the effect with the triplet 'Soul', 'Heaven', 'God', giving the same kind of effect as 'wish, deserve, or suffer' in the clinching couplet in 'Juvenal XIII'.

Henry Higden's *A Modern Essay on the Thirteenth Satyr of Juvenal* (1686), written in Hudibrastic verse, is directly influenced by Oldham's imitation, and borrows rhyme-words and ideas freely. However, Higden 'aimed to abate something of his [Juvenal's] serious Rigour, and express his sense in a sort of Verse more apt for Raillery' (b2[r]). Juvenal argues that religious beliefs are considered foolish; one is mocked if one expects anyone to 'believe that some divinity is to be found in temples or in altars red with blood' (ll. 36–7). Higden keeps close to the Latin and even weakens it with 'believes a Power Divine / Inhabits every Church and Shrine' (p. 8). Oldham turns the line into a piece of self-incriminating rhetoric in the manner of the 'Satyr Against Vertue' and the 'Jesuits'. People will laugh when you

> Preach up a God, and Hell, vain empty names,
> Exploded now for idle thredbare shams,
> Devis'd by Priests, and by none else believ'd
> E're since great *Hobbes* the world has undeceiv'd.

(ll. 57–60)

In 'Garnet's Ghost', the Jesuit similarly mocks religion:

> That frivolous pretence, that empty name:
> Meer bugbare-word, devised by Us to scare
> The senseless rout to slavishness and fear,
> Ne're known to aw the brave, and those that dare.

(ll. 98–101)

Oldham displayed, especially in the 'Jesuits', a talent for elaborating the rhetoric of villainy. Rochester's rakish role both in poetry and in life evidently fascinated Oldham. His first satiric poem, 'A Satyr Against Vertue' (July 1676), was 'Suppos'd to be spoken by a Court Hector at Breaking of the Dial in Privy Garden', which refers to Rochester's celebrated prank of 25 June 1675. The poem seems to have been admired by Rochester, who visited the poet at Croydon; Oldham went on to write a number of obscene or rakish poems under the influence of the Court wits. However, these verses ('Sardanapalus', 'Upon the Author of the Play call'd Sodom' and 'A Dithyrambique') possess an ambivalence not to be found in Rochester; the celebration of vice in Oldham is either openly or potentially ironic. The mockery of religion, virtue or sobriety gave Oldham scope to explore with dramatic vividness the rhetorical excesses of the Hobbesian free-thinker and to play out the roles of Marlovian heroes and villains without committing himself to their villainy.

Oldham's imitations of Juvenal share with the Latin poems a rather factitious moral stance. The stoicism of the thirteenth satire is undermined by the satirist's evident enjoyment of the perjurer's agonies of conscience. Oldham evidently relished these passages and indulges his favourite style of rant:

> And, if the wakeful Troubles of his Breast
> To his tossed Limbs allow one moments Rest,
> Straightways the groans of Ghosts, and hideous Screams
> Of tortur'd Spirits, haunt his frightful Dreams:
> Strait there return to his tormented mind
> His perjur'd Act, his injur'd God, and Friend:
> Strait he imagins you before his Eyes,
> Ghastly of shape, and of prodigious size,
> With glaring Eyes, cleft Foot, and monstrous Tail,
> And bigger than the Giants at *Guild-hall*,
> Stalking with horrid strides across the Room,
> And guards of Fiends to drag him to his Doom.
>
> (ll. 363–74)

However, when Juvenal introduces a more dignified note of stoic reflection, Oldham allows a plainer more Horatian tone to emerge:

> Thus, we by sound Divinity, and Sense
> May purge our minds, and weed all Errors thence:
> These lead us into right, nor shall we need
> Other than them thro' Life to be our Guide.   (ll. 305–8)

Oldham sometimes introduces a colloquial idiom, approximating Juvenal rather more to Horace:

> All people, sir, abhor (as 'tis but just)
> Your faithless friend . . .
> Besides, your Case for less concern does call,
> Because 'tis what does usually befal.   (ll. 7–8, 13–14)

The London setting of 'Juvenal III' not only gives Oldham the opportunity for vivid realism, but allows him to develop the plain style of comedy with greater effect. Juvenal complains that the Greek immigrants are play-actors and flatterers; a Greek is always ready 'to take his expression from another's face, to throw up his hands and applaud if his friend gives a good belch or pisses straight' (ll. 105–7). Oldham presents a scene from Restoration comedy:

> Thus he shifts Scenes, and oft'ner in a day
> Can change his Face, than Actors at a Play:
> There's nought so mean, can scape the flatt'ring Sot,
> Not his Lord's Snuff-box, nor his Powder-Spot:
> If he but Spit, or pick his Teeth; he'l cry,
> *How every thing becomes you? let me die,*
> *Your Lordship does it most judiciously:*
> And swear, 'tis fashionable, if he Sneeze,
> Extremely taking, and it needs must please.   (ll. 156–64)

Horace's satire on the bore not only demanded a plainer style on grounds of decorum, but, in its plot, suggests the repartee of comedy. The hounded poet calls the bore 'a familiar Fop' (l. 3), a 'Coxcomb' (l. 9), and 'my wheadle' (l. 55), declares 'The Devil take me now' (l. 91), and invokes the licence of the stage to his aid:

> Wou'd I were like rough *Manly* in the Play,
> To send Impertinents with kicks away!   (ll. 24–5)

Oldham casts the bore in the appropriate role of an affected, vain fop who pretends to wit:

> I'm grown the envy of the men of Wit,
> I kill'd ev'n *Rochester* with grief, and spight . . .
>
>   (ll. 67–8)

He looks for an introduction to the poet's patron, and declares:

> Gad, Sir, I'll die, if my own single Wit
> Don't Fob his minions, and displace 'em quite,
> And make your self his only Favourite.   (ll. 133–5)

Oldham may have been remembering Oldfox ('an old impertinent Fop') who plagues Manly in *The Plain Dealer* (III. i.) or Novel whom Manly threatens and expels from the room in Act II, sc. i. Horace's friend, 'who knew him [the bore] perfectly well', with a 'wicked wit pretends not to understand' Horace's nods and winks. Oldham keeps close to the Latin and yet manages to preserve the comic style already established: his friend 'knew the Fellow's humor passing well' but

> He, naughty Wag, with an arch fleering smile
> Seems ignorant of what I mean the while.   (ll. 169–70)

The turn which he gives Horace here can be appreciated by contrast with Sprat's earlier version:

> But my *unmerciful* malitious friend,
> Seem'd not to understand what I intend.[26]

Sprat's imitation has historical interest: it anticipates some of Oldham's technique of modernization and even influences his wording occasionally.[27]

   The original of Oldham's most ambitious imitation, 'Horace His Art of Poetry', had already been translated by Jonson (whose version appears in Brome's *Horace*), Boileau, and the Earl of Roscommon. By 'putting Horace' into 'modern dress', and by making use of 'English names of Men, Places, and Customs', Oldham achieves a freshness and originality only to be found earlier in Rochester's 'Allusion', although the example of Boileau certainly helped him. Where Horace advises the avoidance of literal translation, Jonson introduces a new emphasis on originality:

> For, being a Poet, thou maist feigne, create,
> Not care, as thou wouldst faithfully translate,
> To render word for word . . .[28]

Jonson's first line has no equivalent in the Latin. Oldham approaches the passage in the same spirit and with greater freedom:

> When you some of their Story represent,
> Take care that you new Episodes invent:
> Be not too nice the Authors words to trace,
> But vary all with a fresh air, and grace.   (ll. 224–7)

This reflects precisely the spirit of the imitation as a whole. The introduction of 'new Episodes' gives the poem a contemporary freshness matched only by Pope's Horatian imitations. While translation forced Jonson tediously to recite the development of stage machinery in Greek drama, Oldham's 'libertine way' made possible the following celebration of the modern stage:

> But since our Monarch by kind Heaven sent,
> Brought back the Arts with him from Banishment,
> And by his gentle influence gave increase
> To all the harmless Luxuries of peace:
> Favour'd by him, our Stage has flourisht too,
> And every day in outward splendor grew:
> In Musick, Song, and Dance of every kind,
> And all the grace of Action 'tis refin'd;
> And since that Opera's at length come in,
> Our Players have so well improv'd the Scene
> With gallantry of Habit, and Machine:
> As makes our Theater in Glory vie
> With the best Ages of Antiquity.   (ll. 342–54)

At this time, most dramatists were lamenting the decline of the stage. Dryden's *Mac Flecknoe* (written *c.* 1678) castigated Shadwell's enormously successful operatic plays, *The Tempest* and *Psyche*; even Rochester, who praised Shadwell in 'An Allusion', ridiculed the Duke's men's money-spinning 'songs and scenes', 'machines and a dull masque', and 'awkward actors'.[29] It is fitting that, in an imitation, Oldham presents a more detached and nationalistic view of the theatre of his time.

Oldham completed paraphrases of two Horatian odes (i. xxxi. and ii. xiv.) and started a third (iv. xiii.). Their excellence makes one wish he had done more. Once again Oldham's use of the translational categories is unusual. Both completed odes are fully modernized; Oldham seems to have used the term 'imitation' only where the scene is transposed to a specifically modern and English situation. The following passage from i. xxxi. might have appeared in 'Juvenal iii':

> Let wealthy Merchants, when they Dine,
>   Run o're their costly names of Wine,
> Their Chests of *Florence*, and their *Mont-Alchine*,
> Their *Mants*, *Champagns*, *Chablees*, *Frontiniacks* tell,

> Their Aums of *Hock*, of *Blackrag* and *Moselle*.
>
> > (ll. 19–23)

The catalogue of wines is suggested by Horace's *vina Syra reparata merce* ('wines bought with Syrian profit'). The list evokes a typical and not a specific picture of the modern world. Oldham responds carefully to the requirements of the 'happy man' theme; he even out-Horaces Horace in cultivating the humble role of the *beatus ille*: *quid . . . poscit . . . vates?* becomes 'What does the Poet's modest Wish require?' The brief prayer for health and sanity in old age is treated with studied plainness:

> Let him in strength of Mind, and Body live,
> But not his Reason, nor his Sense survive:
> His Age (if Age he e're must live to see)
> Let it from want, Contempt, and Care be free.
>
> > (ll. 40–3)

The second couplet has no equivalent in the Latin and may have a personal application.

The other ode (*Eheu fugaces*), on the inevitability of death, displays the advantages and disadvantages of Oldham's method of liberal paraphrase. On the negative side, he is inclined to expand Horace to the point of being over-explicit. At its best, the version has much in common with Oldham's best satiric style. We must all cross Lethe, says Horace, both rich and poor. Alexander Radcliffe's translation gives us the plain-style equivalent:

> This irksom Shore must entertain
> The greatest Prince that e'er shall reign:
> > As great a welcom shall be there
> > Made to the meanest Cottager;
> > > Distinctions are in vain.[30]

Oldham's sixteen-line version dismisses the conventional classical Hades, expatiates on the 'vast stock of humane Progeny' which crawl on the 'Earth's spacious Ball' like 'swarms of Insects', and concludes with a piece of satire in the traditional manner of 'complaint':

> The busie, restless *Monarch* of the times, which now
> > Keeps such a pother, and so much ado
> > > To fill Gazettes alive,

And after in some lying Annal to survive;
Ev'n He, ev'n that great mortal Man must die,
And stink, and rot as well as thou, and I,
As well as the poor tatter'd wretch, that begs his bread,
And is with Scraps out of the Common Basket fed.

(ll. 25–32)

Congreve's dignified neoclassical imitation of the same lines reminds us how strongly Oldham was moved to introduce his favourite manner:

The Rich, the Great, the Innocent and Just,
    Must all be huddled to the Grave,
With the most Vile and Ignominious Slave,
    And undistinguished lie in Dust.[31]

In the magnificent final stanza, Horace describes how the rich man's heir will waste his inheritance, broach old wines (*caecuba*), and *tinget pavimentum superbo / pontificum potiore cenis* ('drench the floor with prouder wine than is drunk at the pontiff's banquet'). Oldham picks up the satiric hint:

And wash these stately Floors with better Wine
Than that of consecrated Prelates when they dine.

(ll. 60–1)

John Tutchin, who appears to have been a disciple of Oldham (he also wrote a memorial elegy on Oldham), published a translation of the ode in his *Poems on Several Occasions* (1685), which owes several phrases to Oldham. His concluding couplet is a variation on Oldham's:

And wash the Stones with better Wine
Than that which makes the *Bishops* ruby Noses shine.

Congreve's 'pamper'd Prelates' may be influenced by Oldham too.

Oldham's imitations of Bion and Moschus were done, according to the author, to show that the 'roughness' of his satires 'was out of choice, not want of judgement' and that he was capable of writing on 'agreeable Subjects'. Moschus' third idyll, the 'Lament for Bion', which Oldham considered 'a piece of as much Art, Grace, and Tenderness, as perhaps was ever offered to the Ashes of a Poet' (Advertisement, *Some New Pieces*), became 'A Pastoral . . .

bewailing the Death of the Earl of ROCHESTER'. The style is certainly plainer and more elegant than in the satires. However, Oldham's use of rhyme and prosody are not noticeably less 'rough'. His norm of correctness in these respects was less classical than Dryden's or even Rochester's. The modernization is more perfunctory; pastoral did not permit vivid particularity:

> Mourn ye sweet Nightingales in the thick Woods,
> Tell the sad news to all the *British* Floods:
> See it to *Isis*, and to *Cham* convey'd,
> To *Thames*, to *Humber*, and to utmost *Tweed*. .
>
> (ll. 16–19)

In the second Greek pastoral, Bion's 'Lamentation for Adonis', Oldham responds to the greater intensity of feeling in the original by giving rein to his more characteristic vehemence. Two lines of Greek[32] describing Aphrodite's roaming the thickets in distressful disarray correspond to the following passage in Oldham:

> But the sad Goddess, most of all forlorn,
> With love distracted, and with sorrow torn,
> Wild in her look, and ruful in her air,
> With garments rent, and with dishevel'd hair,
> Through Brakes, through Thickets, and through pathless
>   ways,
> Through Woods, through Haunts, and Dens of Savages,
> Undrest, unshod, careless of Honor, Fame,
> And Danger, flies, and calls on his lov'd name.
>
> (ll. 37–44)

His characteristic cumulative rhetoric carves a way through the delicate 'Art, Grace, and Tenderness' of the Greek. The goddess laments that she is immortal and cannot follow her beloved. Oldham expands a sentence to a sixteen-line soliloquy in which her thoughts roam in eschatological speculations in the manner of heroic drama, concluding with

> If I by death my sorrows might redress,
> If the cold Grave could to my pains give ease;
> I'd gladly die, I'd rather nothing be
> Than thus condemn'd to immortality:
> In that vast empty void, and boundless wast,

We mind not what's to come, nor what is past.
Or life, or death we know no difference,
Nor hopes, nor fears at all affect our sence:
But those who are of pleasure once bereft,
And must survive, are most unhappy left:
To ravenous sorrow they are left a prey,
Nor can they ever drive despair away.   ((ll. 99–110)

Oldham's version of Virgil's eighth eclogue returns to a form of
translation favoured by Ben Jonson; the version is more faithful
than paraphrase but a few references are modernized (Spenser for
Sophocles, '*Lightfoot*' for 'Hylax', and the Duke of York's Dutch
wars for Pollio's Illyrian campaign). The Jonsonian technique of
combining literalism with native idiom is also used: 'Nut-scramble'
(*sparge nuces*), 'Daffadill' (*narcissus*), 'True-love-knots' (*Veneris
vincula*), and 'Church-yards' (*sepulchris*). Two translations of the
eclogue, published soon after his death by Stafford and Chetwood,[33] are more conventional.

A final group of shorter poems on love and wine comprises
versions of an Anacreontic, Catullus VII, 'Petronius'' *Foeda est in
coitu*, and three of Ovid's elegies (*Amores*). These poems reflect an
aspect of Oldham's admiration for Rochester. The paraphrase of
'τὸν ἄργυριον τορεύων'[34] is partly influenced by Rochester's 'Upon
His Drinking a Bowl' (which is itself indirectly from the Greek but
directly from Ronsard).[35] Rochester's outrageous imagination
transforms the bowl:

Make it so large that, filled with sack
    Up to the swelling brim,
Vast toasts on the delicious lake
    Like ships at sea may swim.   (ll. 5–8)

This surely suggested Oldham's:

I lack no Pole-Star on the Brink,
To guide in the wide Sea of Drink,
But would for ever there be tost;
And wish no Haven, seek no Coast.   (ll. 36–9)

Oldham's hyperbolical fancy here receives its stimulus from the
Earl; the Greek has only 'the deepest cup you may' ('ποτήριον . . .
ὅσον δύνῃ βαθύνας). Other verbal echoes conclusively establish

Rochester's influence.[36] Oldham uses this style brilliantly from the beginning:

> Make me a Bowl, a mighty Bowl,
> Large, as my capacious Soul,
> Vast, as my thirst is; let it have
> Depth enough to be my Grave;
> I mean the Grave of all my Care,
> For I intend to bury't there . . .   (ll. 1–6)

All this too from 'the deepest cup you may'! One might call the style mock-metaphysical rather than mock-heroic.

The well-known fragment of 'Petronius', *Foeda est in coitu et brevis voluptas*[37] is treated by Oldham with his usual freedom yet without abandoning the principle of consecutive translation. The anonymous translation in 'Dryden's Miscellany' (1684) and Old-mixon's 'imitation' are much less daring. Oldmixon is plainer and more elegant:

> Fruition is at best but short,
> A silly fulsom fleeting sport,
> Which when we've perfectly enjoy'd,
> We're quickly weary, quickly cloy'd.[38]

The anonymous translator tries to retain the brevity of the Latin, with poor results:

> 'Tis but a Short, but filthy Pleasure,
> And we soon nauseate the enjoy'd treasure.   (p. 217)

Oldham expands the opening, adding a more explicit unpleasantness:

> A squirt of slippery Delight,
> That with a moment takes its flight.   (ll. 5–6)

The Latin asks us not to behave like beasts in love, 'for [then] love droops and the flame dies'. Oldham's exuberant version of this line extends the metaphor in another mock-conceit:

> For when in Floods of Love we're drench'd,
> The Flames are by enjoyment quench'd.   (ll. 13–14)

In his versions of Ovid's *Amores*, Oldham enters the poetic space elegantly inhabited by the Court Wits, especially Rochester and Sir

Charles Sedley. The translation of the fifth elegy of the second book can be compared with Sedley's, which was published in 'Dryden's Miscellany' (1684). In 'An Allusion to Horace', Sedley is considered to have

> that prevailing art,
> That can with a resistless charm impart
> The loosest wishes to the chastest heart.   (ll. 64–6)

Oldham never pretended to this kind of subtlety, and his expanded version lacks Sedley's graceful and delicate wit. However, Oldham's expansions once again give him the opportunity of heightening the passions with conceits and intense diction. Sedley is at his best in the pointed closed couplet:

> Happy's the man that's handsomely deceiv'd,
> Whose *Mistress* swears and lies, and is believ'd.[39]

Oldham's version of the next couplet (omitted by Sedley) shows him in his best vein:

> Cruel the Man, and uncompassionate,
> And too indulgent to his own Regret,
> Who seeks to have her guilt too manifest,
> And with the murd'ring secret stabs his Rest.
>   (ll. 16–19)

His second couplet does not directly translate the cryptic Latin (*cui petitur victa palma cruenta rea*) but develops its point effectively from the word *cruenta* ('bloody'). Ovid describes the secret messages exchanged between his mistress and the other man; Sedley removes the details and simply refers to 'signs . . . conveying the glad message of thy Love'. Oldham develops the details wittily:

> I saw the conscious Board, which writ all o're
> With scrawls of Wine, Love's mystick Cypher bore:
> Your Glances were not mute, but each bewray'd,
> And with your Fingers Dialogues were made.   (ll. 26–9)

Compare Marlowe's translation:

> Not silent were thine eyes, the boord with wine
> Was scribled, and thy fingers writ a line.[40]

Oldham's added conceits remind one of the metaphysicals; Donne's 'mystique language of the eye and hand' and 'Alphabet of flowers' come to mind aptly, since 'Natures lay Ideot' may itself be influenced by Ovid.[41] The three translators show their respective strengths in a passage describing the lady's pleasing guilty blush:

> A scarlet blush her guilty face arayed.
> Euen such as by *Aurora* hath the skie,
> Or maides that their betrothed husbands spie.
>
> > (Marlowe, ll. 34–6)

> Her face she cover'd with a Conscious red:
> Like a Cloud guilded by the rising Sun,
> Or Virgin newly by-her Love undone.
>
> > (Sedley, ll. 32–4)

> While conscious shame her Cheeks with Blushes fir'd:
> Such lovely stains the face of Heav'n adorn
> When Light's first blushes paint the bashful Morn.
>
> > (Oldham, ll. 53–5)

Marlowe keeps close to the Latin, favouring native diction, but relishes the music of a name ('*Aurora*' for *Tithoni conjuge*). Sedley conforms to Rochester's image of him ('mannerly obscene'); he begins by elegantly refining on Ovid's first simile, only to transform his pre-coital blush (*sponso* visa *puella nova*) to a post-coital glow. Oldham, by the use of personification ('the bashful Morn'), neatly extends the first simile to take in the second. As in so many of his versions, he allows his poetic fancy greater freedom than is usual in Augustan translation and paraphrase in the seventeenth century.

Oldham is probably the most adventurous and various of Augustan classicists. He informs his models with his own 'masculine' wit without departing from their sense. His skill in elaborating the 'passions' is equally effective in his vehement satiric versions and in the more lyrical or amatory middle style. He usually intensifies feeling by using dramatization, grotesque imagery, cumulative rhetoric, hyperbole and downright native idiom. The acerbic and unruly rhetoric of the 'Jesuits' is a regular source of highly charged moments, but the demands of decorum usually prevail and effectively control his excesses. His methods of paraphrase and imitation opened the way for Pope and Dr Johnson.

NOTES

1 'The "Imitation" in English Poetry . . .', *RES*, 25 (1949), 124–40.

2 Quotations from Oldham's *Poetical Works*, forthcoming Oxford edn, edited by H. F. Brooks with my collaboration.

3 See Advertisement, *Satyrs upon the Jesuits*, and C. H. Cable's 'Oldham's Borrowing from Buchanan,' *MLN*, 66 (1951), 523–7.

4 See H. F. Brooks, 'Oldham and Phineas Fletcher . . .', *RES*, 22 (1971), 410–22, and 23 (1972), 19–34.

5 He has versions of Bion, Moschus and an Anacreontic ode; and a 'Praise of Homer'.

6 These include Persius, Aulus Gellius, Diodorus Siculus, Plato, Strabo, Clement of Alexandria, S. Augustine, Suidas, Lucan, Pliny, Casaubon, Lactantius, Minutius Felix, and of the moderns Barclay and Varenius.

7 George Watson (ed.), *Of Dramatic Poesy and Other Critical Essays*, 2 vols (London, 1962, I, 69. Cf. Carew's 'To Ben Johnson', ll. 39–46.

8 *Works*, ed. C. H. Herford, Percy and Evelyn M. Simpson, 11 vols (Oxford, 1925–52), VIII, 567.

9 Both 'allusions' are spoken by the poet in his own person.

10 See *Complete Works*, ed. M. Summers (1933), IV, 3.

11 Watson, I, 265, 41.

12 Watson, I, 52.

13 ll. 469–70: *placida resoluta quiete/saepe videt quod amat.*

14 l. 630: *incertae tanta est discordia mentis.*

15 ll. 483–4: *gaudia quanta tuli! quam me manifesta libido / contigit! ut iacui totis resoluta medullis!*

16 Watson, I, 41.

17 *Miscellany Poems* (1697), C3^r – C3^v, C7^r – C7^v, C8^v.

18 See Raman Selden, 'Juvenal and Restoration Modes of Translation', *MLR*, 68 (1973), 481–93.

19 See Rachel Trickett, *The Honest Muse* (Oxford, 1967), 102: 'imitation had chastened and dignified Oldham's violent style'.

20 Cited by H. F. Brooks, 'Poems of John Oldham', in H. Love (ed.), *Restoration Literature* (London, 1972), 182.

21 Oldham had earlier translated Boileau's *Le Lutrin*, Canto I

(July 1678) and had, in the same year, transcribed Dryden's *Mac Flecknoe*.

22 Watson, II, 149.

23 For discussion of the term see Raman Selden, 'Roughness in Satire from Horace to Dryden', *MLR*, 66 (1971), 264–72.

24 See W. S. Anderson, *Anger in Juvenal and Seneca*, University of California Publications in Classical Philology, 19, no. 3 (1964), 127–96, and Raman Selden, *English Verse Satire, 1590–1765* (London, 1978), 30–1.

25 Cf. Juvenal, X. 153: *montem rumpit aceto*.

26 *The Poems of Horace* (ed. Alexander Brome, London, 1666), 231. For the attribution to Sprat, see H. F. Brooks, 'Contributors to Brome's *Horace*', *N&Q*, 174 (January–June 1938), 200–1.

27 Sprat's French dancing (p. 228) anticipates Oldham's reference to St André, the French dancing master (l. 70). Sprat's 'A Bailiff' (p. 231) becomes Oldham's 'a brace of Bailiffs' (l. 191). Other verbal echoes include: 'all wayes to shake him off I tri'd', p. 228 (cf. Oldham's 'I try all ways / To shake him off', ll. 16–17); 'Have you / No mother Sir, nor other kindred', p. 229 (cf. Oldham's 'Have you / A mother, Sir, or Kindred living', ll. 73–4); 'Strange and unusual this which you relate', p. 230 (cf. Oldham's ''Tis mighty strange . . . what you relate', l. 143). See also Brooks, 'The "Imitation" . . .' (see n. 1 above). Oldham tells us, in the Advertisement, that he did not see Sprat's version until his own was completed. He seems to have been disingenuous.

28 *Works*, VIII, 313.

29 David M. Vieth (ed.), *The Complete Poems of John Wilmot, Earl of Rochester* (New Haven, Conn., and London, 1968), 91, 92.

30 *The Ramble* (1682), 57.

31 *Complete Works*, IV, 3.

32   ἁ δ᾽Ἀφροδίτα
      λυσαμένα πλοκαμῖδας ἀνὰ δρυμὼς ἀλάληται
      πενθαλέα νήπλεκτος ασάνδαλος . . .

('Aphrodite, with her locks unbound, roams the thickets, sorrowful, unkempt, barefoot')

33 *Virgil's Eclogues Translated By Several Hands* (1684), published also in *Miscellany Poems* (1684). Chetwood's version makes use of Oldham's rhyme-words.

34 J. M. Edmonds (ed.), *Elegy and Iambus . . . with the Anacreontea* (London and New York, 1931), II, 23.

35 Vieth, quoting Curt Zimansky, 52.

36 Compare Rochester's 'But carve thereon a spreading vine' with Oldham's 'Draw me first a spreading Vine'. Rochester's 'Cupid and Bacchus' may have suggested Oldham's '*Bacchus* and soft *Cupid*' (The Greek has 'ὅμου . . . Λυαίῳ / Ἔρωτα καὶ Βαθύλλον').

37 *Anthologia Latina*, Teubner edn, ed. F. Buecheler *et al.* (1964), I, ii, 171.

38 *Poems on Several Occasions* (1696).

39 *Works*, ed. V. de S. Pinto (London, 1928), I, 96. Pinto also prints a version from f. 56 of BM Add. MS. 34, 744, combining sixty-five lines from Oldham and twenty from Sedley.

40 *Works*, ed. C. F. Tucker Brooke (Oxford, 1910), 587.

41 In fact, the more direct source is Tibullus, I. vi., which in turn seems to have influenced Ovid's lines. Compare Tibullus' *nutu, digitoque liquorem . . . mensae* with Ovid's *nutibus . . . vino / mensa . . . digitis.*

9

THE ART OF ADAPTATION

SOME RESTORATION
TREATMENTS OF OVID

Harold Love

During the closing decades of the seventeenth century, translation and the closely related craft of imitation established themselves, in a way that was both unprecedented and never to be repeated, as the central preoccupation of English poetry. Dryden's Juvenal and Persius (1693) and Virgil (1697), taken with the translations that appeared in *Fables* (1700) and the first five of the Tonson miscellanies, amount to well over half his poetic output and show him at the height of his powers. Rochester's corpus of translated and adapted verse is slight by comparison but includes such masterpieces as 'O Love! how cold and slow to take my part', 'After death nothing is', his two crucial experiments in the free imitation of French models, 'Timon' and 'A Satyr against Reason and Mankind', and the stricter, and even more influential, 'An Allusion to Horace'. John Oldham produced no single version as dazzling as Dryden's or Rochester's at their best; but his four books published between 1681 and 1684 present a fascinating record of a gifted poetical alchemist hard at work in the laboratory of linguistic transmutation with, once again, well over half his verse being derived from alien models. It is thoroughly symptomatic of the temper of the age that Thomas Creech, who was a specialist translator, producing complete English versions of Lucretius, Horace, Theocritus and Manilius but hardly any original work, should none the less have been accepted as one of its leading poets. His Lucretius of 1682 attracted laudatory verses from, among others, John Evelyn, Nahum Tate, Thomas Otway, Joseph Arrowsmith, Richard Duke and Aphra Behn, the last of whom hails the translator as a second Rochester.[1] Critics, also, showed a keen concern with theories of translation, pride of place after Dryden's discussions in the prefaces to *Ovid's Epistles* (1680) and *Sylvae* (1685) going to the Earl of Roscommon's *An Essay on Translated Verse* of 1684.

Where Dryden, Rochester, Oldham and Creech led, there were any number of lesser poets eager to follow, whose shorter-breathed talents found a home in the Tonson miscellanies and their many imitators and in composite translations such as *Ovid's Epistles*, the Dryden Juvenal and the *Metamorphoses* of 1697 and 1717. After 1700 the flow of new translations appears to have intensified, culminating in Pope's Homer. There is naturally dross as well as gold to be encountered among the lesser translators of the period; but it is still possible to claim that their powers, whether great or small, were actively elevated rather than being depressed by the prospect of putting a foreign original into English. Horace was particularly fortunate in this respect: Congreve's version of *Odes* I.ix and Sedley's of II.viii are arguably their finest achievements in the lyric mode.[2] In Dryden's case, where the poet was a great one, the translated verse taken as a body may well represent the outstanding success of its kind in the language, with the best of it – the sixth satire of Juvenal, say, his versions of Lucretius on the fear of death and the nature of love, or 'Of the Pythagorean Philosophy' – standing level in terms of quality with the very best of his original work. It seems pertinent therefore to enquire why, during these years, the creative tide should have run so powerfully in favour of an art which most other ages have regarded as secondary and servile.

We are dealing, of course, with a time which for well-understood reasons had the profoundest reverence for the classics and was prone to see Greek and Roman civilization as in many ways superior to its own. But this had been just as much the case a century earlier and was to remain the case for over a century to come, without translation ever diverting poetic energies away from original composition to the extent it did in the decades 1670–1700. For this to happen required that poets should want to translate in preference to writing original verse, and that readers should want to buy their translations, and it is only in the second case that reasons readily suggest themselves. In London, which was always the largest market for the products of the book trade, the greater spaciousness of middle-class living conditions following the great post-fire rebuilding, allied with rising literacy and leisure, especially among women, were leading to an overall expansion of the market for literature from which translations naturally benefited. Such readers will rarely have been able to read the classics in the original languages, but will have been drawn to them not only by their prestige and intrinsic interest but by a well-founded suspicion that they provided a kind of literary code for keeping ideological debate beyond the understanding of the uneducated – a matter well understood by Dryden.[3] It is also likely that those who did read the ancient languages now did so with less fluency than had been the case with the generations educated before the 1650s, as pedagogical standards in the grammar schools and universities were in a state of continuing decline which was not to be arrested for many decades to come. Among more immediate influences was that of enterprising publishers, especially Jacob Tonson who built the fortunes of the most successful house of the era very much on the commissioned translation offered to the world first in a lordly folio, then in a steady reiteration of octavos and duodecimos. In this, and his successful promotion of editions of Shakespeare and Milton, Tonson was probably creating taste quite as much as following it; while the economics of the subscription system allowed for payments of unprecedented generosity to favoured translators. After the political changes of 1688–9, it is also fair to say that translation formed a highly convenient common ground for a Whig publisher, who knew how to sell books and was prepared to pay authors handsomely to write them, and a group of poets, led by Dryden, who were predominantly Tory or Jacobite in their sympathies. But the Tonson translations and their successors were never intended merely to fill vacant shelf-space in the new crop of town and country houses. Their aim is patently to be read; to be read, moreover, by a public who could not be relied upon to know the originals or to be capable of unriddling a pregnant obscurity by looking up the Latin or Greek. Their language is unfailingly clear and idiomatic. Their aim – possibly to a fault – is always to be effective and approachable English poems.

For all of these reasons and others which will readily suggest themselves, there is no difficulty in accounting for an immense vogue for translation and adaptation reaching its peak at the turn of the century. But it is a characteristic of vogues that they do not succeed in harnessing the most deeply seated poetic energies of an era, whereas, with the translations under discussion, the distinguishing point is not their numerousness but that, by the standards that prevailed before and after, they are so consistently good. To discover the imperative that made poets of the 1690s wish not merely to transmit the meaning of an alien original to their age and nation but to make this the principal goal of their own creativity, we have to look beyond the obvious social influences to a much profounder linking of minds across languages and cultures. Our evidence for its precise nature must be the poems themselves and what the translators made of them, using as our sample some of the Restoration versions of Ovid's *Amores* and *Metamorphoses*.

*

The modes of translation available to a Restoration poet were basically seven in number. The first was the crib translation, or in Dryden's term 'metaphrase', in which the aim was one of 'turning an Authour word by word, and Line by Line, from one Language into another', irrespective of any aesthetic awkwardness or violations of native idiom that might result.[4] The second was a mode, usually just as faithful in its communication of lexical meaning, in which the poet tried in addition to convey something of the verbal texture of his original by using abnormally long lines or unusual dislocations of syntax. The third, and predominant, mode was a freer one in which the ideas of the original were given in phrase by phrase paraphrase rather than exact verbal translation – versions of the author's sense rather than his words as such – and in which a conscious effort was made that language, idiom and verse form should be indistinguishable from those of an original poem of the day. The fourth mode, perfected by Dryden working along lines earlier advocated by Denham and Cowley, involved a much freer handling of the poetic materials of the source and gave the translator liberty to incorporate images and ideas of his own devising; but still presented itself (sometimes quite misleadingly) as a representation in English of a Roman or Greek original. The fifth and the sixth modes were the strict and free forms respectively of the 'imitation', in which references to the original poet's times were replaced by allusions to contemporary English life. The stricter imitations, as Harold Brooks has pointed out in his classic paper on the early history of the genre, are often no more than 'modernized translations' denying themselves even the liberties claimed by the more radical translators.[5] The freer imitations may be further subdivided into those – among which Howard Weinbrot would number explicit parodies – which count on readers possessing prior knowledge of the work imitated, and which therefore have to maintain a fairly close parallelism,[6] and a final class of reconstructions *ad libitum* out of the rubble of demolished originals. This last approach is most often found when the author being imitated is French, for the Restoration imitator, bold as he was in his reworkings of Boileau, was not normally prepared to take major structural liberties with Horace or Juvenal.

Of these seven modes, the first, the literal-minded crib translation, was hardly ever attempted by serious poets of our period. Dryden likened it to 'dancing on Ropes with fetter'd Leggs'.[7] The most notable exception, Shadwell's labouredly scholarly translation of the tenth satire of Juvenal, published in 1687 in parallel text with detailed explanatory notes, seems to have been undertaken chiefly in order to refute accusations by Dryden and the anonymous author of *Poeta de Tristibus* (1682) that the translator knew no Latin.[8] Its preface contains the only serious plea from a major writer of the period for strict fidelity in translation; but it is a plea that patently springs less from critical principle than from Shadwell's violent, and who is to say unjustified, animus against the '*Cock Translator*', Dryden.[9] There was likewise, apart from the specialized case of the Cowleyan pindaric, virtually no interest in the second mode in which the attempt is made to mimic the phonetic or syntactical qualities of the original languages. If any such ambition is to be encountered in the poetry of Dryden and his contemporaries, it is only to the extent that the closed, antithetical Ovidian distich of a hexameter followed by a pentameter had served as an influence on the development of similar tendencies in the English couplet.[10] Examples of an earlier aesthetic of translation which had actively encouraged such mimicry are Golding's Elizabethan and Sandys's Caroline translations of the *Metamorphoses*. Golding's galloping fourteeners give some sense of the linear drive of the original metre, albeit their ebullient, clodhopping rhythms could not be less suggestive of Ovid's seamlessly euphonious hexameters. Sandys, whose translation was praised for its accuracy by Oldham and apparently consulted by Dryden when

he made his own versions of parts of the same work, used an
exceptionally elliptical syntax of the kind it is usual to call Latinate,
though it is likely that a native love of 'strong lines' and the
difficulties of translating in as close as possible an approximation to
the lineation of the original also exerted an influence. The following
from Book xv is a fair sample of the result:

> So change our bodies without rest or stay:
> What wee were yester-day, nor what to day,
> Shall bee to morrow. Once alone of men
> The seeds and hope; the womb our mansion: when
> Kind Nature shewd her cunning; not content
> That our vext bodies should be longer pent
> In mothers stretched entrailes, forth-with bare
> Them from that prison, to the open aire.[11]

Such language suggests something of the compression of Latin;
but, by such omissions as that of an essential 'neither' from the
beginning of the second line and an even more necessary 'we' from
the second position in the third, made things very difficult for those
English readers who were not able to look over to the original to
discover what Ovid was really saying. Moreover, Sandys's dislocations of syntax do not perform the binding function created by
the separation of adjectives from nouns and the unpredictable
placing of subjects and objects with regard to verbs that is
characteristic of Latin poetry. Their effect is to shatter the sentence
rather than knit it.

The very different attitude of the Restoration poets can be shown
by juxtaposing a few lines from Rochester's translation from the
same Roman's *Amores* II. ix which will also serve to introduce the
third mode:

> O Love! how cold and slow to take my part,
> Thou idle wanderer about my heart.
> Why thy old faithful soldier wilt thou see
> Oppressed in my own tents? They murder me.
> Thy flames consume, thy arrows pierce thy friends;
> Rather, on foes pursue more noble ends.[12]

Rochester's language, while catching the Ovidian manner remark-
ably well, shows little metrical or syntactical influence from the
Latin. It is true that his task is an easier one than Sandys's had been in

that his original is written in self-contained distichs, not run-on hexameters. But it will be clear, even at the outset, that one of Rochester's leading priorities was that the poem should not be in any way recognizable as a translation apart from the fact that the author has told us so. Encountered without title, it would be accepted in its own right as a fine English love poem, much as 'All my past life is mine no more' has been accepted as an original lyric despite its origin as a verse expansion of a passage in Hobbes's *Leviathan*.[13] The elegy is in fact a perfect example of the concept of translation as paraphrase as it was preached, though not practised, by Dryden. Essentially it is a careful reworking of each of the ideas of the original, usually on a couplet for distich basis, but one which is always prepared to sacrifice strict semantic fidelity to its original in the interest of securing a natural, poetically effective English idiom. Thus we find on inspection that the opening line is rather a counterpart to, than a translation of, *O numquam pro re satis indignande Cupido* (given by Guy Lee, still a little freely, as 'Cupid, contempt's far more than you deserve'[14]) and that, having taken this liberty in order to get his poem off to a striking start, Rochester was forced to readjust the sense of the following lines so that the dealer of the wound is no longer Cupid in person (*quid me . . . laedis?*) but the women whom the poet can not help loving ('They murder me.'). In the third couplet, however, Rochester not only returns to Ovid's original image, but shows that, when not under the constraint of making his translation of interest to English readers as an English poem, he can in fact paraphrase with great precision. Ovid's distich is *Cur tua fax urit, figit tuus arcus amicos? / Gloria pugnantes vincere maior erat.* The only real liberties taken by Rochester are that the first line is no longer a question and that, in the second, a strong implication becomes a straight-out admonition. Otherwise he is as faithful to his original as we could fairly expect a verse translation to be and remain poetry, which is sadly not the case with Guy Lee's 'Is it always friends your torch and arrows pierce and burn? / There'd be more glory in overcoming resistance.'

Rochester, in other words, is a competent and conscientious paraphraser, but one whose first allegiance is to English idiom and to the rhythms, as his ear conceived them, of the English pentameter couplet. There are only three instances where he fails to maintain the correspondence of couplet to distich, lines 21–6, 27–30 and 56–60, and it is only in the first of these that he allows ideas of his own to infiltrate the poem, thus modulating briefly into the fourth mode. Here the successive images of ships laid up in dock and of a retired gladiator exchanging his sword for a practice foil are replaced by the distinctively Restoration 'The harassed whore, who lived a wretch to please, / Has leave to be a bawd and take her ease', and the active service of the amorous soldier is declared, without Ovidian warrant, to have taken place 'in Celia's trenches'. But these departures are no more than fairly minor personal flourishes added to a translation elsewhere faithful to the principles of the third mode, in which, to borrow a definition from Dryden, 'the Authour is kept in view by the Translator, so as never to be lost, but his words are not so strictly follow'd as his sense, and that too is admitted to be amplyfied, but not alter'd'.[15] In the other two instances cited, two couplets are used to translate a single distich, producing a somewhat periphrastic but not significantly distorted version of what is stated by Ovid.

Similar principles and a similar general fidelity to the sense of the originals inform John Oldham's Ovidian translations with the qualification that Oldham, lacking or having no interest in culti-vating Rochester's gift of lucid conciseness, was far more prone to call on Dryden's let-out clause of amplification. Following him with the Latin, especially in his imitations of *Amores* II. iv, v, and x, where he very frequently requires two couplets to deal with the sense of a single distich, one is continually encountering filler-lines, which have no precise counterpart in Ovid but at the same time do not represent any clearly distinguishable addition to his meaning. In II. iv, for instance, a single distich *non est certa meos quae forma invitet amores; / centum sunt causae cur ego semper amem*, which might be translated in crib style: 'It's not any particular kind of beauty that arouses my passions; there are a hundred reasons for my always being in love', is expanded by Oldham to:

> 'Tis not one Face alone subdues my Heart,
> But each wears Charms, and every Eye a Dart:
> And whereso'er I cast my Looks abroad,
> In every place I find Temptations strow'd . . .[16]

Here Oldham finds an excellent English equivalent for the hexameter of Ovid's distich; but in two goes at the pentameter, neither of which really hits the nail on the head, only succeeds in becoming diffuse. Against this, however, must be set the real triumphs of translation that can spring from his willingness to embroider the strict verbal sense of his originals:

> One with her soft and wanton Trip does please,
> And prints in every step, she sets, a Grace:
> Another walks with stiff ungainly tread;
> But she may learn more pliantness abed,
> This sweetly sings; her Voice does Love inspire,
> And every Breath kindles, and blows the fire:
> Who can forbear to kiss those Lips, whose sound
> The ravish'd Ears does with such softness wound?
> That sweetly plays: and while her Fingers move,
> While o'er the bounding Strings their touches rove,
> My Heart leaps too, and every Pulse beats Love:
> What Reason is so pow'rful to withstand
> The magick force of that resistless Hand?[17]

These thirteen lines of English verse are extracted from a mere six Latin ones. A Rochester would undoubtedly have wanted to reduce this number; but it would be hard to deny that Oldham has here succeeded admirably in Dryden's ideal of making the author speak as he would have done 'had he liv'd in our Age, and in our Country'.[18] In any case, it must be accepted that one of the charms of these translations is a certain sense of felicitious improvisation, or, to borrow Rochester's words in praise of Shadwell, 'great mastery, with little care'. Oldham's verse generally delights through its idiomatic bite and rhetorical exuberance rather than its verbal fine detail. It is also only fair to say that, as Harold Brooks's eagerly awaited critical edition will make clear, Oldham's finest achievements as a translator are in his versions of Horace and Juvenal rather than his attempts at Ovid.[19]

*

From what has been said, it should be clear that Rochester and Oldham in their versions of Ovid, whether presented as translations or as conservative imitations, share a body of common assumptions about the relationship of the language of a translation to that of its original, and that the two most important of these assumptions are the paraphrastical ideal, as promulgated by Dryden in the preface to *Ovid's Epistles*, and a belief that their English should flow as naturally and idiomatically to readers of their own nation as Ovid's

Latin had to Roman ones. Indeed, their aim can be seen as one of restoring the kind of excitement that must have been felt when Ovid was read by contemporaries as a contemporary. Dryden, on the other hand, soon developed far more radical views than those of his 1680 preface, while still claiming to be a translator rather than an imitator. In the preface to *Sylvae: or, the Second Part of Poetical Miscellanies* (1685), after a nod to Roscommon, he presents a charter for a translator which must be one of the most liberal ever framed:

> Yet withall, I must acknowledge, that I have many times exceeded my Commission; for I have both added and omitted, and even sometimes very boldly made such expositions of my Authors, as no *Dutch* Commentator will forgive me. Perhaps, in such particular passages, I have thought that I discover'd some beauty yet undiscover'd by those Pedants, which none but a Poet cou'd have found. Where I have taken away some of their Expressions, and cut them shorter, it may possibly be on this consideration, that what was beautiful in the *Greek* or *Latin*, wou'd not appear so shining in the *English*: And where I have enlarg'd them, I desire the false Criticks wou'd not always think that those thoughts are wholly mine, but that either they are secretly in the Poet, or may be fairly deduc'd from him: or at least, if both those considerations should fail, that my own is of a piece with his, and that if he were living, and an *Englishman,* they are such, as he wou'd probably have written.[20]

Dryden is here arguing for liberties which he had specifically rejected only five years previously. In his defence of his new approach, he asserts that the task of a translator 'is to make his Author appear as charming as possibly he can, provided he maintains his Character, and makes him not unlike himself', supporting his case with an analogy from painting where it is not enough 'to draw the Out-lines true, the Features like, the Proportions exact, the Colouring it self perhaps tolerable' without being able to make these things graceful 'by the posture, the shadowings, and chiefly by the Spirit which animates the whole'.[21] The requirements of readers may also be of weight alongside fidelity to the poet. Later in the same preface, in comparing his versions of Lucretius with those of Creech, he explains that he has taken greater liberties in order to make him 'as pleasing as I could', whereas Creech as an interpreter of the whole poem, not just select episodes, would have become too voluminous had he employed Dryden's method.[22]

Dryden is not always as daring in practice as his theory allowed him to be; but there are a great many passages among his translations where a genuine imaginative transformation has taken place in which the texture of thoughts, images and feelings characteristic of the original has been replaced by something distinctively different and just as distinctively his own. With the precedents of Rochester and Oldham before him, it was hardly to be doubted that he would try his hand at one of the *Amores* and that the result would be a *tour de force*; however two aspects of the version of II. xix that appeared in *Miscellany Poems* (1684) make it inappropriate to represent our fourth mode in the present discussion. The first is that its singularities have already been carefully explained by H. T. Swedenberg Jr in his notes to Volume II of the California edition; the second that, exceptionally for Dryden, it is really an imitation rather than a translation both in its extreme verbal liberties and its substitution of an English milieu. References to lying rough on bulks, Whetstone whores, orange wenches and city cuckolds take us straight into the social world of Restoration comedy, while its speaker is clearly no sophisticated Roman debauchee but the malicious, sharp-tongued rake of that comedy. A more characteristic example of Dryden's practice as a translator, and of our fourth mode, is his other great Ovidian *tour de force*, the version of Book XV of the *Metamorphoses* that appeared in *Fables* as 'Of the Pythagorean Philosophy'.

In the course of this dazzling demonstration of sustained rhetorical energy, we find Dryden seizing with obvious pleasure on the account, running from lines 214 to 236 in the Latin, of the cycle of human life from birth to death as a process of unceasing change. The words which were earlier given in Sandys's translation, *fuit illa dies, qua semina tantum / spesque hominum primae matris habitavimus alvo*, present the translator with the task of expressing the sense of six nouns, two verbs, three qualifying words and a relative. Golding in his rough and ready Elizabethan way, and with the advantage of his long line, manages to fit in all of them with the exception of the adjective *primae*:

> The day hath beene, wee were but seede and only hope
>   of men,

And in our moothers woomb wee had our dwelling place as
    then . . .[23]

but in the process totally fails to clarify Ovid's meaning. Sandys,
allowed less room to manoeuvre, manages with some spasmodic
contortions of syntax to translate Ovid's twelve Latin words into
twelve English ones (Once alone of men / The seeds and hope; the
womb our mansion . . .) but in doing this leaves the reader in even
deeper confusion as to which of the many possible senses of *semina*
and *spes* Ovid had in mind. But at least the two early translators had
made an effort, however perfunctory, to find an English counterpart for each of Ovid's significant words. Dryden's priorities are
different. He feels no obligation to find a substitute for *primae matris
habitavimus alvo* and this phrase simply disappears from his version:

> Time was, when we were sow'd, and just began
> From some few fruitful Drops, the promise of a Man . . .[24]

One will note for a start that this is poetry, where Golding and
Sandys had supplied us only with doggerel. It is also in its use of
'promise' for *spes*, rather than the bare and ambiguous 'hope',
better translation. The interpretation of *semina* as seminal fluid
shows him a worse translator but an inspired practitioner of his
own carefully defined theory of re-creation through translation. It
is most unlikely that the Latin word was meant to have the physical
specificity that Dryden gives it. He has simply assumed the liberty
of selecting from the range of lexical possibilities available to him
the one which would be most vivid for readers of his own time and
nation. In doing so he gives Ovid's ideas a concrete appeal to the
senses which is valid and valuable in English poetry, but which was
generally alien to Ovid, and particularly so in this section of the
Metamorphoses.

Dryden now takes a single phrase, *artifices natura manus admovit*,
and expands it into four lines:

> Then Nature's Hand (fermented as it was)
> Moulded to Shape the soft, coagulated Mass;
> And when the little Man was fully form'd,
> The breathless Embryo with a Spirit warm'd . . .
>
> (ll. 326–9)

The misleading position of 'fermented as it was', which belongs grammatically with 'Mass' not 'Hand', is an uncharacteristic awkwardness that mars an otherwise brilliant piece of poetical expansion. Ovid's image of nature at work with her 'cunning hands' (in the Loeb translation) involves no more than a conventional personification. She could be any kind of craftsman working with any kind of raw material. Dryden, taking up a second possible implication of the sowing image of the opening line, makes her a cook working dough into one of those French loaves in the shape of a human form. The addition of spirit to the physical mass is presented as the equivalent of cooking the dough to make it rise. This carefully articulated image points, in a somewhat subversive way, towards seventeenth-century speculations on the chemical basis of vital processes, several of which drew on the analogy of fermentation;[25] but its most important effect is to relate the ideas of the poem to a vividly realized domestic environment. This tendency reappears in lines 336–41 with the exception that we have now moved from the kitchen to the nursery:

> He next essays to walk, but downward press'd
> On four Feet imitates his Brother Beast:
> By slow degrees he gathers from the Ground
> His Legs, and to the rowling Chair is bound;
> Then walks alone; a Horseman now become
> He rides a Stick, and travels round the Room . . .

The delightful domestic image of the small child learning to walk with its 'rowling chair' and hobby horse is performed with no more warrant from the Latin than *mox quadrupes rituque tulit sua membra ferarum, / paulatimque tremens et nondum poplite firmo / constitit adiutis aliquo conamine nervis*.[26] All the human detail is Dryden's. In the following lines, a single word, *spatium*, one of whose possible Latin meanings would be race-course, though its primary sense in Ovid is of a period of time, encourages him to develop the hobby-horse image so that the growing man becomes a post-horse and his life a succession of stages:

> In time he vaunts among his youthful Peers,
> Strong-bon'd, and strung with Nerves, in pride of Years,
> He runs with Mettle his first merry Stage,
> Maintaines the next abated of his Rage,

But manages his Strength, and spares his Age.
Heavy the third, and stiff, he sinks apace,
And tho' 'tis down-hill all, but creeps along the Race.

(ll. 342–8)

Dryden's technique throughout this passage is one of interpolating images with an immediate physical appeal into a highly abstract original. These images, in turn, provide material for further expansion and elaboration and may, as we have seen, be sustained for a dozen lines or more. In this last respect they have an important structural function to which I will be returning shortly.

But Dryden's imagery is by no means all pictorial. Throughout his verse, his most successful effects are often suggestions of movement, dimensionality or physical effort presented without any sharp visual focus. A passage intermediate between those just cited, describing the birth of the formed embryo, creates a power-ful sense of muscular struggle linked to an almost demonic purposiveness:

But when the Mothers Throws begin to come,
The Creature, pent within the narrow Room,
Breaks his blind Prison, pushing to repair
His stiffled Breath, and draw the living Air . . .

(ll. 330–3)

Once again, none of the physical suggestiveness of this passage is contained in the original; neither is the notion of the womb as a prison, which seems to have been suggested by Sandys's in other respects much more accurate translation:

Kind Nature shewd her cunning; not content
That our vext bodies should be longer pent
In mothers stretched entrailes, forth-with bare
Them from that prison, to the open aire.

It is hard to see in what sense Dryden can be seen as having translated Ovid 'closely enough' in passages such as these.[27] Only a conviction of such total rapport with his author that he could think with his thoughts and feel with his feelings can have permitted him to offer the poem to his public as a version of Ovid rather than a brilliant original fantasia on Ovidian themes. And yet we also know from parallel cases what Dryden's reply to such a criticism would have been: that he is making Ovid as interesting and as poetical in English as he had been for his first readers in Latin.

What he does not attempt to justify in theory, but which can be justified to a degree from its effects in his practice, is his enriching of Ovid's largely abstract language with visual and physical imagery. The problem here is that many of the best effects of the original are not easily transferable to English because they depend on verbal patternings made possible by the flexible syntax of Latin. While Dryden's reworking of Ovid's language robs it of a characteristic quality of high generality, it also permits English readers to encounter something analogous to the 'bound' quality of the Latin verse statement – the sense of words, often longitudinally remote from each other, being linked and patterned as part of an intricate web of grammatical affinities. English with its rigid syntax and lack of inflections can only attempt such effects at the risk of incomprehensibility, and it requires the genius of a Milton or the eccentricity of a Sandys to make any worthwhile use of the expressive possibilities latent in word order which are so richly exploited by the Roman poets. But something closely related to this 'bound' quality can be achieved through sustained patterns of imagery of the kind that have just been analysed. Dryden, therefore, in what may appear to be his most radical departure from his original, is simultaneously working to find an equivalent – an *English* equivalent – for a central and untranslatable poetic effect. It is unlikely that this was a conscious process but its force is real – and not only in the passage chosen here for analysis.

★

To look at a handful of translations from Ovid is not to encounter anything like the range of achievement of the Restoration translators, or even Restoration translators of Ovid; but it may be enough to suggest a provisional answer to the question posed at the beginning of the first section: what was it that made these poets regard translation not simply as a profitable and necessary chore, but as a vehicle for their highest creative powers? Our clue lies in the fact that, while all three writers discussed strive urgently to make their translations fresh, contemporary and above all English, they none the less retain an intense respect for the integrity of their originals. Their aim is not to replace these originals but merely to provide their unchanged and immortal souls with up-to-date bodies. Their choice of paraphrase in preference to word for word translation was itself, paradoxically, an indication of this respect. As Dryden stressed, the crib version must inevitably destroy the poem in the process of extracting its meaning: only the translator prepared where necessary to depart from his author's words can have any hope of transmitting his poetry. In Oldham's and Rochester's cases, moreover, we are dealing with careful and conservative paraphrasers. Oldham, specifically rejecting the liberty of free paraphrase claimed by Cowley and his followers, assured the readers of his imitation of the *Ars poetica* that despite his use of 'English *names of Men, Places, and Customs, where the Parallel would decently permit*', he had been '*religiously strict*' to his author's meaning.[28] (Harold Brooks finds this claim 'rather too strong' but agrees that it 'illustrates the principle of his method'.)[29] Dryden, as we have just seen, laid claim to a freedom in paraphrase rejected by Oldham but in ways that spring from an uncommonly deep understanding of his sources and that sometimes bring him through superficial liberties back to a deeper fidelity. It is also significant that he almost always rejects the notion of relocating a Roman poem in an English social world. In these three poets, and in many of their contemporaries, it is possible to sense an exceptionally close community of attitudes between the translators and their originals. This rapport does not involve any kind of belief that their world is another Rome or Greece: this would have explained their fidelity but not their equally insistent modernity. Neither do they display much concern for pious antiquarianism or the apeing of classical manners. The issue is rather one of seeing in the world of the classical poets, and above all in the Rome of Horace, Virgil and Ovid, a society which operated on the same general principles as their own and in which poetry was written to perform the same or at least very similar social functions.

There were many good grounds for such a belief. Augustan Rome and polite Restoration London share many important things in common, among them a rhetorical ideal of literary language, a passional theory of personality, a tolerantly experimental attitude towards sex, a measured scepticism in matters of religion, and an uneasy political relationship with autocratic rulers who had come to power in the aftermath of a catastrophic failure of collective self-rule. But our concern must now be with effects rather than with possible reasons. Reading the Restoration translators one detects that the two cultures involved in any act of translation, the donor and the receiver, are here in an unusually exact equilibrium in which differences in language, manners and the externals of social being have come to be seen as matters of accident rather than of essence. As a result of this, the world of Roman poetry, but particularly that of its satire and love elegy, can be presented with a vivid immediacy that is quite another thing from the marbled remoteness with which it was to be endued by most subsequent translators. Moreover, because the poems and the poetic genres of the classical poets, once clothed in a new national dress, can still perform the tasks of persuasion, celebration or reproof that they were created to perform, there is that much less urgency for poets to be at work on wholly original verse. The real reason why translation and imitation had become valid means of creativity for the best poets of the age is simply that the perceived social functions of literature could be perfectly well performed by translations and imitations. Once the nature of those functions began to change, as it did in the early decades of the following century, translation no longer held the same attraction.

To leave our subject at this point is to leave many fascinating questions unasked about the varieties of balance, tension and reciprocity between intersecting cultures that may become manifest in the act of translation and the ways in which differing ideals of this relationship have succeeded each other in English literature over the last four centuries. But for the moment it must be enough to assert that it is only rarely that translations are written that are also poetry of the highest calibre and that the age of Dryden was one such age.

NOTES

1 Not all are present in the earliest editions. Further verses once attributed to Waller and Dryden are now believed to have been composed with fraudulent intent by Jacob Tonson.

2 Reprinted in Harold Love (ed.), *Restoration Verse* (Harmondsworth, 1968), 200–2 and 203–4 respectively.

3 Witness his tussle with Tonson over the dedication of the Virgil. W. J. Cameron's 'John Dryden's Jacobitism' in Harold Love (ed.), *Restoration Literature: Critical Approaches* (London, 1972), 277–308 draws on its author's experience as an editor of the

1688–97 volume of the Yale *Poems on Affairs of State* series to give a plausible account of the political inferences that might have been drawn from the translation by an intelligent reader at the time of its first appearance.

4 Preface to *Ovid's Epistles* in *The Works of John Dryden* (Los Angeles, 1956–), I, 114.

5 'The "Imitation" in English Poetry, especially in Formal Satire, before the Age of Pope', *RES*, 25 (1949), 138. Points made in this paper are taken up in Howard D. Weinbrot, 'Translation and Parody: Towards the Genealogy of the Augustan Imitation', *ELH*, 33 (1966), 434–47 and Leonard A. Moskovit, 'Pope and the Tradition of Neoclassical Imitation', *SEL*, 8 (1968), 445–62.

6 Weinbrot, 435 and *passim*. Cf. Brooks, 139: 'Cowley had advocated imitation as meeting the need of those to whom an alien language and setting were obstacles, preventing them from reading or at least from thoroughly appreciating the original. Swift, Pope, and Johnson intended their readers to have the original in mind, and to get an added enjoyment from the comparison.'

7 *Works*, I, 116.

8 See *The Vindication of the Duke of Guise*, in George Saintsbury (ed.), *The Dramatic Works of John Dryden* (Edinburgh, 1882), VII, 180 and Harold Love (ed.), *Poeta de Tristibus: or, the Poet's Complaint* (Los Angeles: Augustan Reprint Society, 1971), 23 and n.

9 Montague Summers (ed.), *The Complete Works of Thomas Shadwell* (London, 1927), V, 291–4. Shadwell's attitude is very different in his theatrical reworkings of Molière.

10 Ovid's use of the distich, which was much closer to the methods of the English heroic couplet than that of earlier Latin and Greek elegiac poets, is carefully analysed in John Barsby's edition of Book I of the *Amores* (Oxford, 1973), 19–23. His example did not, however, encourage metrical or phonetic mimicry so much as incite poets to develop their own medium for writing an Ovidian kind of poetry in English.

11 *Ovids Metamorphosis Englished, Mythologiz'd, and Represented in Figures* (Oxford, 1632), 496.

12 The text is that of David M. Vieth (ed.), *The Complete Poems of John Wilmot, Earl of Rochester* (New Haven, Conn., 1968), 35.

13 This does not seem to have been pointed out, though many readers of Hobbes must have observed it. The passage concerned is on p. 97, lines 22–7 of C. B. Macpherson's edition (Harmondsworth, 1968).

14 Guy Lee (tr.), *Ovid's Amores* (London, [1968]), 83. As the textual tradition of the *Amores* is an uncomplicated one, I have also accepted this as my source for the Latin, though ideally an attempt should have been made to identify the editions consulted by the translators.

15 *Works*, I, 114. In line 27 of the Latin (*si tamen exaudis pulchra cum matre rogantem*) Rochester reads *pulchra cum matre* as modifying *rogantem* rather than *exaudis*. But this would seem to be an honest mistake rather than a wilful departure.

16 *Poems and Translations. By the Author of The Satyrs upon the Jesuits* (London, 1683), 100

17 *Poems and Translations*, 101–2.

18 *Works*, I, 116.

19 Oldham himself speaks disparagingly in the preface to *Satyrs upon the Jesuits* (1681) of 'The Passion of Byblis', translated from *Metamorphoses* IX, though it is certainly no worse than most of the contributions to *Ovid's Epistles* which had inspired him to the attempt. The same preface includes a deferential reference to Sandys; yet it must have been unmistakably evident to Oldham that he and his age had discovered an infinitely better way of conveying the experience of Ovid to English readers.

20 *Works*, III, 3–4.

21 *Works*, III, 4.

22 *Works*, III, 14.

23 W. H. D. Rouse (ed.), *Shakespeare's Ovid Being Arthur Golding's Translation of the Metamorphoses* (London, 1961), 299.

24 James Kinsley (ed.), *The Poems of John Dryden* (Oxford, 1958), IV, 1726. This (ll. 324–5) and subsequent excerpts are from this edition.

25 Most notably by van Helmont in his *Ortus Medicinae* (1648), though his notion of 'fermentation' was not, of course, our post-Pasteurian one. See Elizabeth Gasking, *The Rise of Experimental Biology* (New York, 1970), 45–6.

26 In the Loeb translation: 'but soon it lifted itself up on all fours after the manner of the beasts; then gradually in a wabbling, weak-kneed fashion it stood erect, supported by some con-

venient prop'. F. J. Miller (tr.), *Metamorphoses* (Cambridge, Mass., 1916), 381.

27 His own words in the Preface to *Fables Ancient and Modern*, in *The Poems of John Dryden*, IV, 1445.

28 *Some New Pieces Never before Publish'd* (London, 1681), a1ᵛ.

29 Brooks, 137.

10

SECURING A REPERTORY

PLAYS ON
THE LONDON STAGE 1660–5

Robert D. Hume

Immediately after the Restoration, securing plays for presentation was a relatively simple task. . . . The theatres in 1660
naturally turned to the large stock handed down from Elizabethan
and Jacobean times. For some years following 1660 the Lord
Chamberlain regulated the division of plays among the principal
companies. . . . Within a short time after the resumption of acting
the professional dramatist, the most productive source of new
plays, became a highly influential element in the offerings of
each company.[1]

Theatre historians have devoted a great deal of attention to the
circumstances in which the theatres reopened in 1660, and to the
organizational infighting which ensued.[2] They have seldom much
concerned themselves with what would be performed in these
theatres. Drama historians, once the problem of 'continuity' with
pre-1642 drama was settled,[3] have tended to hare off in the
direction of the 1670s, searching along the way for anticipations of
'heroic drama' and 'comedy of manners'. Scant attention has been
spared for the repertory of the early 1660s. Scholars generally seem
to assume (as did the editors of *The London Stage*) that the
companies simply split up the old plays to tide them over until a
rapidly rising new generation of professional playwrights could
take up the slack. In fact, the 'tidy division' theory has been
decisively demolished by Gunnar Sorelius.[4] And no professional

playwright was to appear before 1668. Obviously some serious misunderstandings of theatrical circumstances at the start of the Restoration are still current. I want therefore to reconsider some little-examined assumptions about the first years of the Restoration theatres, especially concerning the difference in circumstances which affected their demand for, and use of, new plays.

THE PROBLEM OF RIGHTS TO OLD PLAYS

The assertion in *The London Stage* that 'the Lord Chamberlain regulated the division of plays' is true only in part. Scholars have so far discovered exactly three orders relating to rights in plays. All of them deal with specific play titles (rather than matters of principle), and two of them come as late as 1668 and 1669. Cibber states that the two companies 'had a private Rule or Agreement' whereby 'All the capital Plays . . . of *Shakespear*, *Fletcher*, and *Ben. Johnson* were divided between them by the Approbation of the Court and their own alternate Choice.'[5] There is no evidence to support this view, however, and indeed the most cursory review of the offerings of the two companies shows at once that Cibber was misinformed. An overwhelming majority of the older plays fell to the King's Company. Sorelius has suggested that the King's Company tried to lay claim to *all* older plays, probably on the basis of its members' affiliations in pre-1642 companies.[6] The inference is plausible, but we lack hard evidence, and some older plays were allowed to the Duke's Company.

Prior to 1642, play manuscripts were treated essentially as physical properties. 'Professional' playwrights were kept on a company payroll, and normally received the proceeds (less expenses) from one night in the initial run, after which the actors owned all further rights.[7] Publication compromised these rights. Hence (except when desperate for money) troupes usually did not countenance publication of scripts which continued in their active repertory, or might well be revived. The celebrated case is the plays of 'Beaumont and Fletcher', most of them jealously guarded from print by the members of the King's Company until 1647, when, despairing of ever being allowed to reopen under the Common-wealth, the surviving actors took what they could get from a publisher.

This brings us to an obvious problem: did rights to plays carry over from Caroline companies to those established in 1660? Most scholars agree with Nicoll's suggestion that Killigrew's Company successfully claimed rights to the old King's Company repertory – a plausible hypothesis, especially in light of the Lord Chamberlain's order of *c*. 12 January 1669, reserving 107 plays 'formerly acted at the Blackfryers' for them. This order comes, however, nearly ten years after the establishment of the Restoration companies.

What prevented Davenant from helping himself to the remainder of the rich stores of Renaissance drama? This question has gone almost entirely unconsidered. A great many old plays had been published. And even if the King's Company got the Lord Chamberlain to agree that they should have exclusive rights to all plays in their pre-Restoration companies' repertories, there should have been plenty of others left for Davenant. How pre-1642 company rights could have been considered paramount is hard to see. The King's Company actors did not have direct connections to all earlier theatre companies. Physical possession of manuscripts seems to have conferred some control over performance rights in the Jacobean and Caroline periods, and as late as 1662 property rights in play manuscripts were apparently considered separate from shares in an acting company or a building.[8] Nevertheless, when the Duke's Company was organized in November 1660, it may well have been without performance rights to any plays whatsoever.

We have two solid pieces of evidence that there was a scramble for play rights in 1660. One is a letter from the publisher Humphrey Mosely to Sir Henry Herbert, stating that he has been 'solicited by the gentlemen actors of the Red Bull' to know what agreement he had made with 'Mr. Rhodes, of the Cockpitt playhouse'. Mosely denies having 'treated with him . . . neither did I ever consent directly or indirectly, that hee or any others should act any playes that do belong to mee. . . . And the same also I doe certify concerning the Whitefryers playhouse and players.'[9]

The second piece of evidence is an order issued through the Lord Chamberlain's office on 12 December 1660:

Sr Will: D'avenant Acting Playes

Whereas Sr William Davenant, Knight hath humbly p^{r}sented to us a proposition of reformeinge some of the most ancient Playes that were playd at Blackfriers and of makeinge them, fitt, for the Company of Actors appointed under his direction and Comand, Viz: the playes called the Tempest, measures, for measures, much adoe about nothinge, Rome and Juliet, Twelfe night, the Life of Kinge Henry the Eyght, the sophy, Kinge Lear, the Tragedy of Mackbeth, the Tragedy of Hamlet prince of Denmarke, and the Dutchesse of Malfy, Therefore wee have granted unto the sayd Sr William Davenant, liberty to represent the playes above named by the Actors under his comand, notwithstandinge any Warrant to the contrary, formerly granted, And it is our will and pleasure and we comand that noe person or persons upon what p^{r}tence soever, shall act or cause to be acted any of those above named Eleven playes. . . . And wee further grant liberty unto the sayd Sr William Davenant to represent by the Actors under his Comand all the playes written by himselfe formerly for the Blackfriers. . . . And we likewise grant liberty to the sayd Sr William Davenant dureinge the space of Two Months after the date hereof to cause to be rep^{r}sented publiquely, by the Actors under his apointment these six followinge playes: Viz: The Mad Lover, the mayd in ye mill, the Spanish Curate the Loyall Subject, Rule a wife and have a wife and Persiles prince of Tyre.   (L.C. 5/137, pp. 343-4)

Certain implications are obvious. (1) Davenant had to petition the King even for rights to his own plays. (2) Davenant had to ask specifically for rights to any older play: with the possible exception of one or two plays that had been in the repertory of Rhodes's troupe in 1659-60, Davenant had no inherited repertory. (3) Davenant was allowed two months' rights to six plays because they had been in the repertory of Rhodes's actors, who had become the core of the Duke's Company, and Davenant needed works his company could perform immediately.

A broader issue is less clear cut. John Freehafer has argued that Davenant was promising to adapt and modernize classic plays no longer regarded as stageworthy; Sorelius believes that the promise was merely to purge them of 'profaneness and scurrility', as directed in the King's order of 21 August 1660. The latter now seems to me the likelier interpretation, though we cannot treat Davenant's staging some of these plays in original form (i.e. without adapting them) as decisive evidence. Such matters were not always closely regulated by the authorities.

One clear sign that the issue of rights to plays had not been settled when the companies were established is some definite instances of direct collision in the first partial season of competition (1660–1). Two cases involve 'two month' plays and perhaps signify no more than the King's Company asserting its claim. Thus *The Mad Lover* (Duke's Company, 9 February) was mounted by their rivals at Vere Street sometime during February or March,[10] and *The Maid in the Mill* (Duke's, 29 January) made an appearance there *c*. March. Much more startling is an episode involving Thomas Heywood's *Love's Mistress*. On 2 March, Pepys went to Vere Street, 'where I found so few people . . . that I went out again'. Proceeding to Salisbury Court he found 'the house as full as could be' for a performance of Heywood's 'new play'. Exactly nine days later Pepys saw the same play at Vere Street – 'which I do not like it some things so well as their acting in Salisbury Court'. Obviously the success of the upstart Duke's Company provoked Killigrew's group into direct rejoinder. The final instance, which is even more interesting, involves *The Bondman*. This was one of six plays named by Downes as part of Rhodes's repertory which was not made part of the 'two month' grant.[11] The implication would seem to be either that the Duke's Company could take it or that it was up for grabs. It was in Davenant's repertory by 1 March; Herbert's records show it at Vere Street *c*. May. But back on 1 March Pepys was commenting: 'above all that ever I saw, Baterton doth the Bondman the best' – perhaps implying earlier production at Vere Street. During the season the King's Company also mounted *The Wild Goose Chase*, *A Wife for a Month* and *Woman's Prize*. It had staged Davenant's own *The Unfortunate Lovers* on 19 November (before the grant to Davenant) and it put on *Aglaura*, *The Spanish Curate* and *Rule a Wife* the following season. This looks very much like a systematic attempt to lay claim to the 'Rhodes' repertory. Only *The Changeling* was apparently left undisputed to the Duke's Company.

We may guess that direct duplication ceased after 1662 because both managers realized that such tactics helped neither company. But the evident confusion, the extreme restrictions on Davenant's company, and the lack of an official order from the Lord Chamberlain to settle the issue are distinctly puzzling, especially since the issue ought to have been hottest just when the two companies were starting up. Not until 20 August 1668 did another official order appear. On that day the Duke's Company was granted exclusive rights to twenty-five old plays.[12] They were not particularly desirable properties, and so far as we know few of them ever got performed. The following January the Lord Chamberlain issued an order confirming that 107 old plays – said to have been acted at Blackfriars – were the property of the King's Company.[13] Judith Milhous speculates that after Davenant's death (7 April 1668) the new managers tried to see what old plays they could get hold of and came up with few of value, though in the process they provoked the King's Company into laying formal claim to its most valued old plays – and perhaps to some others. This seems likely enough, although by this time both companies had built up substantial repertories of new plays on which to draw.

The collisions, and the order of 12 December, tell us that there was indeed an immediate problem over rights to plays in 1660. Given the extreme limitations placed on the Duke's Company we have to ask how Davenant proposed to operate, and why he apparently did not make more strenuous efforts to secure rights to old plays. Sorelius goes so far as to wonder if Davenant 'may even have failed to realize the value of the old plays'.[14] This I doubt. Davenant was an experienced manager and he had learned his trade in the theatres which had spawned those old plays. Denied access to them, he capitalized initially on two years' uncontested advantage in possessing a scenic theatre, and starting in 1663 he mounted a flock of new plays. Given his long-standing commitment to scenery and spectacle, necessity probably just fed his natural inclinations.

THE REPERTORIES IN 1660–1 AND 1661–2

By my count, the King's Company mounted at least thirty-nine old plays during the 1660–1 season – and this count is probably on the low side, since our performance records are incomplete. Against this profusion of riches from Shakespeare, Jonson, Fletcher and other eminent writers, what could Davenant offer? We have certain record of only fourteen plays performed by the Duke's Company this season – four of them 'two month' plays and three of them Davenant's own. We are probably safe in accepting the usual assumption that Davenant's company did not perform as frequently as Killigrew's during this first year, and it probably opened about two months later, so it needed fewer plays. None the less Davenant cannot have been in an altogether comfortable position. He certainly did make good use of the plays reserved to him in the grant of December 1660. Within a decade all eleven of the plays granted outright are recorded in the Duke's Company repertory (as published or adapted), most of them within three seasons. We have record of Duke's Company productions of four of the six 'two month' plays.[15] Curiously, Davenant seems to have been able to keep permanent rights to both *The Mad Lover* and *The Maid in the Mill*, despite King's Company productions of them in the spring of 1661. He was also able to keep *The Changeling* and *The Bondman* from Rhodes's repertory, though four other Rhodes plays reverted to the King's Company.

At the most optimistic count we have direct or inferential evidence of only fifteen old plays (plus Davenant's own) legally available to the Duke's Company. We have records of six to eight others mounted by Davenant in these first five years for which we have no idea of the legal rights.[16] These are Webster and Rowley's (?) *The Thracian Wonder* (5 February 1661?),[17] Heywood's *Love's Mistress* (2 March 1661), Fletcher's *The Little Thief* (2 April 1661),[18] *Love's Quarrel* (6 April 1661),[19] Ford's *'Tis Pity* (9 September 1661),[20] Glapthorne's *Wit in a Constable* (23 May 1662), and (according to Downes) at an uncertain date before June 1665, Brome's *Sparagus Garden* and Middleton's *A Trick to Catch the Old One*. These plays range in date of original production from 1599 to 1638 and they had been the property of five different companies (omitting one of unknown auspices and one about which we know nothing). All save *The Thracian Wonder* (and possibly *Love's Quarrel*) had been published before 1642. Why these plays? We can only guess. Perhaps Davenant struck an unrecorded bargain with Killigrew. Or perhaps he was hoping that Killigrew would ignore his using these unconsidered trifles, though in two instances we have definite proof of counter-productions at Vere Street (*Love's Mistress* and *The Little Thief*). We must also consider the evidence that Killigrew mounted *Hamlet* in November 1661, the grant to Davenant the previous December notwithstanding.[21]

The principal event of the first season was of course the opening of Davenant's Lincoln's Inn Fields theatre in late June 1661. Its scenery was a great wonder, and Davenant's *The Siege of Rhodes* emptied the other theatre. A week or so into its run, Pepys went to

Vere Street and commented: 'strange to see this house, that use to be so thronged, now empty since the opera begun—and so will continue for a while I believe' (4 July). Everyone knows how the King's Company, unable to compete successfully against this innovation the following year, had to reply in kind and started constructing the fancy new Bridges Street theatre. We must beware, however, of letting hindsight make events seem more inevitable than they were. We now see that the Restoration scenic theatres simply continue the development of the Caroline private theatre tradition,[22] which seems logical given the relatively exclusive nature (and high prices) of the Restoration theatres, not to mention tastes for scenery developed abroad by banished cavaliers. We do need to remember, none the less, that Killigrew's company had shown no signs of wanting to employ changeable scenery until forced to do so.

The pattern of competition remained essentially unchanged in 1661–2. The King's Company relied on a long string of revivals; the Duke's Company got by on only a few plays.[23] During this season Davenant was, to be sure, enjoying the considerable advantage of the Lincoln's Inn Fields theatre. He got excellent mileage out of a fancy new production of his own, *The Wits*, 'never acted yet with scenes', which were 'admirable', or so Pepys tells us (15 August). *Hamlet* and *Love and Honour* (the latter using the King's and the Duke of York's coronation robes) seem to have been good draws during the autumn. In the winter and spring, Davenant made his first cautious excursions into new plays.

Limited as our performance calendar is, it suggests quite strongly that neither company initially felt much need for new plays. In 1660–1 the only new plays were the two parts of Davenant's *The Siege of Rhodes*, used to open Lincoln's Inn Fields in June. They had, of course, been given semi-public performances at Rutland House five years earlier. During 1661–2 the Duke's Company's only new plays were Cowley's *Cutter of Coleman Street* (December) and *The Law Against Lovers*, Davenant's own melding of *Measure for Measure* and *Much Ado* (February). Cowley's play was merely a revamping of his *Guardian* (1642). It had received only a college performance before the closing of the theatres and ought not to have belonged to any professional troupe. It had, however, been published in 1650, and it had been acted 'several times . . . privately during the troubles, . . . as it has been lately too at *Dublin*' (1663 preface), which leads me to wonder if the revision was in part a safeguard against objections from Killigrew. This hypothesis is strengthened by the peculiar later history of the play. It stayed in the Duke's Company's repertory during the 1660s, usually billed as *The Guardian*. (On 5 August 1668 Pepys reported: 'to the Duke of York's House and there saw "The Guardian", formerly the same, I find, that was called "Cutter of Coleman street".') Lack of performance at Blackfriars notwithstanding, *The Guardian* was included in the January 1669 list of plays belonging to the King's Company – but some three weeks later it was performed at court by the Duke's Company, in whose repertory it remained.

During 1661–2 the King's Company mounted two genuinely new plays and one which may have been new. The honour of being the first newly written play produced on the Restoration stage evidently belongs to William Killigrew's sprawling tragi-comedy *Selindra* (March 1662); the second was Sir Robert Howard's *The Surprisal* (April). Sir William Bartley's (Berkeley's?) *Cornelia* (*c*. June 1662?) is lost, but was dubbed 'a New Play' by Herbert (who collected double fees for new plays). About *Cornelia* and its author we know almost nothing (it was described as 'too witty for the vulgar sort' in a contemporary piece of doggerel). We should note, however, that the other two plays came from friends of the management – the patentee's brother, and a close friend and theatre shareholder.

For two seasons the King's Company had relied on its classics while Davenant turned to scenery. The result was no contest, but Davenant could not operate indefinitely without a substantial number of new scripts. The monopoly granted in 1660 might well have inhibited the production of new plays – a phenomenon with which eighteenth-century scholars are all too familiar. We have the inequitable division of the older plays to thank for the strong impetus given to the production of new plays in this period. The chances seem good that, 'uninterrupted', the Caroline theatre would have evolved more or less in the directions taken in the sixties and seventies. The principal innovations of the Restoration theatre (actresses and changeable scenery) were commonplaces in the Caroline Court theatre, and would presumably have eventually been adopted by the public theatres – a movement Davenant had attempted to spearhead in 1639.[24] Given his longstanding fascination with scenery, Davenant would probably have proceeded quickly with a scenic theatre in any case. Would another patentee, given half of the pre-1642 plays by his own 'alternate choice', have plunged into the expense and risk of a scenic theatre? Quite possibly not. But what compelled Davenant to turn fairly quickly to new plays was, very simply, lack of old ones.

THE NEW PLAYS, 1662–5

We should not be surprised at the slowness with which new plays appeared on the Restoration stage. Even had Davenant and Killigrew been clamouring for fresh scripts, they would probably not have found many. Competent playwrights take time and practice to develop. The older generation were mostly dead, and those not dead (notably James Shirley) remained inactive. Davenant adapted and translated, and Killigrew revised old work, but neither wrote any new plays after 1660.

The acute dearth of experienced playwrights gives the lie to *The London Stage*'s assertion that 'within a short time' professional playwrights were proving a 'productive source of new plays'. Dryden was the first professional playwright to appear after 1660, and he seems to have signed a contract with the King's Company *c*. May 1668.[25] His first two plays (*The Wild Gallant*, 1663, and *The Rival Ladies*, 1664) were failures. *The Indian Queen* (1664) was credited largely to Sir Robert Howard. *The Indian Emperour* (1665) succeeded, as did *Secret-Love* (1667), but Dryden's contract probably reflects his hand in a pair of major successes, *The Tempest* (with Davenant) and *Sir Martin Mar-all* (with Newcastle) later in 1667.[26] And Dryden is, quite clearly, the only professional playwright of the 1660s. Shadwell had his first play mounted in 1668; Behn in 1670; Crowne and Settle in 1671; Ravenscroft in 1672. A theatre manager peering into his crystal ball in the late spring of 1665 might have hoped for a new generation of Massingers, Bromes, and Shirleys, but they were not yet visible.

The obvious sources of fresh scripts in the early 1660s were foreign plays which could be translated and manuscripts from the earlier period. Davenant did make use of translations from divers hands – *Ignoramus* (from Latin), *The Valiant Cid*, *Pompey* (two versions?), *Heraclius*, *Worse and Worse*, *'Tis Better than It Was*, all mounted by 1665. Killigrew had no need for such scripts,[27] but he does seem to have acquired control of most or all of the available manuscripts – Humphrey Mosely being the principal source. Whether Killigrew acquired these rights simply as part of the older repertory, or by special agreement to keep them out of Davenant's hands, we do not know. Alfred Harbage studied the whole subject in detail and has offered strong arguments to show that a number of Restoration plays are adaptations of such manuscripts – among them Dryden's *Wild Gallant* and Wilson's *Cheats* in the years at issue here.[28] If Harbage is correct (and I believe he is), these old manuscripts were still proving a fruitful source of 'new' plays some thirty years after 1660.

Newly written plays start to become a significant part of the repertory during the season of 1662–3. The King's Company was not able to open Bridges Street until May, but the eight new plays mounted at Lincoln's Inn Fields suggest that Davenant felt he could no longer get by on his minimal repertory. The plays he put on are testimony to the scarcity of scripts – three translations, one *mélange* of Davenant's own devising (*The Playhouse to be Let*), and a topical bit of fluff (*A Witty Combat*).[29] Beyond these oddments the Duke's Company mounted Porter's *The Villain*, a popular exercise in blood and thunder; Tuke's *The Adventures of Five Hours*, a trend-setting 'Spanish romance' based on Calderon; and Stapylton's *The Slighted Maid*, an old-fashioned tragi-comedy. The King's Company replied with four new plays of its own: Robert Howard's *The Committee*, a popular city comedy with topical trimmings; James Howard's *The English Mounsieur* (one of the earliest gay-couple plays),[30] Dryden's *Wild Gallant* and Wilson's *Cheats*. Once again Killigrew was not knocking himself out to mount new plays.

The pattern of 1662–3 is quite precisely repeated in 1663–4 in both numbers and the nature of the scripts involved. In 1664–5, however, a distinctly startling reversal occurs. Consider the following table of new plays produced by each company:

	1660–1	1661–2	1662–3**	1663–4***	1664–5[31]
King's	0	3	4	5	7****
Duke's	[2]*	2	8	10	4

* *The Siege of Rhodes* (in two parts).
** omits Henry Howard's *The United Kingdoms* (*c.* 1662–3), which is unassignable, though most Howard family plays went to the King's Company.[32]
*** omits *The Exposure* (anon.), auspices unknown.
**** includes Killigrew's *The Parson's Wedding* (written *c.* 1641?) and *Thomaso* (prepared for production; no definite performance record), but not *Elvira* (anon.), auspices unknown.

Davenant scored a major success with Orrery's *Henry the Fifth* in August at the end of the 1663–4 season; Killigrew thereupon chose to reply with the same author's *The Generall*, a script on which he had been sitting for about two years. To judge from Pepys, the Duke's Company did very nicely this season with only two major new productions – a revival of *Macbeth* in the autumn and Orrery's *Mustapha* in the spring.

The figures tabulated above show nineteen new plays for the King's Company and twenty-six for the Duke's before the closing of the theatres on account of plague in June 1665. The totals are twelve and twenty-two respectively before the pivotal season of 1664–5. Closer analysis reveals greater disparity than these numbers alone suggest. Of the nineteen new plays staged by the King's Company, seven are by various members of the Howard family; three by their brother-in-law Dryden; and three by Killigrew family members. One was by actor-sharer John Lacy, another by the Earl of Orrery, backed by the recommendation of Charles II. In other words, at least fifteen of the nineteen plays are by friends, relatives and 'insiders'.[33] By contrast, twenty-one of twenty-six Duke's Company plays are by 'outsiders'. Davenant staged five of his own plays; the rest he got where he could. The King's Company was essentially a closed shop, and we may guess that some of those nineteen plays were produced more as favours to friends than out of urgent need for new scripts.

The reversal of figures in 1664–5 is striking and significant. It suggests a decided turn on the part of the King's Company toward reliance on new plays as a competitive device. Following the reopening of the theatres in 1666–7, the companies' overall offerings are very closely matched – approximately twenty-two new plays each up to 1670. We know that, throughout this first decade, premières (or just new productions) tended to draw large audiences – something Pepys testifies to again and again. Except by word of mouth, this cannot have reflected interest in particular authors, since authors' names were not put in playbills. Killigrew seems to have found by 1664–5 that he had to match Davenant in new plays, his advantage in old plays notwithstanding. Many of the pre-1642 plays remained popular for decades, and when the two companies united in 1682 the managers – Duke's Company stalwarts – eagerly set to work reviving 'the several old and Modern Plays, that were the Propriety of Mr. *Killigrew*'.[34] Of the eleven Downes names, only *The Plain-Dealer* is not an 'old' play. During the 1680s, with no competition, the United Company managers could get by with almost no new plays. In the highly competitive sixties and seventies this proved impossible.

The Lincoln's Inn Fields production of *Macbeth*, *c*. November 1664, is a clear indication of the route the Duke's Company would pursue under Davenant and his successor Betterton – a path leading to the construction of the fancy Dorset Garden theatre in 1671 and the spectacular 'English operas' in which Betterton specialized. Anticipating Vanbrugh by some forty years, Killigrew too seems to have dreamed of capitalizing on Italian opera. Talking to Pepys as early as 2 August 1664, Killigrew boasted of plans (never fulfilled) for four operas a year, with 'the best Scenes and Machines, the best Musique, and everything as Magnificent as is in Christendome; and to that end hath sent for voices and painters and other persons from Italy'.

The rhymed heroic play and the 'gay couple' love chase certainly have demonstrable antecedents in the old plays, but with *The Indian Queen*, *The English Mounsieur* and *The Comical Revenge* in 1663 and early 1664 we find a new tone and attitude. *The Adventures of Five Hours* has many features of Caroline tragi-comedy, but the imitations it spawned (*The Rival Ladies*, *Elvira*, *Flora's Vagaries*) quickly reflect the new atmosphere. To expect radical innovations in plays in 1660 is unrealistic: there were no new plays in 1660. Change in plays could occur only after writers had a chance to assimilate changes in public theatre conditions, and by 1663 we can see clear signs of innovation and experiment. Actresses aside, the theatre of 1660–1 was very close to that of Charles I. But the monopoly, the unequal division of plays and the use of scenery in the public theatres quickly created very different circumstances.[35]

Davenant was committed to fancy productions, not to new plays. His success with *Macbeth*, *The Tempest* and other old plays suggests that the unequal division of old plays is one of the crucial determinants of English drama in the 1660s. Another is the absence of professional playwrights. No writer made a living in the theatre between 1660 and 1665. Only Dryden did so before 1670. The first new plays of the Restoration are amateur efforts; only in 1668 and thereafter did the theatres start to develop and utilize professional writers. No judgement of the sixties plays should be made without acknowledgement of this fact. Initially the emphasis was on having theatres at all, and then on scenery. The eighteen-month hiatus for plague in 1665–6 further slowed the re-development of professional playwrights. Only in 1667 do we really start to see the Carolean theatre operating as it was hinted at in 1664–5 and as it was to be in the glorious seventies. During the past fifteen years, scholars have come to understand that the 1670s and 1690s are essentially distinct periods.[36] We need likewise to recognize that the 1660s are something of an isolated freak – a period of largely amateur experimentation prior to the re-establishment of a professional tradition in the 1670s.

NOTES

1 William Van Lennep, Emmett L. Avery and Arthur H. Scouten (eds), *The London Stage, 1660–1800: a calendar of plays*, 5 pts; *Part 1: 1660–1700* (Carbondale, Ill., 1965), cxliii–cxliv.

2 See particularly Leslie Hotson, *The Commonwealth and Restoration Stage* (London, 1928), chs 5 and 6; Allardyce Nicoll, *A History of English Drama, 1660–1900*, revised edn, 6 vols (Cambridge, 1952–9), I, Appendix A; John Freehafer, 'The Formation of the London Patent Companies in 1660', *Theatre Notebook*, 20 (1965), 6–30; Gunnar Sorelius, 'The Early History of the Restoration Theatre: Some Problems Reconsidered', *Theatre Notebook*, 33 (1979), 52–61. For the best account of the implications of the Patent grants and the competitive circumstances of the two companies see 'The Organization and Management of the Patent Companies, 1660–1668', ch. 1 of Judith Milhous, *Thomas Betterton and the Management of Lincoln's Inn Fields, 1695–1708* (Carbondale, Ill., 1979).

3 See particularly Alfred Harbage, *Cavalier Drama* (London, 1926; reprinted New York, 1964).

4 'The Rights of the Restoration Theatrical Companies in the Older Drama', *Studia Neophilologica*, 37 (1965), 174–89. I am indebted to Sorelius's discussion, which supersedes Allardyce Nicoll's 'The Rights of Beeston and D'Avenant in Elizabethan Plays', *RES*, 1 (1925), 84–91, and Hazelton Spencer's 'The Restoration Play Lists', ibid., 443–6. For a helpful analysis of the companies' repertories in a broader context, see Sorelius's excellent (and too little used) '*The Giant Race Before the Flood*': *Pre-Restoration Drama on the Stage and in the Criticism of the*

Restoration, Studia Anglistica Upsaliensia, 4 (Uppsala, 1966), 33–53.

5 Robert W. Lowe (ed.), *An Apology for the Life of Mr. Colley Cibber*, 2 vols, (London, 1889), I, 91.

6 'Rights of the Restoration Theatrical Companies', 181, 188.

7 This discussion is largely based on Gerald Eades Bentley, *The Profession of Dramatist in Shakespeare's Time 1590–1642* (Princeton, N.J., 1971).

8 See Philip H. Highfill, Jr, Kalman A. Burnim and Edward A. Langhans, *A Biographical Dictionary of Actors, Actresses, Musicians, Dancers, Managers, and Other Stage Personnel in London, 1660–1800*, 16 vols, in progress (Carbondale, Ill., 1973–), II, 135.

9 Joseph Quincy Adams (ed.), *The Dramatic Records of Sir Henry Herbert* (New Haven, Conn., 1917), 90.

10 Unless otherwise indicated, performance information is noted in the *London Stage* calendar.

11 John Downes, *Roscius Anglicanus* (London, 1708), 18. I except Davenant's own *Unfortunate Lovers*. The others were *The Wild Goose Chase, A Wife for a Month, Woman's Prize, Aglaura* and *The Changeling*.

12 P.R.O. L.C. 5/139, p. 373. The titles are printed in *The London Stage*, Pt I, 140.

13 P.R.O. L.C. 5/12, p. 212. For the titles see *The London Stage*, Pt I, 151–2.

14 'Rights of the Restoration Theatrical Companies', p. 189.

15 *The Mad Lover, The Maid in the Mill, The Spanish Curate* and *Rule a Wife*. Only the King's Company seems to have mounted *The Loyal Subject*, and we have no record of any production for *Pericles*.

16 In all probability the Duke's Company did perform a number of plays of which we have no record in these two seasons. Sir Henry Herbert's claim that they 'did Act Diuers stage Playes . . . to witt 10 new playes and 100 revived Playes' (*Dramatic Records*, 110) between 5 November 1660 and 6 May 1662 can, however, safely be dismissed as a considerable exaggeration.

17 Deduced from a MS. date in a British Library copy by Edward A. Langhans ('Restoration Manuscript Notes in Seventeenth Century Plays', *RECTR*, 5 [November, 1966], 13), and assigned to the Duke's Company because the King's Company performed *Argalus and Parthenia* on this day. We cannot be

certain, however, that this is a performance rather than an acquisition date.

18 Subsequently performed 15 March 1662 by the King's Company.

19 Essentially nothing is known of this play, but it is probably a revival. For discussion see Judith Milhous and Robert D. Hume, 'Lost English Plays, 1660–1700', *Harvard Library Bulletin*, 25 (1977), 5–33, No. 4.

20 Company uncertain. The play was acted at Salisbury Court on this date – the only recorded performance in the period. This could be either the Duke's Company temporarily out of Lincoln's Inn Fields or a minor company.

21 The evidence is Pepys, 27 November 1661: 'to the Theatre and there saw "*Hamlett*"'. At this time Pepys consistently calls Vere Street 'the Theatre' and Lincoln's Inn Fields 'the Opera'. The identification may, of course, merely be a slip on his part.

22 A point well made by Colin Visser in 'The Killigrew Folio: Private Playhouses and the Restoration Stage', *Theatre Survey*, 19 (1978), 119–38.

23 During 1661–62 the King's Company is known to have staged forty-two different plays – three new ones, eighteen revivals previously unrecorded, and twenty-one of the plays mounted in 1660–1. Because of incomplete records these figures are probably low, especially that for plays carried over from 1660–1. Our best source is Herbert, and of course he does not record plays after the initial revival. By contrast, we have only twelve known titles for the Duke's Company in 1661–2: two new plays, four revivals previously unrecorded, and six plays already mounted in 1660–1.

24 For the terms of Davenant's original 1639 Patent see Gerald Eades Bentley, *The Jacobean and Caroline Stage*, 7 vols (Oxford, 1941–68), VI, 304–9.

25 Charles E. Ward, *The Life of John Dryden* (Chapel Hill, N.C., 1961), 57.

26 Both of these collaborations were mounted by the Duke's Company. Dryden may have been signed up by the King's Company in part to keep him from working for their rivals.

27 *The Lyar* (*c.* 1661), from Corneille, is the only translation staged by the King's Company in these years. It was not a success.

28 'Elizabethan-Restoration Palimpsest', *Modern Language Review*, 35 (1940), 287–319.

29 Assigned to the Duke's Company on the basis of a MS. cast in the Ohio State University copy.

30 On this play see Robert D. Hume, introduction to the Augustan Reprint Society facsimile (Los Angeles: Clark Library, 1977).

31 For assignment of *All Mistaken* to this season, see Robert D. Hume, 'Dryden, James Howard, and the Date of *All Mistaken*', *Philological Quarterly*, 51 (1972), 422–9.

32 *The Faithfull Virgins* (assigned to spring 1663 in *The London Stage*) should be dated *c.* 1670. See Judith Milhous and Robert D. Hume, 'Two Plays by Elizabeth Polwhele: *The Faithfull Virgins* and *The Frolicks*', *Papers of the Bibliographical Society of America*, 71 (1977), 1–9.

33 Three of the remaining plays are by Sir William Bartleys, John Wilson and Richard Rhodes; the fourth is the anonymous *Labyrinth* (May 1664).

34 *Roscius Anglicanus*, 39.

35 How different the audiences were is hard to determine. For a recent argument stressing continuity from the tenuous evidence available, see Kenneth Richards, 'Theatre Audiences in Caroline and Early Restoration London: Continuity and Change', *Das Theater und sein Publikum* (Vienna, 1977), 162–87. On the post-1660 audience see Emmett L. Avery, 'The Restoration Audience', *Philological Quarterly*, 45 (1966), 54–61, and Harold Love, 'Who were the Restoration Audience?' *Yearbook of English Studies*, 10 (1980), 21–44.

36 A point decisively made by A. H. Scouten in 'Notes Toward a History of Restoration Comedy', *Philological Quarterly*, 45 (1966), 62–70.

THE 'GREATEST ACTION'

LEE'S 'LUCIUS JUNIUS BRUTUS'

Antony Hammond

Everyone interested in the work of Nathaniel Lee remarks in some puzzlement at the persistent lack of critical attention to him. Although a good edition of his *Works* was published over a quarter of a century ago,[1] there have appeared since only a few good articles and one book-length study – and that in the Twayne's English Authors Series,[2] that respectable cemetery for writers who somehow are not famous enough to interest ordinary publishers.

A further puzzlement is that amongst authors of general studies of the literature or drama of the Restoration, responses to Lee persist which have been literary-historical small change for the better part of the century.[3] This essay is offered as a gesture towards setting the record somewhat straighter with regard to one of the finest tragedies written in English since the death of Shakespeare, *Lucius Junius Brutus*.

It is almost universally conceded that Lee was a highly uneven dramatist.[4] The pressures of producing professional work in the 1670s and 1680s can hardly be exaggerated, and almost all playwrights found it impossible to sustain their best level. Lee, however, was spectacularly erratic. He wrote altogether thirteen published plays (rumours of works composed during his stay in Bedlam have not yet been substantiated). Of these thirteen, two are collaborations (with Dryden); two are occasional plays of political and satiric intent; five, alas, are either apprentice work or else largely attempts to rehash what had been successful in the better plays. The remaining four, however, are thoughtful, careful, well-written explorations of serious dramatic and political themes in language which is often exciting and powerful: *Sophonisba*, *The Rival Queens*, *Caesar Borgia* and *Lucius Junius Brutus*.[5]

The Restoration was in general, like the Elizabethan age before it, acutely concerned with the nature of the political ruler. After the collapse of the republican experiment at the end of the Commonwealth, political science turned back to consider the ruler himself as the basis of government. What sort of man the ruler was, and what sort of attitude the subject must adopt towards him, were central questions. The drama was a natural vent for the expression of public interest in these matters.

The heroic drama adopted an ethical stance towards sovereignty: the ruler was *ipso facto* always right, and subjects likewise owed him absolute loyalty. When the ruler was a nasty man or worse, the subject suffered, but it was his duty to endure that suffering, since rebellion would strike at the root of the entire moral code of heroism and destroy the political fabric woven from it. Naturally, if no one ever disobeyed these principles there would never have been any heroic drama, but what counted was the way in which the principles were violated and how they were reaffirmed by the dramatic action. Lee's mind was not, however, attracted by this intellectualized version of behaviour. Instead he chose to explore in his finest plays the nature of the flawed ruler and the effects of that kind of ruler upon society. Armistead rightly identifies *Sophonisba* as the first play in which Lee takes up this theme.

> Melting at Capua I in pleasures lay,
> And for a Mistriss gave the World away

says Hannibal bitterly early in that play (1.i.104–5). Hannibal, and Massinissa in *Sophonisba*, Alexander in *The Rival Queens* and Caesar Borgia are all prone to lose sight of their regal nature and duties when diverted by other, often sensual, aspects of their personalities.

The flawed hero is of course not new, even in heroic drama. Dryden built an entire dramatic ethos out of the man 'irregularly great': Almanzor pre-eminently, but also Montezuma in *The Indian Emperour*, and later his own Antony, among others. However, in Dryden's plays the function of the action was (in general) to show how the ethical code extended to accommodate the talents of such men. Lee was more concerned with the dramatic possibilities of tragic resolutions to such personal conflicts.

Sophonisba is a beautiful and elegantly structured heroic play in which the imperatives of heroic military behaviour in three great men are tested against their other emotional components. *The Rival Queens* is a much more complete study of the flawed hero. Alexander the Great is the archetype of the military genius, whose gifts as a soldier are not identical to those needed by a ruler. His deficiencies lead to an insoluble political dilemma and a powerful tragic conclusion. *Caesar Borgia* explores a similar theme; in it Borgia, a man of extraordinary talents, but also of profoundly crippling weakness, is steered into certain kinds of action by Machiavel. Borgia is heroic, but also vicious; Machiavel, no mere villain, has the goal of restoring Roman greatness and thinks that, if Borgia's luxuriousness can be controlled, he will be a man equal to the task. Machiavel sets up conspiracies to achieve this end, but in fact disastrously unleashes Borgia's violence and destructive power, rather than his beneficent qualities.

There are thus three tragedies exploring different aspects of a similar theme. In *Sophonisba* degrees of weakness are set off against each other; in *The Rival Queens* the hero's weakness leads to a tragic catastrophe; in *Caesar Borgia* the attempt to control the hero's weakness by external action leads to disaster. The next step is clearly to examine a hero who was himself aware of the siren song of personal feeling and who would not allow himself to fall victim to it; a man who sought political probity by extinguishing his softer side – a development of Scipio in *Sophonisba*, in fact. The tragedy in this case is that he falls into a parallel error on the other side. By extirpating human emotion he becomes inhuman, irrational, destructive. This is Lucius Junius Brutus.

The reputation of *Lucius Junius Brutus* as a work of Whig propaganda is now so firmly entrenched that it might seem a hopeless task to try to expunge it. Yet the attempt must be made, for to read it in such a light is the way to ensure misunderstanding it. It is well known that the play was banned, after three (or six)[6] performances, on 11 December 1680 by the Lord Chamberlain; the grounds were that he had been 'informed' that the work contained 'very Scandalous Expressions & Reflections vpon yᵉ Government'.[7] It is clear from the wording that the Chamberlain was acting upon a complaint, not first-hand knowledge, and that he had not troubled to verify the objections to the play. Yet ever since, almost without exception,[8] critics have been content with the notion that it is a pro-Whig, anti-monarchical play.[9] It is hard to conceive of a worse authority for such an opinion than that of a government official who had neither read nor seen the work.

Of the two classes of evidence that might be called in to support such a reading, external evidence is largely wanting. Lee was indeed thought for a time to be a writer in the Whiggish camp. However, he was also a friend and collaborator of Dryden (not a man noted for republican sympathies!) during the period in question. Part of the difficulty is that it is not possible to establish a firm date for the violently anti-Catholic propaganda play, *The Massacre of Paris*. Hume thinks it was late, about 1680-1,[10] but it is even more likely that it was written in 1679,[11] and, if so, Lee's active Whig phase, if it ever occurred, might not have been more than a few months in duration. The prologue to *Theodosius* (probably summer 1680) is full of topical allusions which are collectively hostile to extreme Whig positions, and the play received royal patronage – hardly likely for the work of an author in opposition to the Government.

Lacking solid external evidence, we must consider the internal evidence instead. Lee's sources for *Lucius Junius Brutus*[12] were chiefly Livy's *History* for the political details, and Madeleine Scudéry's *Clelia* for the love-interest; he also took some details from Plutarch and was greatly impressed by Machiavelli's *Discourses* on the First Decade of Livy:

> nothing ever presented it self to my Fancy with that solid pleasure as Brutus did in sacrificing his Sons. Before I read Machivel's Notes upon the place, I concluded it the greatest Action that was ever seen throughout all Ages on the greatest Occasion.[13]

Alas, Lee's prose is almost as crabbed as his verse is lucid and eloquent. The Preface as a whole is actually a dedication to Dorset (no republican he!) and is largely an attempt to defend the seriousness of Lee's artistic intentions. 'There are some Subjects that require but half the Strength of a great Poet, but when Greece or old Rome come in play . . . the Poet must elevate his Fancy with the mightiest Imagination', and the critic of such a work must also be 'Longin throughout or nothing'. In consequence, 'I was troubled for my dumb Play' since 'a sparkish Generation, that have an Antipathy to Thought' had resolved to mislike it. When Lee talks of the greatness of the action in this context, it is surely evident that he means not 'morally most superior', but great in the sense of offering a dramatic opportunity to a thoughtful playwright. What Lee wished to do was to transmit to his audience the aesthetic possibilities of the historical event, that which had stirred his fancy with such solid pleasure; as in Aristotle's phrase, 'There are things which we see with pain so far as they themselves are concerned, but whose images, even when executed in very great detail, we view with pleasure.'[14]

The plot of *Lucius Junius Brutus* is fairly simple; a summary will help to clarify the discussion. It begins on the eve of Lucrece's rape, an event which provides Brutus with the occasion to throw off the guise of his insanity and to lead the rebellion. He feels obliged to separate his son Titus from his bride Teraminta, since she is Tarquin's bastard daughter. His actions provoke increasing dis-affection amongst the nobles, chiefly Collatinus (who was related to Tarquin and has been stripped of all office) and Tiberius, Brutus' younger son. They form a plot and by use of the unwilling Teraminta inveigle Titus into it. The plot is discovered; Titus, who had already changed his mind about collaborating, is sentenced with the rest of the conspirators, and, despite the pleas of both the Senate and the women, Brutus holds to his purpose and has him executed.

Three positions towards political power are expressed in the play. The monarchist malcontents stand exclusively for their own self-interest, disguised as the 'Tory' attitude of loyalty towards the King. Really what this group supports is the *status quo* which assured them of their social distinctions, their privilege as nobles. This group cannot conceive that Brutus is not similarly motivated; Tiberius puts it down to pride:

> Now, by the Gods, I hate his upstart pride,
> His Rebel thoughts of the Imperial Race,
> His abject Soul that stoops to court the Vulgar,
> His scorn of Princes, and his lust to th'People.
>
> (III. i. 21–4)

The other, extreme 'Whig' position amounts to mob-rule, anarchical when not self-centred, unreasoning, rash. The mob and their scatty leader Vintidius represent this extreme:

look you, Sirs, I am a true Commonwealths-man, and do not
naturally love Kings, tho they be good; for why should any one
man have more power than the People? Is he bigger, or wiser
than the People? Has he more Guts, or more Brains than the
People? What can he do for the People, that the People can't do
for them selves? Can he make Corn grow in a Famine? can he
give us Rain in Drought? or make our Pots boil, tho the Devil
piss in the Fire?   (II. i. 41–8)

Between these extremes, neither of which is entirely devoid of
principle, but whose principles are altogether too close to self-
interest for comfort, stands the man of fierce and passionate
principle, the man who will sacrifice his own interest freely – will
go out of his way to do so rather than allow any suspicion that he
might be corrupt: Brutus. Emotions of any kind, including
parental affection and love, are subordinate in him to the ideal of
political integrity. His language is full of dignified nobility, as in his
address after the death of Lucrece:

> You that were once a free-born People, fam'd
> In his Forefathers days for Wars abroad,
> The Conquerors of the World; Oh Rome! Oh Glory!
> What are you now? What has the Tyrant made you?
> The Slaves, the Beasts, the Asses of the Earth,
> The Soldiers of the Gods[,] Mechanic Laborers,
> Drawers of Water, Taskers, Timber-fellers,
> Yok'd you like Bulls, his very Jades for luggage,
> Drove you with Scourges down to dig in Quarries,
> To cleanse his Sinks, the Scavengers o'th'Court:
> While his lewd Sons, tho not on work so hard,
> Employ'd your Daughters and your Wives at home.
>   (II. i. 194–205)

At stirring rhetoric Brutus is without equal, but no one man can
construct a new society. Brutus must have help and obviously
cannot draw on the disaffected monarchists for support. So he
gives his trust to Vintidius. Yet his first political action was to work
a confidence trick on Vintidius and his rabble, by persuading them
– through the sheer force of his personality – that portents were
visible in the heavens. He thus knows that Vintidius is a bubble-
brain, and a vicious one to boot, as can be seen from the brutal

lynching he conducts in Act II. No regime is going to be better than its servants, and Brutus' decision to employ Vintidius is ominous to the audience, who have by the early part of Act III a clear insight into the weakness of the extremists on either side.

Another dimension of Brutus' dilemma is made manifest in the persons of Titus and Teraminta. In Act I Titus is ordered by Brutus to sever his relationship with her; at first he is horrified, but later feels obliged to accede, and the lovers part in a restrained, moving scene at the end of Act II. Brutus admits that his decision has been made on expedient, political grounds, not on personal ones: Teraminta, he says, is 'chastly good, most sweetly fram'd, / Without the smallest Tincture of her Father' (II. i. 324–5). Yet because she would appear to the world as a representative of the Tarquins, her relationship with Titus is politically unacceptable to him.

It is important that we should be persuaded of the reality of the lovers' affection for each other, and Lee expends a good deal of his talent for sensuous, sentiment-laden verse on them to convey this reality.[15] Two crucial issues arise from it. First, it is necessary for Titus to feel deeply enough for Teraminta to join the conspiracy against Brutus in order to save her life: in III. ii., she is forced by this threat to plead with Titus to join the plot. She expects him to refuse and reacts with horror when he embraces Tarquin's cause to save her life. The moral depth of both lovers in their dilemma is clearly shown. Yet, secondly, both of them are political innocents, entirely out of their depth in the political jungle into which they have been willy-nilly tossed. No provision for such people is made by any of the three political positions the play presents, which is a calamitous indictment of the political approach to social issues. The failure of the new republic to protect them, their unnecessary deaths, is a criticism of Brutus' principles (and of Brutus himself); the implication grows upon the reader that the Romans have, in their attempt to establish a new government built upon firm principles, really only exchanged one kind of tyranny for another.

This is a surprising conclusion, especially in view of the effort Lee makes to build up the positive side of Brutus' character. But it is an inescapable one. Nobody is going to be greatly distressed at the just deserts which Tiberius and his unpleasant associates meet. We may also wearily accept that cretins like Vintidius will inevitably play a part in political affairs. But Titus and Teraminta are something else. The dreadful temptation offered to the audience is to write off their sufferings in an expedient light, as unfortunate but necessary casualties in the creation of the great edifice which is Roman republicanism. But to do so is to commit an elementary blunder in the debate of ends and means, a blunder that Lee, son of a clergyman, could hardly have made unwittingly.

Curiously, it is a blunder that Armistead makes, for all his attempt to impose upon the play an ideological structure derived from the Christian political ethic of the Renaissance. 'By favoring Rome through Brutus,' he writes, 'Providence compensates for the tragic deaths of Titus and Teraminta and gives the piece a comedic [sic] shading'.[16] This is simply grotesque. The conclusion of *Lucius Junius Brutus* is stark and terrible, in no way coloured by comedy. Does the implied future harmony of Verona 'compensate' for or make 'comedic' the deaths of Romeo and Juliet? The notion is ethically indecent in any society which has rejected human sacrifice as a way of securing divine favour. Armistead notices that, like the monarchists, who celebrate their compact with an exceptionally horrible ritual murder (a kind of parody of transubstantiation in an anti-Eucharist) which shocks even Vintidius into outrage, Brutus opens his bid for power by requiring his associates to swear loyalty in a blood-ritual with Lucrece's dagger and concludes it with these abhorrent sacrificial executions. He might have remembered Machiavel's wry conclusion at the end of *Caesar Borgia*:

> No Power is safe, nor no Religion good,
> Whose Principles of growth are laid in Blood.

Machiavel has learned painfully of the truth of his *sententia*, though he is not the tragic focus of *Caesar Borgia*; Brutus does not learn, and that is a fearsome thing.

Armistead maintains that in Titus and Teraminta there is no 'viable alternative' to Brutus' kind of politics, on the grounds that 'man is no longer capable of living in the natural harmony they embody'.[17] This of course suits his reading of the play, but claims rather more than the work itself shows: why cannot man live in harmony, if these two people do? In any event, Titus and Teraminta are (like many of the secondary characters in Lee's best plays) chiefly symbolic. Teraminta is daughter to Tarquin – but a 'natural' daughter, in whom the evil of tyranny is purged. Titus is the scion of the noble republican; their marriage represents figuratively the only real solution to the power struggle: namely that both sides must learn to live in harmony (as is true of all political jars). Brutus, however, moves first to separate and then to destroy this symbolic union, while remaining satisfied throughout that he is acting in Rome's best interests. It casts a dreadful blight over the future of the new state.

How does the noble Brutus come to act so contrary to the true interests of his people? The answer is that ultimately he trusts no one's judgement but his own. The reasons for this are dramatic, and well expressed by Lee. First Brutus is shown feigning madness, then perceiving in the affront to Lucrece the opportunity for decisive action (I.i.94ff.). His tools must be the foolish plebs, and he immediately seeks occasion to win them to his side by an exercise in deceit. The first obstacle he meets is, unluckily and ominously, Titus' secret marriage to Teraminta. At the scene in which Lucrece recounts her rape, Brutus alone scornfully rejects grief and lamentation, and rouses the Romans to revenge. By the end of Act I, then, he is confirmed in his opinion that he alone, in his resolution, can provide the opportunity for a decent government to be created. And he is undoubtedly right.

Yet Lee begins to sow the seeds of doubt at the very moment Brutus seems most entirely right: his endorsement of Vintidius, his treatment of Titus, his confidence trick on the plebs – all are signs of a confusion of ends and means in him. In coping with the monarchists as time goes on, and defending his allies such as Valerius, Brutus gradually grows more monolithic, less adaptable, more rigid in his opinions. We cannot altogether blame him, as he must act in an atmosphere dominated by a sinister crescendo of conspiracy. This atmosphere is excellently evoked by Lee as Acts III and IV proceed, and caught brilliantly at the opening of Act IV in an image of Shakespearian vividness:

> *Tiberius*   Hark, are we not pursu'd?
> *Vitellius*   No, 'tis the tread
>   Of our own Friends, that follow in the dark.

The ghastly ritual sacrifice by the conspirators follows. Which of us could guarantee to keep our heads in such a crisis? Brutus confesses his 'Philosophy seems at a stand' in these perplexities (IV.i.286), though he does not think of taking advice from anyone to help him. As the putative Father of his Country, the revolt of his own sons against him is freighted with terrible significance. He forgives them as a father, but as Rome's Consul is determined to execute the letter of the law (IV.i.305–11).

The fragmentation of his personality implied is ominous: he immediately begins to prevaricate with both Titus and Teraminta, assuring her (l. 438) that he will 'not be cruel', and at line 578 promising Titus to take care of Teraminta. Neither of these promises will be kept. Act V deepens the sense of his isolation from reason and reality; he casts himself in the role of divine avenger, as Valerius' awestruck reaction makes clear:

> why, he's no more a man;
> He is not cast in the same Common mould,
> His Spirit moves not with our Springs and wards.
> He looks and talks, as if that Jove had sent him
> To be the Judge of all the under World.
>
> (v.i.8–12)

The horror begins as Titus is confronted with the wounded Teraminta and learns from her that Brutus was responsible (v.i.75). The disgust evoked by the abominations of the conspirators is shallow compared to the distress engendered by Brutus' fall from honour and probity; by now the defiant curses of Tiberius begin to seem almost justified:

> Enjoy the bloody Conquest of thy Pride,
> Thou more Tyrannical than any Tarquin,
> Thou fiercer Sire of these unhappy Sons,
> Than impious Saturn or the gorg'd Thiestes . . .
>
> .   .   .
>
> But end, Barbarian, end the horrid vengeance
> Which thou so impiously hast begun,
> Perfect thy Justice, as thou, Tyrant, call'st it.
>
> (v.i.115–25)

Brutus indeed purposes his own bloody ritual (v.ii.6–30), giving a dreadful catalogue of the benefits he hopes to obtain therefrom. The pleadings that follow leave him unmoved; the unkindest cut, and finest dramatic irony, is that Titus himself is persuaded to believe in the justice of Brutus' actions (v.ii.182–6). Brutus is still magnificent, in his inhumanity:

> Peace, Consul, peace: let us not soil the pomp
> Of this Majestick Fate with Womans brawls.
>
> (v.ii.191–2)

But he shows no sign now that he is aware of the enormity of his actions; he is not stoic in the face of a personal catastrophe: rather he is transported beyond human feeling in his enthusiasm for his principles.

This, then, is his central hamartia: in his fearless honesty towards the ideal of republican government (in itself, in terms of the play, an obvious good by comparison with the corrupt monarchy it replaces) he forgets that the state is made up of the people who live in it. In his rigidity of purpose he becomes an unreliable judge, as well as a cruel man in his desperate crisis, and tramples upon the real in support of his vision of the ideal. It is a kind of hubris that he suffers from: the belief that he is incorruptible and that his judgement is inevitably correct. He is a tragic figure for this reason, that his belief in himself outruns what we can accept as right or just, and his moral nature becomes deeply flawed without his growing aware of it. The tragedy is thus twofold: for him, that though the best man – indeed the only man capable of bringing Rome out of its crisis – he is placed in a position where he is encouraged to think himself absolute. The tragedy is also Rome's, whose new dawn is streaked red with the blood of injustice. Brutus himself remains, for all his failure, an always commanding and partly sympathetic figure, a tragic hero in the finest and most terrible sense.

How can such a sensitive study of the cost of political power have been thought propaganda for republicanism, or Whiggism, or any other -ism? There are in it, of course, allusions to contemporary events, most notably in the Jesuitical behaviour of the priests. But there is no plausible way of seeing the entire work as an allegory on events of the period. Rather, the play's political basis is curiously similar to that of *Venice Preserv'd*: that however justified a rebellion may be, it will inevitably bring injustice and suffering to the innocent in its train. The suffering of Titus and Teraminta is undoubtedly a sign for the times. But it is not their tragedy.

It is Brutus, the greatest figure in the state, who is most diminished in his moral being by the actions he takes. A tragedy could of course have been made of a ruler who is aware that he is inevitably involved in corruption by the mere act of taking power, as Shakespeare illustrated in the *Henry IV* plays. But Lee preferred the harder and obviously riskier course of leaving the hero unaware of his failure, leaving the anagnorisis to the audience while the hero persists blindly in his hamartia. The classical restraint of the play's style (so foreign to the usual assessments of Lee's extravagance) matches the restrained dignity of the tragic theme and produces a play which for sustained subtlety of political thought is without equal in the Restoration, and a poetic tragedy which deserves recognition as a major masterpiece.

NOTES

1 Thomas B. Stroup and Arthur L. Cooke (eds), *The Works of Nathaniel Lee*, 2 vols (New Brunswick, N.J., 1954–5).

2 J. M. Armistead, *Nathaniel Lee* (Boston, Mass., 1979). Twayne's English Authors No. 270.

3 For example, in James Sutherland's *English Literature of the Late Seventeenth Century*, Oxford History of English Literature, VI (Oxford, 1969), 71–5, where all the old clichés – Lee's 'hysterical emphasis' and 'natural extravagance' – are trotted out again.

4 One exception is Armistead, who scarcely mentions qualitative differences in the plays he discusses.

5 Apart from Armistead's essay on *Sophonisba* (*Durham University Journal*, 71 (1978), 35–43) which is incorporated into his book as the chapter on that play, and the critical introductions to the two plays published in the Regents Restoration Drama series (*The Rival Queens*, ed. P. F. Vernon (Lincoln, Nebr., 1970); *Lucius Junius Brutus*, ed. John Loftis (Lincoln, Nebr., 1967)), the only major article is David Vieth's 'Psychological Myth as Tragedy: Nathaniel Lee's *Lucius Junius Brutus*' (*Huntington Library Quarterly*, 39 (1975), 57–76). Vieth touches on a number of points discussed in the present essay, but his main focus is on the Freudian interpretation of the relationship between Brutus, his sons, and Teraminta. It is a fascinating alternative reading of the play.

6 Loftis, in his edition (pp. xii–xiii), summarizes the evidence and concludes that six is the likelier number.

7 P.R.O., L.C. 5/144, p. 28.

8 Vieth, op. cit., 58–60, surveys the notion coolly and critically. Armistead, in his chapter on the play (pp. 130–43) also treats it dismissively.

9 Loftis, op. cit., xviii, writes of its 'vehement Whiggism', and Robert Hume, in his *The Development of English Drama in the*

Late Seventeenth Century (Oxford, 1976), speaks of it as 'vehemently upholding constitutional principles which the Stuarts considered inimical at best' (p. 344). These are only two of the most recent, and authoritative, of such comments.

10 See 'The Satiric Design of Nat. Lee's *The Princess of Cleve*', *JEGP*, 75 (1976), 120–2.

11 Hume's arguments for the late date are in fact partly based on the assumption that *Lucius Junius Brutus* is Whig propaganda. My view is that Lee wrote *Massacre* immediately after the breaking of the Popish Plot and the murder of Godfrey; that he wrote it hastily as a deliberate popular-polemical piece, in disappointment after the failure of *Caesar Borgia*. Armistead (op. cit., 95–8) also dates it before 1680.

12 Detailed in Stroup and Cooke, II, 317–18.

13 Quoted from the Dedication; Stroup and Cooke, II, 321. All subsequent quotations from the play are taken from this edition.

14 *Poetics*, ch. 6. Translated by Gerald F. Else (Ann Arbor, Mich., 1967), 20.

15 Vieth, op. cit., concentrates much attention upon the imagery, though his focus is different from mine.

16 Armistead, op, cit., 139.

17 ibid., 138.

12

CONGREVE AS A SHAKESPEAREAN

T. W. Craik

Congreve is, by general agreement, one of the most conscious stylists among the writers of comedy in English, and his literary expression has received much attention. In this essay I shall confine myself to a single aspect of it, his echoes of Shakespeare. Some of these echoes have the nature of allusions and depend for their full comic effect on their recognition by the audience. Others – by far the greater number – are verbal reminiscences, conscious or unconscious, sometimes evidently prompted by the speaker's character or circumstances, and at other times seemingly springing from Congreve's familiarity with Shakespeare's plays in general and a few of them in particular.

The fact that this aspect of Congreve's style has not – as far as I am aware – been examined as a whole, though some individual examples have been noted by his editors, shows that it is far from being developed into a mannerism. He never makes his *dramatis personae* quote from Shakespeare directly, as Belinda quotes from Cowley, Sir Sampson from Dryden and Millamant from Waller and from 'natural, easy Suckling'.[1] Even his few direct and pointed allusions are integrated into his dialogue, and are uttered by speakers quite unconscious of the Shakespearean origin of their expressions. To attempt to identify them, and still more those of which Congreve himself may not have been fully conscious, is not without such dangers as Johnson humorously points out in the Preface to his edition of Shakespeare:

I have found it remarked, that, in this important sentence, *Go before, I'll follow*, we read a translation of, *I prae, sequar*. I have been told, that when *Caliban*, after a pleasing dream, says, *I cry'd to sleep again*, the author imitates *Anacreon*, who had, like every other man, the same wish on the same occasion.[2]

Nevertheless, for the sake of the light which these verbal reminiscences may throw on Congreve's reading, his memory and sometimes his dramatic art, the dangers seem worth risking.

In *The Way of the World*, Sir Wilfull Witwoud's first appearance, at Lady Wishfort's house, is marked by the recurring phrase 'No offence'. He salutes Mrs Marwood, saying, as he does so, 'No Offence, I hope'. His half-brother Witwoud remarks: 'This is a vile Dog, I see that already. No Offence. Ha, ha, ha, to him; to him *Petulant*, smoke him.' Petulant thereupon accosts Sir Wilfull, using the phrase for the third time with ironical intent; presently Sir Wilfull is goaded into asking him 'Do you speak by way of Offence, Sir?', and, when giving his name to Mrs Marwood, adds pointedly, 'No offence to any Body, I hope.' At this stage Mrs Marwood introduces him to his half-brother, who acknowledges him coldly; Sir Wilfull reacts indignantly, and Witwoud, evidently with tongue in cheek, replies 'No offence, I hope, Brother.' At this, Sir Wilfull delivers the retort direct: ''Sheart, Sir, but there is, and much offence.' This is the last time the word is used for nearly eighty lines, though it reappears (with the effect of a running joke) at Lady Wishfort's entrance, and again in Sir Wilfull's drunken scene in Act IV.[3]

Only one of Congreve's editors annotates 'No offence', finding it 'possibly reminiscent of Falstaff's attempts to excuse his insults to Hal (*2 Henry IV*, II.iv.302, 305, 307: 'No abuse, Hal, o' mine honour').[4] The device of repetition may owe something to this scene, though it should be noticed that Falstaff's insults belonged to the past and not to the present. However, at the climax of Congreve's exchange it is another scene in Shakespeare that is recalled:

Horatio   These are but wild and whirling words, my lord.
Hamlet   I am sorry they offend you, heartily;
   Yes, 'faith, heartily.
Horatio   There's no offence, my lord.
Hamlet   Yes, by Saint Patrick, but there is, Horatio,
   And much offence too.[5]

The echo is surely one of which Congreve was conscious and also one which he expected his audience to recognize. (*Hamlet* was in the repertory, Betterton, who played Fainall in Congreve's comedy, acting the Prince.) The humour lies in the incongruity between the two speakers and between the two senses in which they use the phrase (for the 'offence' that Hamlet means is his uncle's crime).

Nothing in the situations or the characterization of this play recalls *Hamlet*.[6] By contrast, throughout *The Double-Dealer*, Maskwell's behaviour owes a great deal to Iago's in *Othello*, a play which was evidently in the forefront of Congreve's mind when writing the scenes in which the villain persuades Lord Touchwood that his nephew Mellefont is trying to seduce Lady Touchwood.[7] This preoccupation, presumably, threw up the incongruous allusions to *Othello* in the wholly comic scenes involving Sir Paul and Lady Plyant. One of Maskwell's early stratagems is to have Lady Plyant persuaded (by Lady Touchwood) that Mellefont loves her. This is done, and Lady Plyant (with her husband in tow) taxes Mellefont with dishonourable behaviour:

> *Lady Plyant*   Have I behaved my self with all the decorum, and nicety, befitting the Person of Sir *Paul*'s wife? Have I preserv'd my Honour as it were in a Snow-House for this three year past? Have I been white and unsulli'd even by Sir *Paul* himself?
>
> *Sir Paul*   Nay, she has been an impenetrable Wife, even to me, that's the truth on't.
>
> *Lady Plyant*   Have I, I say, preserv'd my self, like a fair Sheet of Paper, for you to make a Blot upon –
>
> *Sir Paul*   And she shall make a Simile with any Woman in England.   (II. i. 252–62)

It is not Lady Plyant's role to make similes (the literary set, in this play, consists of the Froths and Brisk), so Sir Paul's admiring comment draws attention to the feeble one she makes here, and hence to the strong Shakespearean metaphor behind it:

> Was this fair paper, this most goodly book,
> Made to write 'whore' upon?[8]

Congreve soon disentangles this misunderstanding – or, rather, leaves it to disentangle itself – and sets Mellefont's friend Careless in pursuit of the virtuous lady. When Careless's love-letter accidentally falls into Sir Paul's hands, it is Sir Paul's turn to make similes; he exclaims, in soliloquy: 'O my Lady *Plyant*, you were Chaste as Ice, but you are melted now, and false as Water' (IV. i. 430–1). Here the echoes of *Hamlet* and *Othello* are not stressed, and though both come from well-known dialogues[9] it would be a quick-minded spectator who would identify them. Congreve seems to have employed them passingly, perhaps instinctively, to exaggerate Sir Paul's passion. Earlier in the same soliloquy he also draws on Shakespeare, this time in *Love's Labour's Lost*, evidently without allusive intent, when Sir Paul is apostrophizing Careless: 'Die and be Damn'd for a *Judas Maccabeus*, and *Iscariot* both.'[10] Here Shakespeare's humorous association of the two Judases is borrowed simply to give a comic heightening. Similarly, Lady Plyant, having already realized that she gave her husband the wrong letter, is made to express her alarm in an idiom of unconscious sexual suggestion derived from Juliet's Nurse: 'I'm all over in a Universal Agitation, I dare swear every Circumstance of me trembles' (IV. i. 397–8).[11] As these borrowings show, Congreve's memory was a reservoir of Shakespearean dialogue into which he could dip easily: how easily can be seen from a single speech of Brisk's when he and Lady Froth are anatomizing their social acquaintances:

> I know whom you mean – But Deuce take me, I can't hit of her Name neither – Paints de'e say? Why she lays it on with a Trowel – Then she has a great Beard that bristles through it, and makes her look as if she were plaistred with Lime and Hair, let me perish. (III. i. 583–7)

Here we have Hamlet addressing Yorick's skull ('let her paint an inch thick'), Celia ironically applauding Touchstone's cliché about the destinies, Sir Hugh Evans voicing his misgivings about the fat woman of Brentford, and Theseus commending Snout's performance as Wall.[12] There is, of course, no compulsion to ascribe all or any of these phrases to Shakespearean reminiscence, but, in view of Congreve's demonstrable habit of mind elsewhere, such reminiscence seems highly possible. The following dialogue between Maskwell and Lady Touchwood, for instance, must derive from *2 Henry IV*:

> *Maskwell* You have already been tampering with my Lady *Plyant*?

> *Lady Touchwood*   I have: She is ready for any Impression I think
>   fit.   (I. i. 406–9)

Lady Touchwood's metaphor, of softening wax in order to set one's seal on it, depends on a transitive sense of the verb 'tamper', but the verb is used intransitively in Maskwell's question.[13] Behind the passage lies Falstaff's plan announced when Bardolph tells him that the army is disbanded after the Gaultree Forest campaign:

> Let them go. I'll through Gloucestershire, and there will I visit Master Robert Shallow, Esquire. I have him already temp'ring between my finger and my thumb, and shortly will I seal with him. Come away.   (*2 Henry IV*, IV. iii. 125–30)

This is an interesting example of Congreve's indebtedness: apart from the one word 'tampering' ('temp'ring') there is no verbal similarity whatever between the passages, and yet the conclusion seems irresistible, because of Congreve's inconsistent use of this word, that he derived his metaphor from Shakespeare.

Sometimes the Shakespearean reminiscence is a matter of Congreve's retaining a single phrase while transposing the remainder into the idiom of his own times. Thus Bottom's unforgettable 'I have a reasonable good ear in music. Let's have the tongs and the bones' (*MND*, IV. i. 26–7) begets Jeremy's reply to Sir Sampson's indignant question (he does not think a servant is entitled to any tastes, literal or metaphorical) 'and Musick, don't you love Musick, Scoundrell?':

> Yes, I have a reasonable good Ear, Sir, as to Jiggs and Country Dances; and the like; I don't much matter your *Sola*'s or *Sonata*'s, they give me the Spleen.   (*Love for Love*, II. i. 371–5)

More usually, however, Congreve's Shakespeareanisms are fleeting phrases which bring little if anything of their original contexts with them. In *The Old Batchelour*, Sir Joseph Wittol repeats Pistol's error of 'Cannibal' for 'Hannibal', and in the next speech but one Captain Bluffe repeats Dogberry's 'Comparisons are odorous'.[14] Later, Bluffe makes a Pistolian use of the verb 'ensue';[15] Heartfree, in love with Silvia against his better knowledge, gloomily foresees himself 'Chronicled in Ditty, and sung in woful Ballad'.[16] and when, near the end of the play, he reacts violently to a taunt of Belinda's, she declares that she has 'only touch'd a gall'd-beast till he winch'd'.[17]

In *The Double-Dealer* Mellefont, setting his friend Careless to keep Lady Plyant out of the scheming Lady Touchwood's way, declares 'I'le observe my Uncle my self';[18] Maskwell, disingenuously letting Mellefont into his intrigue to get him disinherited, says 'I am to turn you a grazing';[19] and Lord Touchwood, resolving to disinherit him, exclaims 'Death I'll have him stripp'd and turn'd naked out of my house this moment, and let him rot and perish, incestuous Brute'.[20] In *Love for Love* Valentine is reported by Jeremy, as is Hamlet by the Gravedigger, to be 'mad for want of his wits';[21] Buckram the lawyer is said by Valentine, as is Cassius by Brutus, to have in 'itching Palm';[22] and Valentine (still in his pretended madness) addresses his father as 'Old Truepenny'.[23] In *The Way of the World*, Fainall (with a materialistic sense alien to Shakespeare's use of the phrase) talks of wearing his horns 'tipt with Gold';[24] and Waitwell, as Sir Rowland, pretending to recognize the handwriting of Mrs Marwood's letter as Mirabell's, declares:

> The Rascal writes a sort of a large hand; your *Roman* hand – I saw there was a throat to be cut presently. If he were my Son as he is my Nephew I'd Pistoll him.[25]

This sort of reminiscence is not confined to Shakespeare. Cowley ('Nay the *mute Fish* witness no less his praise') may be behind Sir Sampson's command to Ben ('To your Element, Fish, be mute, Fish, and to Sea');[26] Bunyan behind Ben's 'For to speak one thing, and to think just the contrary way; is as it were, to look one way, and to row another';[27] Marston (unless there is some intervening reference which has not been traced) behind Petulant's 'Carry your Mistress's Monkey a spider'.[28] Mirabell's famous metaphor on Millamant's arrival – 'Here she comes i'faith full sail, with her Fan spread and her Streamers out, and a shoal of Fools for Tenders' – seems to be Congreve's heightening of Dryden's metaphor on Jacintha by conflating it with Milton's on Dalila;[29] Dryden's *Mac Flecknoe* is echoed in Foresight's abuse of Sir Sampson the traveller ('*Ferdinand Mendez Pinto* was but a Type of thee, thou Lyar of the first Magnitude').[30] Echoes of Jonson are too numerous to be listed here,[31] but a couple may be mentioned: Lady Plyant's complaisant response to Sir Paul's grovelling request to kiss her hand ('My Lip indeed, Sir *Paul*, I swear you shall'), and (one reminiscence leading to another) Sir Paul's urging of Cynthia to transmit the Plyant family features to her offspring ('our House is distinguish'd by a Languishing Eye, as the House of *Austria* is by a thick Lip').[32]

But it is Shakespeare who most frequently comes to Congreve's mind as he writes, and to ours as we read. In *The Way of The World* Petulant talks of throat-cutting in Nym's laconic vein;[33] in *Love for Love*, Sir Sampson's back-slapping salutations to Foresight as 'old *Ptolomee*', 'old *Nostrodamus*', 'old *Merlin*', and so on, are in the exuberant style of the Host of the Garter Inn.[34] As Brian Gibbons points out, 'the marvellously particular and complete identities of the comic characters [in *The Way of the World*] owe much to Shakespeare's example'; he traces aspects of Lady Wishfort to Juliet's Nurse and to Falstaff, and of the revelling Sir Wilfull Witwoud to Sir Toby Belch.[35] One of Sir Wilfull's drunken protestations, to Millamant, 'If I drunk your Health to day, Cozen – I am a *Borachio*', is Shakespearean in the spirit as well as in the letter. It not only carries an (unconscious?) echo of Falstaff's 'I am a rogue if I drunk today', but also allows us a Shakespearean glimpse into Sir Wilfull's fuddled brain as he triumphantly produces the newly learned term of abuse that his aunt has just bestowed on him.[36]

In his tragi-comedy *The Mourning Bride* Congreve again turns towards Shakespeare, not in the characterization – all these figures breathe only the rarefied air of heroic drama – but in the language. The language is, of course, prevailingly as 'heroic' as the characterization, thus making the Shakespearean echoes, when they occur, the more obvious. *Romeo and Juliet*, as Shakespeare's tragedy of young lovers, is the play on which Congreve chiefly draws. In the second act Almeria's situation, betrothed to Garcia against her will, is so similar to Juliet's, betrothed against her will to Paris, that she naturally applies Juliet's macabre imagery to it:

> Or wind me in the Shroud of some pale Coarse
> Yet green in Earth, rather than be the Bride
> Of *Garcia*'s more detested Bed.[37]

When the action presently shifts to the burial vault, *Romeo and Juliet* continues to furnish imagery and diction. Almeria's attendant says:

> the Iron Grates that lead to Death
> Beneath, are still wide stretch'd upon their Hinge,
> And staring on us with unfolded Leaves.

And Almeria replies:

> Sure, 'tis the Friendly Yawn of Death for me . . . .
>
> . . .
>
> Death, grim Death, will fold
> Me in his leaden Arms, and press me close
> To his cold clayie Breast.[38]

However, when Almeria apostrophizes her love Alphonso (whom she supposes lost at sea) and Osmyn ascends from the tomb with the line 'Who calls that wretched thing, that was *Alphonso*?', the seeming apparition of a ghost suggests a different Shakespearean tragedy. Almeria exclaims: 'Angels, and all the Host of heaven support me!' and urges her confidante to 'speak to it quickly, quickly'.[39] Osmyn makes a speech identifying himself, for our information, as Alphonso, and rejoicing that Almeria herself is not a ghost but a living woman: 'It is *Almeria*, 'tis, it is my Wife!'[40] After some time, *Romeo and Juliet* re-surfaces with Osmyn-Alphonso's 'inauspicious Stars',[41] and, Congreve now being again tuned in to Shakespeare's wavelength, Zara shortly demands 'Haste me to know it'[42] and immediately afterwards exclaims: 'O Heav'n! my Fears interpret / This thy Silence'.[43] Zara is the Moorish queen, in whose army the disguised Alphonso has taken service, and whose unreturned passion for him provides most of the play's strongest moments. Meanwhile, Alphonso, languishing in prison, foresees his desperate gestures when Almeria shall marry Garcia; his speech owes something to Romeo's passion over the banishment which will prevent his consummating his marriage to Juliet:

> Then will I . . .
> Break on the flinty Ground my throbbing Breast,
> And grovel with gash'd Hands to scratch a Grave.[44]

It is the non-consummation of his own marriage to Almeria that has just been Alphonso's theme. This scene is shared by Almeria; and Zara, discovering the lovers together, exclaims: 'Perdition catch 'em both, and Ruine part 'em'.[45]

Towards the end of the play, poison becomes a prominent vehicle of the intrigue, and *Romeo and Juliet* resumes its prominence as a source of imagery and diction. Zara, killing herself with one of the two bowls of poison which she intended to share with Alphonso, cries: 'This, to our mutual Bliss when joyn'd above', and then: 'O friendly Draught, already in my Heart!'[46] Almeria, in her turn, believing that the headless body before her (actually her villainous father's, in Alphonso's disguise) is her husband's, decides to take the poison but finds the first bowl empty and cries

> O noble Thirst! and yet too greedy to
> Drink all – O for another Draught of Death.[47]

Besides these reminiscences which are prompted more or less directly by the situations, there are possibly others. When Zara (intending thereby to save Alphonso's life) proposes to substitute a private strangling for a public execution, the King's favourite Gonsalez shrewdly remarks:

> Methinks this Lady's Hatred to the *Moor*
> Disquiets her too much.[48]

Later, having through a misfiring stratagem killed the King with his own hand, Gonsalez apostrophizes himself in terms very like Hamlet's to Polonius: 'O Wretch! O curs'd, and rash, deluded Fool!'[49] Another verbal reminiscence is, unexpectedly, of *2 Henry VI*, one of the less familiar of Shakespeare's plays: 'Confusion, all is on the Rout!'[50] Possibly (as perhaps in the case of the resemblance to Marston's *Malcontent* noted above) some other writer's borrowing of the phrase intervened; however, the scene (in which Young Clifford finds his father dead on the battlefield) contains some of the most memorable verse of the play, and so Congreve may have remembered it for himself.

His favourite plays, it would seem, were what one would expect: for tragedy, *Romeo and Juliet, Julius Caesar, Hamlet* and *Othello*; and for comedy, *Love's Labour's Lost, A Midsummer Night's Dream, Much Ado about Nothing, As You Like It, Twelfth Night, The Merry Wives of Windsor* and the Falstaff scenes of the English histories. Not all of these held the stage in Congreve's time, and it is notable that when Congreve uses allusion allusively it is with reference to those plays – *Hamlet* and *Othello* – which were secure in the theatre. He was himself evidently a reader of Shakespeare. This is further borne out by the handful of Shakespearean allusions in his surviving letters. 'Of my philosophy I make some use' he writes in 1704 (to Joseph Keally), referring to his lack of an official appointment: the metrical word order shows that he is adapting Cassius.[51] In another letter of the same year to the same correspondent he follows a couple of Falstaffian reminiscences with a distorted and witty one of Othello:

> I am grown fat; but you know I was born with somewhat a round belly. I find you are resolved to be a man of this world, which I am sorry for, because it will deprive me of you. However, think of me, as I am nothing extenuate.[52]

Finally (again writing to Keally) he applies a quotation from *The Merry Wives of Windsor* to their fat friend Robert Fitzgerald's proposed Irish voyage:

> Robin talks of going every day. I would have him stay till the weather is a little settled; for if he should be cast away, you know your water swells a man; and what a thing were he if he were swelled?[53]

Both these last quotations illustrate Congreve's thorough familiarity with Shakespearean idiom. In the new sense which he gives to the line from *Othello*, he uses 'nothing' with the Elizabethan meaning 'not at all'; and in quoting Falstaff from memory he substitutes for 'the water' the idiomatic 'your water' – possibly because of yet another spontaneous recollection, this time of the Gravedigger in *Hamlet*.[54]

NOTES

1 *The Old Batchelour*, IV. iii. 144–5; *Love for Love*, V. i. 381; *The Way of the World*, IV. i. 52–3, 63, 80 (stage direction), 98–9, 101, 104–5, 153. Quotations are from Herbert Davis (ed.), *The Complete Plays of William Congreve* (Chicago and London, 1967).

2 W. Raleigh (ed.), *Johnson on Shakespeare* (Oxford, 1908), 35.

3 *The Way of the World*, III. i. 484–527, 605; IV. i. 386, 444.

4 Brian Gibbons (ed.), *The Way of the World* (London, 1971), III. i. 64n.

5 *Hamlet*, I. v. 133–7. Quotations are from Peter Alexander (ed.), *William Shakespeare; The Complete Works* (London, 1951).

6 There is only one other verbal reminiscence, Witwoud's 'Hum, a hit, a hit, a palpable hit, I confess it' (II. i. 353), which combines Osric's 'A hit, a very palpable hit' and Laertes's 'A touch, a touch, I do confess't' (*Hamlet*, V. ii. 273, 277).

7 'Lord Touchwood How! give me but Proof of it, Ocular Proof,

that I may justifie my Dealing with him to the World, and share my Fortunes. *Maskwell* O my Lord! consider that is hard . . .' (IV.i.562–5). Cf. *Oth.*, III.iii.364, 401–12. '*Lord Touchwood* Honest *Maskwell*! . . . Give me thy hand – my Nephew is the alone remaining Branch of all our ancient Family; him I thus blow away, and constitute thee in his room to be my Heir' (V.i.53–9). Cf. *Oth.*, III.iii: 'All my fond love thus do I blow to heaven' (449); 'Now art thou my lieutenant' (482).

8 *Oth.*, IV.ii.72–3. In the ensuing dialogue between Lady Plyant and Mellefont there are further burlesque echoes of *Othello* when she bids him 'give me Mathemacular Demonstration, answer me directly', and exclaims 'oh! the Impiety of it!' (II.i.302–3, 304). Cf. *Oth.*, III.iii.364: 'give me the ocular proof'; IV.i.191–2: 'But yet the pity of it, Iago! O, Iago, the pity of it, Iago!'.

9 *Hamlet*, III.i.135–6: 'be thou as chaste as ice, as pure as snow, thou shalt not escape calumny'; *Oth.*, V.ii.137: 'She was false as water'.

10 *The Double-Dealer*, IV.i.417–8; *Love's Labour's Lost*, V.ii.588–91: '*Hol. Judas I am – Dum.* A Judas! *Hol.* Not Iscariot, sir. / *Judas I am, ycliped Maccabaeus.*'

11 *R.&J.*, II.iv.156–7: 'Now, afore God, I am so vex'd that every part about me quivers. Scurvy knave!'

12 *Hamlet*, V.i.189–90; *AYL*, I.ii.94: 'Well said; that was laid on with a trowel'; *Merry Wives*, IV.ii.169–72: 'By yea and no, I think the oman is a witch indeed; I like not when a oman has a great peard; I spy a great peard under his muffler'; *MND*, V.i.164: 'Would you desire lime and hair to speak better?'

13 For the etymology and history of the word, see *OED*, 'Tamper', *v.*[1]. Congreve retained the text as given here when he prepared the collected edition of his *Works* (London, 1710).

14 *The Old Batchelour*, II.i.176, 179; *2 H 4*, II.iv.157: 'Compare with Caesars, and with Cannibals'; *Ado*, III.v.16: 'Comparisons are odorous'.

15 *The Old Batchelour*, III.i.258–60: 'Tell him, I say, he must refund – or Bilbo's the Word, and Slaughter will ensue'. Cf. *Merry Wives*, I.iii.30: 'Why, then, let kibes ensue.'

16 *The Old Batchelour*, III.i.80. Cf. *AYL*, II.vii.147–9: 'the lover

. . . with a woeful ballad / Made to his mistress' eyebrow', and
1 H 4, II. ii. 44–5: 'An I have not ballads made on you all, and
sung to filthy tunes, let a cup of sack be my poison.'

17 *The Old Batchelour*, v. ii. 46. Cf. *Hamlet*, III. ii. 236–7: 'Let the
galled jade wince, our withers are unwrung.'

18 *The Double-Dealer*, I. i. 135. Cf. *Hamlet*, III. ii. 77–8: 'Even with
the very comment of thy soul / Observe my uncle.'

19 *The Double-Dealer*, II. i. 402–3. Cf. *R.&J.*, III. v. 189: 'Graze
where you will, you shall not house with me.'

20 *The Double-Dealer*, III. i. 100–102. Cf. *Oth.*, IV. i. 177: 'Ay, let her
rot, and perish, and be damn'd to-night.'

21 *Love for Love*, IV. i. 33. Cf. *Hamlet*, v. i. 154.

22 *Love for Love*, IV. i. 238. Cf. *Caes.*, IV. iii. 10.

23 *Love for Love*, IV. i. 268. Cf. *Hamlet*, I. v. 150.

24 *The Way of the World*, III. i. 646–7. Cf. *Ado*, v. iv. 44: 'Tush, fear
not, man; we'll tip thy horns with gold.' In Fainall's previous
speech (III. i. 636–7), the horns were likened to a snail's. Cf.
AYL, IV. i. 47–55.

25 *The Way of the World*, IV. i. 601–3. Cf. *Tw.N.*, II. v. 34: 'Pistol
him, pistol him.'; III. iv. 27–8: 'I think we do know the sweet
Roman hand.' One letter scene evidently recalled another.

26 *Love for Love*, v. i. 417–8. Cowley, *Davideis*, I. 820.

27 *Love for Love*, III. i. 385–7. Cf. Bunyan, *The Pilgrim's Progress*,
Part I, where Mr By-ends tells Christian 'my grandfather was
but a waterman, looking one way and rowing another, and I
got most of my estate by the same occupation.'

28 *The Way of the World*, IV. i. 375. Cf. Marston, *The Malcontent*,
I. iii. 40–1, where Malevole says he lives 'with killing of spiders
for my lady's monkey.'

29 *The Way of the World*, II. i. 323–4. Cf. Dryden, *An Evening's
Love*, II. i. 43: 'Yonder she comes, with full sails i' faith!';
Milton, *Samson Agonistes*, ll. 710–21, especially l. 718: 'Sails
fill'd, and streamers waving.'

30 *Love for Love*, II. i. 236. Cf. *Mac Flecknoe*, ll. 29–30: 'Heywood and
Shirley were but types of thee, / Thou last great prophet of
tautology.'

31 See, for examples from *The Way of the World*, Ian Donaldson,
The World Upside Down (Oxford, 1970), 154, n. 1.

32 *The Double-Dealer*, IV. i. 195, 239–40. Cf. *The Alchemist*, IV. i.
33–5: '*Mammon* Madam, with your pardon, / I kiss your

vesture. *Dol* Sir, I were uncivil / If I would suffer that; my lip to you, sir'; and 54–6: 'There is a strange nobility in your eye, / This lip, that chin! Methinks you do resemble / One o' the Austriac princes.'

33 *The Way of the World*, I.i.425–7. Cf. *Henry V*, II.i.20–23.

34 *Love for Love*, II.i.174–84. Cf. *Merry Wives*, II.iii.25–6 (to Dr Caius): 'What says my Aesculapius? my Galen?'

35 Brian Gibbons (ed.), *The Way of the World*, xxvii, xxviii.

36 *The Way of the World*, IV.i.409–10; *1 H 4*, II.iv.145. Congreve has emphasized the word (itself of Shakespearean origin for him, one supposes, since it is the name of a follower of Don John's in *Ado*, who plays on it with his phrase 'like a true drunkard,' III.iii.98) by having it repeated by Lady Wishfort and Sir Wilfull on its first appearance some twenty lines earlier (IV.i.589–91).

37 *The Mourning Bride*, II.i.76–8. Cf. *R.&J.*, IV.i.84–5: 'Or bid me go into a new-made grave, / And hide me with a dead man in his shroud'; IV.iii.42–3: 'Where bloody Tybalt, yet but green in earth, / Lies fest'ring in his shroud.'

38 *The Mourning Bride*, II.ii.11–14, 20–2. Cf. *R.&J.*, V.iii.47: 'Thus I enforce thy rotten jaws to open.' V.iii.102–3: 'Shall I believe / That unsubstantial Death is amorous . . .?'

39 *The Mourning Bride*, II.ii.35–6, 42. Cf. *Hamlet*, I.iv.39 ('Angels and ministers of grace defend us!'); I.v.92 ('O all you host of heaven!'); I.i.42 ('Thou art a scholar; speak to it, Horatio.')

40 So in *Works* (1710, 1719); the Quartos of 1697 and 1703 have 'It is *Almeria!* 'tis my Wife!' In converting the line (like many others) to regular blank verse, Congreve echoes Romeo's 'It is my lady; O, it is my love!' (*R.&J.*, II.ii.10).

41 *The Mourning Bride*, III.i.175. Cf. *R.&J.*, V.iii.111.

42 *The Mourning Bride*, III.i.189. Cf. *Hamlet*, I.v.29.

43 *The Mourning Bride*, III.i.193. Cf. *Oth.*, V.ii.77: 'O, my fear interprets! What, is he dead?'

44 *The Mourning Bride*, III.i.350, 352–3. Cf. *R.&J.*, III.iii.68–70: 'Then mightst thou speak, then mightst thou tear thy hair, / And fall upon the ground, as I do now, / Taking the measure of an unmade grave.'

45 *The Mourning Bride*, III.i.402. Cf. *Oth.*, III.iii.91–2: 'Excellent wretch! Perdition catch my soul / But I do love thee.'

46 *The Mourning Bride*, V.ii.202–3. Cf. *R.&J.*, V.iii.119–20:

'Here's to my love! O true apothecary! / Thy drugs are quick.
Thus with a kiss I die.'

47 *The Mourning Bride*, v.ii.255–6. Cf. *R.&J.*, v.iii.163–4: 'O
churl! drunk all, and left no friendly drop / To help me after?'

48 *The Mourning Bride*, IV.i.202–3. Cf. *Hamlet*, III.ii.225: 'The
lady doth protest too much, methinks.'

49 *The Mourning Bride*, v.ii.68. Cf. *Hamlet*, III.iv.31: 'Thou
wretched, rash, intruding fool, farewell!' The assonance of
'deluded' and 'intruding' is particularly interesting. Davis,
who notes the reminiscence (*Works*, 1967), comments 'Gonzales
[*sic*], with his fighting son and his clever plot, brings to mind
Polonius', though he would doubtless agree that their personalities are quite different.

50 *The Mourning Bride*, v.ii.17. Cf. *2 H 4*, v.ii.31: 'Shame and
confusion! All is on the rout.'

51 John C. Hodges (ed.), *William Congreve: Letters and Documents*,
(London, 1964), 28. Cf. *Caes.*, IV.iii.142–3: 'Of your philosophy you make no use, / If you give place to accidental
evils.' In a later letter to Keally (p. 51), the same allusion is
made, this time in prose (with reference to an attack of gout):
'I make use of my philosophy, and love you as ever.'

52 *Letters and Documents*, 32. Cf. *2 H 4*, I.ii.176–8: 'My lord, I
was born about three of the clock in the afternoon, with a
white head and something a round belly'; and, for 'a man of this
world', Falstaff's words to Pistol (v.iii.96): 'I pray thee now,
deliver them [the tidings] like a man of this world.' The
allusion to Othello's 'speak of me as I am; nothing extenuate'
(v.ii.345) was noted by Montague Summers in his edition of
Congreve's *Works* (London, 1923), 1,238.

53 *Letters and Documents*, 38. Cf. *Merry Wives*, III.v.14–15.
Incidentally, the editor's note on a letter from Congreve's friend
Charles Mein (p. 63) misinterprets Mein's use of 'pass'd some
careers' through not recognizing it as a Shakespearean allusion
to *Henry V*, II.i.122–3: 'The King is a good king, but it must
be as it may; he passes some humours and careers.'

54 *Hamlet*, v.i.166: 'and your water is a sore decayer of your
whoreson dead body.'

13

THE FUTURE OF
DRYDEN BIBLIOGRAPHY

W. J. Cameron

The appearance, over forty years ago, of Hugh Macdonald's *John Dryden*[1] was a landmark in the bibliography of late seventeenth-century English literature. It was both an epitome and an expansion of the published work of A. E. Case, T. J. Wise, P. J. Dobell and others, and of unpublished work, particularly of George Thorn-Drury. Is there a need, after four decades of scholarship and of bibliographical work on Dryden and his contemporaries, for a new bibliography? If so, what form should this author bibliography take? Before we address these particular questions, perhaps it would be wise to look at developments in the tradition of author bibliographies in general.

THE 'BUSINESS OF BIBLIOGRAPHY'

An anonymous reviewer in *The Times Literary Supplement* (1966) asserted that the bibliographical usefulness of author bibliographies was 'beginning to be challenged' and opined that their days 'may be numbered'.[2] The occasion for this Olympian pronouncement was the reviewer's notice of William B. Todd's Burke bibliography which had recently appeared in the series known as the Soho Bibliographies.[3] The reviewer disapproved of author bibliographies in which the so-called 'degressive principle' was used, because they provide only one of the parallel threads of the warp, and (seemingly) only portions of some of the cross threads in the web of historical studies in bibliography. When John Carter, a member of the editorial board of the Soho Bibliographies, challenged the 'dark prediction' of the reviewer, and accused him of negating the degressive principle, the reviewer retorted with a doctrinaire statement: 'The business of bibliography is to relate the finished article to the means of production', and asserted that an author bibliography can only consider a book in isolation from all others being produced by the printer at approximately the same time. He then intemperately suggested that the invoking of the degressive principle 'looks very like the rationalization of laziness or ignorance and at best it is a defence of prejudgment.'[4] Carter had quoted Falconer Madan's own description of the principle, identified and named by him in 1909, as 'varying a description according to the difference of the period treated or of the importance of the work to be described' and had approvingly quoted another (unnamed) commentator who described it as 'Newtonian in its simplicity, Einsteinian in its weight'. Exaggeration on both sides of the controversy thus obscured the reasonableness of the reviewer's original demand for a 'rationale of degression'. Todd very wittily demonstrated that, if the reviewer's demands were to be met, his simple author bibliography might be limited to 192 volumes and the necessary analytical work would be reported in 779,401 pages – that is, in a publication over twice the size of the entire British Museum catalogue. The validity of the degressive principle can be conceded on this utilitarian basis, but more soberly we can agree with Todd's observation: 'A certain discrimination must ever prevail over all matters, including those subject to bibliographical treatment, else we lose all sense of value or significance.'[5] The sprightly controversy still leaves us with some doubt about the rationale of, or practices covered by, the 'degressive principle' so vaguely described by Madan, but so clearly applied in Todd's bibliography of Burke. The *textual* value of the first in a sequence of editions justifies 'full headings, transcriptions, and notes'; authorized reprints 'an abbreviated reference'; and other reprints and translations 'a short-title entry'. The first of these three divisions contains operational definitions; such definitions for the other two can be inferred from observation of Todd's practice. The same is true for a large number of equally useful author bibliographies, but no one has attempted to synthesize the principles of abbreviation that the degressive principle implies.

In 1949, Fredson Bowers very successfully synthesized the principles of bibliographical *description* as practiced by 'the main stream of tradition',[6] and firmly asserted that descriptive bibliography was possible only by applying the results of *analytical* or *critical* bibliography. To isolate his particular area of concern, he 'divorced from descriptive bibliography any consideration of cataloguing',[7] and excluded other kinds of bibliographical work thus: 'I have not concerned myself with the form of checklists, finding lists, or catalogues of special fields or subjects. These most useful aids to scholarship also differ in their aims from the analytical purposes of full-scale descriptive bibliography.'[8]

When dealing with modern books, Bowers admits that 'the closer we come to contemporary authors, the more nearly does the production of a definitive bibliography become impossible in some respects'.[9] However, he still believes that, eventually, his 'definitive', 'full-scale' descriptive bibliography will be desirable and even possible as time goes by. No one would question the desirability of competent analytical or critical bibliography where circumstances warrant it, but common sense should question the desirability of recording the results *always* in the form of a 'definitive' or 'full-scale' descriptive bibliography. Bowers himself advocates the application of a form of the degressive principle:

> Although most bibliographies must limit the full form of description as set up in this book, there seemed every reason to attempt to consider in detail a complete description of large scope such as would be found in an ideal intensive bibliography. According to the material treated, and the purpose and means of a bibliography, omission or condensation of details can thereupon be made as seems necessary or advisable.[10]

By emphasizing the desirability of the 'ideal intensive bibliography', and by divorcing 'enumerative' from 'analytical and critical' bibliography, Bowers has in the last sentence reduced the degressive *principle* to mere expediency. It is, of course, unfair to expect Bowers to have synthesized the principles of degressive practice as well as those of his ideal bibliographical description. However, because no one has attempted on the same scale to establish the principles of other kinds of bibliography, even those of library cataloguing, the subtle interrelationships among varieties of 'enumerative' bibliography and the degree to which the results of analytical and critical bibliography ought to be incorporated into them has been almost completely neglected.[11]

David Foxon illustrates very well the kind of dilemma posed by Bowers's highly successful divorce of 'bibliographical description' from other forms of bibliographical recording. In a very interesting pamphlet he delivers a plea for 'a form of bibliography which lies between the descriptive and enumerative as they are at present conceived'.[12] He aims some well-deserved critical blows at the ill-considered acceptance of some descriptive conventions that have resulted from the idiosyncracies of individual scholars rather than from a rational analysis of general need.[13] More cautiously, but more significantly, he expresses doubts about the general utility of the Greg-Bowers tradition of descriptive detail. He also expresses anxiety about 'the lowest common denominator of cataloguing'[14] which computer technology might foster. Presumably he feared inadequate description and arbitrary arrangement of catalogue entries. Perhaps his most relevant observation for our present purpose is that textual criticism 'will inevitably lead to a more complete bibliographical analysis than the normal methods of bibliographical description can record, and it will almost certainly be better expounded in continuous prose (with the help of tables or diagrams) than in notes to a description'.[15]

Foxon's own descriptive practices in his bibliography of separately published poems of the first half of the eighteenth century[16] exemplify what he rather facetiously called 'a short-title catalog with frills'.[17] He thus attempted to establish a standard for bibliographical description considerably less detailed than that of Greg and Bowers, but well above that 'lowest common denominator': a standard that would serve the purpose of the 'form' or 'genre' bibliography with which he was primarily concerned. The influence of British Library cataloguing practice, and of short-title cataloguing practice[18] can be detected in his bibliography, but practices suitable for embodying the results of analytical and critical bibliography are also incorporated. As no attempt at a 'full' or 'complete' description is intended, the degressive principle is almost unnecessary, although Foxon does follow it in the abbreviated listings for some collected editions.

Foxon's approach to creating a bibliography lying between the descriptive and the enumerative could be put into better perspective if we broke completely with Bowers's approach (with its concomitant degressive principle) and attempted to synthesize principles of bibliographical *identification* (the implied aim of 'enumerative' bibliography) and substituted a concomitant 'ingressive principle'.

Bowers was excused above for not having synthesized the principles of degressive practice. It would be just as unfair at this point to expect a synthesis of the principles of ingressive practice. A parody of Bowers's description of the first practice should be sufficient to explain the second: 'According to the material treated, and the purpose and means of a bibliography, addition or augmentation of details can thereupon be made as seems necessary or advisable.' The 'ingressive principle' is thus the obverse of the 'degressive principle'. Both will need to be more clearly defined or described when applications of the two principles have been gathered, analysed, and synthesized.

Macdonald's bibliography of Dryden and Drydeniana can be taken to be an example of the application of the first, but a new bibliography of Dryden and Drydeniana would have to be created in order to provide an example of the application of the second. This would consist of entries containing the minimum amount of bibliographical data necessary and sufficient to *identify* (not *describe*) each book, complemented in each entry by appropriate descriptive details derived from bibliographical analysis deemed necessary or advisable for the particular book.

The bibliography would be created on the assumption that it is indeed feasible to establish a standard bibliographical entry for an enumerative bibliography that would provide the necessary and sufficient descriptive detail suitable for most books, for most times and for most purposes, and then augment that information for particular books, for particular times and particular purposes.

James M. Osborn's important review of Macdonald's bibliography judiciously pointed out some of its author's idiosyncrasies, failings and limitations,[19] but Osborn paid the bibliography the compliment of using it as a basis for providing a list of holdings of Dryden's publications in ten major US libraries.[20] Osborn's major criticism of Macdonald as a bibliographer was that he did not cite the location of the books he described. Most of his other criticisms were summed up in the statement that 'there are very few books listed in the bibliography (unique items excepted) on which further investigation is not required.'[21] The criticism implies that Macdonald had not provided the kind of 'full description' that Bowers was to advocate so strongly a decade later.[22] Also implicit is mild disapproval of Macdonald's use of the degressive principle. Osborn seems to have been chiding Macdonald for underrating the importance of some of the books he described, and to be suggesting a more thorough treatment of both important and not-so-important books. Despite his severity about Macdonald's descriptive practices, Osborn was fully appreciative of the bibliography as an aid to the biographer and literary historian. He probably underestimated the value of Macdonald as an aid to the textual editor and annotator. If we were to judge Macdonald's bibliographical expertise by applying our proposed standard of bibliographical *identification* plus the ingressive principle, Macdonald would deserve a much higher commendation. As Bowers has himself done some fine bibliographical analysis of early editions of Dryden's plays,[23] we might test this opinion by summarizing what both Osborn *and* Bowers were able to add to Macdonald in identifying separate editions and issues of these plays.

Macdonald provided entries for 130 editions or issues of the twenty-eight plays; Osborn suggested the addition of six, plus a possible nine others.[24] Bowers adds two editions,[25] demotes two Macdonald entries from 'edition' to 'issue',[26] raises a Macdonald footnote to the status of an issue,[27] rejects Osborn's attempt to establish two issues of 73a, and provides a wide range of examples of the bibliographical significance of press-variants which do not warrant the distinguishing of 'issues'.

Three of Osborn's suggested additions are based on cancel leaves undetected by Macdonald (71b, 74a, 76e); and six on variant states of formes within the book ('69j', 70b X and Y, '73ai' and '73aii', 78a, 80a, and 91aii). All these would have been found in Macdonald's notes, not in separate descriptions, if he had detected the differences. Four are based on variant imprints which would have been distinguished in a short-title catalogue similar to Wing's ('68iii', 80g, 86e, 87d). The only real evidence of the value of full title-page transcription would be the 'trial printing' (i.e. a variant state of a title-page) of 86a and the correction of a Latin quotation (a variant state of the title-page?) in 88a. Neither is significant for the textual editor. Both are perhaps interesting to the historian of printing.

Bowers very properly distinguishes among a plethora of states of various formes, including those from which title-pages were printed, and the bibliographical features that would warrant a separate entry in a bibliographical catalogue (i.e. editions and issues). Neither of his additions to the list of editions can be distinguished by title page transcription or collation. Title-page dates have led to a confusion between editions and issues in all other cases.

Neither Osborn nor Bowers demonstrates major shortcomings in Macdonald which can be attributed to his admittedly erratic use of 'full' description and of the degressive principle. Their additional information could be accommodated by adding six abbreviated entries on the degressive principle and by supplying additional notes to existing entries, most of which could be abbreviated without losing accuracy of identification. Where Macdonald is most deficient is in omitting pagination information from truncated descriptions of later editions overly reduced according to the degressive principle.

Despite Osborn's views about the deficiencies of Macdonald's bibliographical descriptions, the identification of most early editions was adequate for the editors of the California edition of Dryden.[28] A search of the textual notes reveals little correction of Macdonald. More detailed identification of cancels, states of particular formes, etc. seldom have significant bearing on the Dryden texts. Some correction in the order of issue of items distinguished by Macdonald is to be found,[29] and other minutiae would need correction in a new edition of Macdonald. But Macdonald has served the editors well – too well in some cases, as his conclusions on textual matters have frequently been adopted without question and his speculations incorporated into the annotations.

The slow but sure progress of the California edition makes it certain that a Dryden bibliography with the major purpose of assisting editors of the text of his writings will not be needed for some time to come. However, when the edition is complete, there will surely be sufficient new information in the very extensive commentary to justify the writing of a much-needed new biography; hence an author bibliography to assist the biographer may well be called for. This, after all, was the major motivation for Macdonald's bibliography:[30]

> I do not believe that we know or can know enough about Dryden to justify another serious biography; but should this be attempted, contemporary pamphlets, however absurd the statements they contain, must at least be consulted, for little information about him is to be got from more reliable sources.

Without having Macdonald's book available to him, Osborn reflected contemporary caution about the possibility of a new biography by attempting to do 'a little preliminary digging' for the next biographer.[31]

Charles E. Ward nevertheless made an attempt to write the first 'serious' biography of the twentieth century; his work appeared in 1961.[32] It did not advance our knowledge of Dryden the man as much as one would like. Although Ward mentions Macdonald only once in his text (to reject a suggestion made in Macdonald's bibliography) there can be no doubt that the biography is heavily indebted to the bio-bibliographical material available in Macdonald. Would a future biographer find a new bibliography of greater use?

AN EXPLORATORY APPROACH TO A BIBLIOGRAPHY OF DRYDEN AND DRYDENIANA

With a clearer formulation of the particular purpose that an author bibliography serves than has been enunciated in the past, and the new approach to bibliographical description suggested above, we might find it worth considering whether it would be justifiable to produce four separate bibliographies:

1 A bibliography of Dryden's writings during his lifetime
2 A bibliography of Dryden's writings during the eighteenth century
3 A bibliography of Drydeniana during his lifetime
4 A bibliography of Drydeniana during the eighteenth century

A new bibliography of Dryden in two parts and a new bibliography of Drydeniana in two parts could in fact be produced with a minimum of expense by means of the *WHSTC* (i.e. *Western Hemisphere Short-Title Catalog*) system now being developed at the University of Western Ontario.[33] This system:

> produces bibliographies, annotated or unannotated, in a variety of arrangements and in a variety of developmental stages. At their most primitive, these bibliographies may be used as check-lists or finding lists. At their most sophisticated, they may supplement or complement, index, rearrange, aggregate, simplify, sophisticate, or even supersede existing bibliographies.[34]

The procedure for building a primitive bibliography is to create a machine-readable list of 'WHUC (i.e. *Western Hemisphere Union Catalog*) addresses'[35] which in effect serves as an index to the *National Union Catalog: Pre-1956 Imprints*.[36] The addresses in the list may be arranged in any desired order. Macdonald divides Dryden's writings by form (poems, miscellanies, collected editions, etc.), but a chronological listing might be of greatest use to a biographer. Macdonald's arrangement is more appropriate for a textual editor. If the machine-readable list (called a 'query file') were annotated at this preliminary stage with references to Macdonald, it would serve as an index to both *NUC* and Macdonald.[37] When the query file is run against the control and main files of the *WHSTC* system, the catalogue records stored in the main files that correspond with the *WHUC* addresses will be printed out between the *WHUC* address and the Macdonald address. We then have a primitive bibliography which relates three kinds of record for the same book – a library catalogue card (*NUC*), a short-title catalogue entry (*WHSTC*) and an entry in an author bibliography (Macdonald). This makes it possible for the bibliographer to decide what the optimal standards for bibliographical description of particular books might be, what would be the best order for individual entries, and what should be included as the most useful kind of annotation. Eventually, the addition of information to the query file could be sophisticated to the point where the bibliography might supersede Macdonald.

To test the potential usefulness of this procedure, a list of 'WHUC addresses' was constructed from *NUC* and sorted by machine into rough chronological order to form an 'annalistic' (rather than a strictly chronological) listing. The draft checklist ran to 281 seventeenth-century items and 379 eighteenth-century items. When references to Macdonald's bibliography were supplied, the seventeenth-century list was expanded to about 300 items and the eighteenth-century list to almost 400. Some clarification of what constituted a 'bibliographically distinct volume' was also made.[38] Running the query file against the *WHSTC* main files produced a bibliography including about one-quarter of the seventeenth-century short-title catalogue entries and about one-fifth of the eighteenth-century entries. These proved to be the Dryden items in the three largest collections in Canada: McMaster University, the University of Western Ontario and the University of Toronto. Most of the items belong in the 1690s, 1730s and 1770s. They may not add up to a comprehensive collection, but they seemed to be sufficient to explore possible future directions for the bibliographer of Dryden.

MINIMUM STANDARDS FOR BIBLIOGRAPHICAL DESCRIPTION

A good deal of thought and practical testing has been put into determining the minimum amount of data that should be transcribed or derived from title-pages to form a 'short-title catalogue' entry for the *WHSTC* and the minimum amount of data that should be derived from the rest of a book in order to provide a concise *identification* of an edition of a work.[39] A necessary and sufficient description of a book, it was assumed, can only be determined after detailed analytical work has been done on several copies of it. The belief that a detailed description of a particular copy can be used as a kind of substitute for the original when comparison between copies is undertaken was frequently found wanting when such analysis *was* undertaken. Ironically, then, minimal identification was found more often than not sufficient to begin the analytical process. The results of analysis could be very succinctly added as a bibliographical annotation to the short-title record.

On the understanding that a biographer using an author bibliography to assist him or her will want an accurate identification of all printed forms in which the author's work was presented to its contemporary readership, we must be careful to add, on the ingressive principle, to the minimum amount of data in the entry any results of simple observation of each book, or of detailed analytical treatment of multiple copies of it. We need to determine the 'frills' that should be added to the 'lowest common denominator' for an entry in an enumerative bibliography. These 'frills' may be references to more detailed discursive reports or to details in other bibliographical descriptions more closely resembling Bowers's ideal, and may differ from one bibliography to another.

In addition to these 'frills', our author bibliography will require collateral bibliographical data from sources other than the book itself (e.g. date of publication) and notes upon the the biographical, rather than subject, implications of the contents of the book.

THE INGRESSIVE PRINCIPLE AS APPLIED TO
BIBLIOGRAPHICAL NOTES

To illustrate the annotation of a short-title catalogue entry in our primitive bibliography, and to contrast the less efficient ways in which Macdonald and other bibliographers or library cataloguers have handled the presentation of the results of analytical and critical bibliography, let us select contrasting examples. First we might choose an item with little or no variation in the title-page and many internal ones. *The Hind and the Panther* should be appropriate.

Macdonald has a single entry (24a) for the first edition of *The Hind and the Panther* with seven sub-entries labelled i-vii. The *WHSTC* entry without the 'Points' and 'Notes' data reads:

[DRYDEN, John]
The hind and the panther
London,
For Jacob Tonson,
1687
4to 145p

This book is exhibited in seventeen entries of *NUC* (D0387006 – D0387028) and Macdonald has greatly influenced the cataloguers who supplied these entries. By means of distinctions supplied by Macdonald, the University of Texas reports an imperfect, unidentified issue (D0387025); and a 'faked copy of the first issue, with the lower third of the last leaf forged' (D0387028). The William Andrews Clark library reports a 'made-up' copy (D0387027) which seems to contain sheets A–Q of the first 'edition' and sheets R–T of the second, with leaf A1 of the second edition and leaves A2–4 of the first.

The 'first issue' of the 'first edition' (Macdonald 24ai) is represented by two entries (D0387006 and 7). The first cites one of two distinctive states of $T1^r$, one of six distinctive states of $U1^r$, and one of three distinctive states of $U1^v$ (if we may freely translate the information given in Macdonald). The second, because it does not use Macdonald's distinctions properly, cannot be so exactly identified. One wonders, however, whether the eight libraries mentioned in the first entry have *exactly* identical copies, and whether the seven mentioned in the second entry might not have copies that should be entered under the first. As Macdonald (p. 323) had assumed that a particular reading on T1^r was the earlier setting of the text, we might expect, by implication, to find on p. 137 of the copies in the second entry, the (corrected?) words:

> Or forc'd by Fear, or by Ambition led,
> Or both conjoyn'd, his Native clime he fled:

Comparison of the seventeen transcriptions of title-page information reveals a surprising number of differences in the library practice of the four who provided the cards for reproduction. The Library of Congress printed cards (D0387007, 10, 17, 25, 28) include the Latin quotation (*pace* Osborn!), the University of Virginia (12) is content with '[Two lines in Latin]', but Harvard (6, 13, 14, 24) and William Andrews Clark (9, 16, 19, 21, 23, 27) just use three periods to indicate its omission. L.C., Harvard and Virginia transcribe Tonson's address (albeit with conventionalized punctuation), but the Clark Library provides the usual three periods to indicate its omission.

As none of these practices makes any difference to the identification of the book, and as the extra information, like Macdonald's title-page transcription, tells the reader of an author bibliography nothing of significance that is not in the *WHSTC* entry (except that the text is a poem in three parts), the *WHSTC* entry could be concisely augmented by annotation to provide the equivalent amount of information: poem divided into three 'books'.

Indeed, by following the ingressive principle, we could add to the short-title catalogue entry for the first edition of *The Hind and the Panther* the following concise bibliographical information in the 'Points' data element of the entry:

Macdonald 24a distinguishes two states of T1^r and 7 states (i–vii) of leaf U1 plus a variant of ii (p. 323). Dearing (California edn., III, 540) believes 24avi is a 'ghost'.

An annotation based on this 'points' information can be supplied in our primitive Dryden bibliography, thus:

T1^r exists in 2 states: A, 'Profit' in line 11; B, 'Ambition' in line 11. U1^r exists in 7 states: A, No Errata; the word FINIS below a rule (i); B, 3-line errata slip pasted in at the foot of the page (ii); C, 3-line printed Errata (iii); D, No Errata, [no word FINIS?] (iv); E, 4-line Errata pasted in at the foot; F, 4-line Errata pasted over the 3-line Errata (v, vi); G, 4-line printed Errata. U1^v exists in 3 states: A, blank (i, ii, vi, [viii]); B, 14-line Tonson booklist (iii, v); C, 3-line Errata and Tonson booklist (iv).[40]

Troilus and Cressida is an appropriately contrasting example of an item with many title-page variants, and few internal ones. Macdonald provides two entries (84ai and 84aii) for the first edition, as does *WHSTC*:

DRYDEN, John
Troilus and Cressida
London,
For Jacob Tonson, and Abel Swall,
1679
4to 69p

DRYDEN, John
Troilus and Cressida
London,
For Abel Swall, and Jacob Tonson,
1679
4to 69p

NUC provides seven entries (D0387790 – D0387796), two of which are for microfilms at the University of Virginia. The L.C. card (92) has the fullest transcription of title-page wording but supplies '[Two lines in Latin]' instead of the quotation. The Clark Library (90) transcribes almost as much of the wording as L.C. but uses three periods to indicate omissions. Yale (93) truncates the title to three words but transcribes the wording of the imprint in greatest detail. Princeton (96) gives no indication that there *is* a Latin quotation, and their truncated imprint is more precisely identified by reference to 'imprint T2a' of Bowers.

Two *WHSTC* entries are provided for the second edition.

DRYDEN, John
Troilus and Cressida
London,
For Jacob Tonson.
1679
4to 69p

DRYDEN, John
Troilus and Cressida
London,
By I. Dawks, for Jacob Tonson.
1695
4to 69p

NUC provides three entries (D0387798, 99, 801) for the '1679' imprint of the second edition and two (802, 803) for the 1695 variant. Bowers infers that 'after a relatively few sheets of the title-forme had been printed [with the false date 1679] the alteration to the 1695 title was accomplished'.[41] Macdonald inconsistently gives the numbers 84ai and 84aii to the variant imprints of the first edition, but 84b and 84c to the variant imprints of the second, thus implying that the 1695 variant state is a third edition.

The title-page of the first edition down to the imprint is in fact exactly the same setting of type for all variants of the title-page, and Yale's short title is sufficient to indicate this. The Clark Library provides information not found in either Macdonald or any of the other five *NUC* entries: 'Caption title: Truth found too late.' This is probably of as much value for identifying the edition and indicating its impact on the contemporary audience as would be a transcription of the sub-title data from the title-page. However, some real complications are to be found in the imprint. Bowers reproduces six variants,[42] three of which are subsumed in *NUC* D0387790, 91 and 92, and three in 93 and 94. One is identified in 96. Macdonald subsumes the first three under 84ai and the second three under 84aii. It would seem practical and reasonable to distinguish two entries in a future bibliography provided that the relationship between the two were made explicit.[43] Here is the suggested 'points' information for the *WHSTC* entries:

Macdonald 84ai. Subsumes three variant imprints (Bowers, *Harvard Library Bulletin*, 3, 1949, 281)

Macdonald 84aii. Subsumes three variant imprints (Bowers, *Harvard Library Bulletin*, 3, 1949, 281)

For the second edition, two entries seem reasonable, without comment in the 'points' field. However, in our primitive bibliography, the 1679 item could be transferred to the 1695 annal, and a relational annotation for each added thus:

Macdonald 84b.   An uncorrected state of the 1695 title page.
Macdonald 84c.   Same edition as previous item.

ARRANGEMENT OF THE BIBLIOGRAPHICALLY AUGMENTED ENTRIES

Bibliographical information added to some of the entries will thus necessitate re-sorting of items into chronological order within the 'annal'. In order to sort *all* items into a chronological sequence, the first non-bibliographical information to be added to each entry should be evidence of publication date. A little thought will establish that, although a biographer will be mainly concerned with dating the stages in the gestation of a particular work by his author, the author-bibliographer will be primarily concerned with dating various stages in the publication of the book containing the work. Our primitive bibliography should therefore be annotated with the circumstantial evidence for dating the appearance of each entry before the public. The evidence will almost always be circumstantial rather than positively unequivocal, and the final settling of the order of publication of particular entries may eventually be the result of limited speculation – the choice of the most likely of a series of hypotheses.

The first annotations to be added to the query file after information about editions and issues could thus be dating information about the books derived from Macdonald. Imprimatur or licensing data for items published between 1662 and 1679, or 1685 and 1695 are an example. *Term Catalogue* dates are another, although Macdonald's application of the degressive principle usually ignores such information for editions later than the first. Stationers' Register entries are relevant to the history of publication and should also be added. Advertisements from newspapers and journals, and the dates of Luttrell's acquisition of a copy of each work are other such snippets. Where Macdonald is deficient, Osborn's additions and those of others can also be incorporated before further original research by the future bibliographer must begin. For dating purposes, too, the existence of a bookseller's book-list in a particular book is often very informative,[44] so such information should also be supplied.

Indeed, so indeterminate have investigations of Dryden's relationship with booksellers been,[45] that we might take one such relationship as an example for demonstrating both the importance and difficulty of providing such obligatory data, and for demonstrating how circumstantial evidence may be used.

Although Macdonald suggests that his item 9c dated 1688 (containing *Annus Mirabilis*, *Astrea Redux*, *To His Sacred Majesty* and *To My Lord Chancellor*) was the first collected edition of Dryden's poems, it can be more reasonably argued that Tonson's first attempt to collect Dryden's fugitive pieces is to be found in *Miscellany Poems* (1684) and *Sylvae* (1685). The 1684 volume included a collected edition of Dryden's three major satires dated 1683.[46] The contents of *Annus Mirabilis* (1688) (Macdonald 9c) seem to imply a glorification of Charles II rather than an attempt to collect fugitive material, and the variant title-page (with 'And an Elegy on the Death of *King Charles* the Second' added) reinforces that impression. The second edition of *Threnodia Augustalis* (1685) was frequently bound up with the new publication.

The combination of the new volume with the March 1685 one can be dated late in February 1688,[47] but it could have been intended to coincide with the much publicized anniversary commemoration on 4 February 1688 for the late King Charles.[48]

Tonson in 1688 must have had stocks of *Religio Laici* (1683) (16c) and *The Hind and the Panther* (1687) (24e) on hand because he was still including them in the aggregate issue of Dryden's works after 1695. But some years later he seems to have made special reprints of *Mac Flecknoe*, *Absalom* and *The Medal* (14b),[49] *Britannia Rediviva* (1688) (27c) and *Heroick Stanzas* (1659) (3f) for issuing with his Charles II aggregation and the two sets of remainders to form a collected volume of poetry. When did he reprint them? He had already 'collected' the three items of 14b by including them in *Miscellany Poems* (1684). Comparison of 14b with the reprinted texts in the second edition of *Miscellany Poems* (1692) (42bi or ii and 43b) reveals that the type setting used for that reprint is identical with that in 14b. To enable him to use the type for both an 8vo and 4to impression, Tonson merely leaded out the false title-pages and made minor adjustments to the type for the text. The other two reprints possibly belong in the same period.

The actual date of publication of the second edition of *Miscellany Poems* has not yet been determined. Post-dating practices suggest that it could have been as early as Michaelmas 1691 and as late as

Michaelmas 1692. However, Jacob Tonson's decision to issue a quarto impression of the three Dryden poems and to reprint the other two items must have been at about the time that he joined the syndicate of vendors of Henry Herringman's publications, some time in or shortly before 1692.[50] Obviously, the future bibliographer will need to investigate very thoroughly the relationship between Herringman and his vendors. Our primitive bibliography tells us that Richard Bentley advertised the 1691 editions of *Secret Love, Amboyna, Evening's Love* and *Marriage A-la-mode* in the November issue of the *Term Catalogues*, and that his book list appears in both *Secret Love* (not noted by Macdonald) and *Amboyna*. Did Tonson and Bentley join the syndicate at the same time? If so, it is very pertinent that a title-leaf for Otway's *Works* (1691) appears as the last leaf of *Secret Love* (1691) and *Oedipus* (1692), just as Tonson's title-leaf for Dryden's *Works* (1691) appears on the last leaf of *Britannia Rediviva* (1688). The circumstantial evidence seems to point to the conclusion that all these reprints probably came out late in Michaelmas term 1691.

This circumstantial evidence, and the dating information derived from our major sources, permit a speculative reordering of the 1691 annal. This portion of the query file would look as follows (for the purposes of the illustration, no explanation of the machine-readable symbols is necessary).

M0605057 691:   /
$Wing M2149
$
D0386643 691:   /
$Macd 90aii
$
D0386515 691:   /
$Macd 88c   Earlier edns 1685
$
L0199189*   :   /
$Macd 117c   Earlier edns 1681, 1685
$
L0199190*   :   /
$Earlier edns or issues 1681, 1685, 1691
$

Lo199190 691:   /
$Wing L873 Earlier edns or issues 1681, 1685, 1691
$

Ho132700 691:   /
$Macd 124 TC Feb
$

Ho403380 691:   /
$Macd 57   SR Oct   TC Feb
$

Wo053972 691:   /
$Macd 136   Osborn: London Gazette April 20
$

Do387634 691:   /
$Macd 71d   TC June   Earlier edns 1668, 1678
$

Do387113 691:   /
$Macd 91ai & ii   Subsumes 2 issues: i, without prologue &
epilogue; ii, with them   London Gazette June 4–8
$

Do387171 691:   /
$Macd 77c   Osborn: TC Nov   Earlier edns 1673, 1684
$

Do387593 691:
$Macd 70d H3^v: Bentley play-list   H4: Title–page Otway's
$Works 1691   Osborn: TC Nov   Earlier edns 1688, 1669, 1679
$

Do386638 691:   /
$Macd 79b   G4^r: Bentley play-list   Osborn: TC Nov   Earlier
$edn 1673
$

Do386949 691:   /
$Macd 75d   Osborn: TC Nov   Earlier edns 1671, 1675
$

Do386412★ 50:   /
$Macd 106a   Published Dec 1691?
$

Do386750 688:   /
$Macd 27c C4^r: Title–page Dryden's Works 1691   Published
$Dec 1691? Earlier edns 1688
$

Do387203 692:   /
$Macd 42bi & 43b   Published Dec 1691?   Earlier edns 1684,
$1685
$
Do387206 692:   /
$Macd 42bii & 43b   Published Dec 1691?   Earlier edns 1684,
$1685
$
Do387158 692:   /
$Macd 14b   Same setting of type as for Miscellany Poems 1692
$Published Dec 1691?   Earlier edn 1682
$

It will be noted that the first six entries still require dating information before being re-sorted into the rest of the sequence. One 1691 item has already been assigned to the 1690 annal, and another to the 1692 one. No attempt has yet been made to add biographical annotation or annotation about the contents of the books. When this part of the query file is printed out to include the short-title catalogue entry between each *WHUC* address and the note that follows it, we will have a draft bibliography which the bibliographer will indeed be able to annotate with the future biographer in mind, especially after a more precise and clearly defined ingressive principle has been synthesized.

A BIBLIOGRAPHY OF DRYDENIANA

Osborn's strictures on Macdonald's treatment of Drydeniana in what he was later to call his 'allusion book' were summed up in the sentence: 'Taken as a whole, the Drydeniana is the least successful section of the book.'[51] One of Osborn's repeated observations was that the selection of items tended to emphasize unfavourable allusions to Dryden. His major objection, however, was that Macdonald did not appear to have settled on a clear distinction between books and pamphlets that should be described in the text and other items that were to be mentioned in the footnotes. It would be worthwhile to list *all* these books and pamphlets in a chronological sequence, and give each entry a new sequential number. One could then give fair appraisal to how well Macdonald has packed into 140 pages items of Drydeniana up to 1747. Osborn in a footnote (p. 314) suggested six items from Macdonald's footnotes that should be given separate entries, and dozens more could be derived from other parts of the book.

A primitive bibliography of Drydeniana was constructed by matching each Macdonald entry against *NUC* and inserting the *WHUC* addresses thus formed into a machine-readable file in roughly chronological order, i.e. to form 'annals' of Drydeniana. Each entry in this query file was augmented with references to Macdonald. The commentary and footnotes of Macdonald were then searched for possible additions. Such additional items were matched against *NUC*, tagged with a page reference in Macdonald, and inserted into the appropriate annal.

Items 158–308 in Macdonald are seventeenth-century books and pamphlets (251 separate entries, including the erratically numbered extra editions of individual items).[52] The preliminary attempt to list those in the footnotes expanded the list by about a hundred items. Items 309–334 are eighteenth-century books and pamphlets (twenty-seven separate items, including extras).[53] *Poems on Affairs of State*, distinguished as seventeen entries (p. 317), were further elaborated into more than twice as many individual volumes, some containing Dryden poems, but most containing Drydeniana. The exercise revealed problems of scope that must be solved before a more elaborate bibliography of Drydeniana can be developed.

Under Macdonald's first item of Drydeniana (158) the author refers the reader to items in the 'Early Editions' section (158 is a reply to 69, and is reprinted in 68b–d). In a *separate* edition of Drydeniana it would obviously be necessary to duplicate such items. The question of how elaborate the bibliographical description should be immediately arises. The ingressive principle might require less detail if the Dryden allusion were not affected by bibliographical variants.

When we come to Macdonald's third item (160), we find that he alludes to three items in his Drydeniana listing, but packs other examples of Shadwell's allusions to Dryden into his commentary, and one into a footnote. He does not mention later editions of the main item. All the unnumbered items probably deserve separate entries in a new separate edition of Drydeniana. But the question of how many later editions of each should be included also arises. Under 161b, Macdonald mentions, describes, but does not number, a later work in which was reprinted the epigram that he is identifying as Drydeniana. In how many later publications did that epigram appear? When we come to *The Rehearsal* (165a–h), we can face more squarely the difficult task of deciding just how many reprints of a particular work ought to be included in a new edition of Drydeniana. *NUC* lists the seven editions before 1700 of *The Rehearsal* for which Macdonald provides entries. It lists twenty-one separate editions during the eighteenth century, of which Macdonald provides entries for the first and fourth. His reasons for the choice are not self-evident. It does not take much reflection before one asserts that the future bibliographer should include *all* such later editions. What was available to a contemporary reader is of considerable interest to the literary historian as well as to other non-textual scholars. From a chronologically ordered file, one can then infer the contemporaneity and longevity of comments on Dryden.

Macdonald's 182 brings up another aspect of the problem. Marvell's verses 'On Paradise Lost' with its allusion to Dryden first appeared in the second (1674) edition of *Paradise Lost*. Dryden's epigram first appeared in the fourth (1688) edition (Macdonald 26) and Macdonald notes: 'Marvell's verses 182 were omitted from this edition, perhaps in deference to Dryden'. Did other, later, editions contain Marvell's verses? Any that did should certainly be added to the future Drydeniana listing. It becomes obvious that our primitive listing based on Macdonald will have to be expanded considerably, just to accommodate reprints of many items.

As bibliographies of many of the authors mentioned in the Drydeniana section have appeared since Macdonald's pioneering effort, it should be possible to derive many new entries from them. Editions of Rochester's *Poems* (cf. Macdonald 196) make a good case in point. Thorpe has distinguished several editions which are so rare that they are not represented in *NUC*.[54] Another example is *Poems on Affairs of State* (pp. 316–322). Macdonald did some fine pioneering work on the 'Sessions of the Poets' genre (cf. 189), and on a major MS. (Harleian 7319) containing such poems (p. 215). Now, however, the existence of both printed and MS. versions of many satirical poems has been established as a result of the Yale edition of *POAS*.[55]

Even the matching of Macdonald references against *NUC* resulted in major advances in the Drydeniana listings. Location of copies for instance, made it possible to revise Macdonald's notes on the scarcity of various items. *NUC* also helped to identify items that were so cryptically described by Macdonald that it was previously almost impossible to follow up on them. 'Elegies of old age 1688 H. Walker' (p. 250, n. 2) is Sir Hovendon Walker's translation of Maximianus Etruscus (M0363958), and 'The Poet Buffoon'd' is *Abstersae lachrymae* (A0031013). In some cases, lacunae and misinformation in Macdonald were also eliminated. For instance, two copies of 193 are listed in *NUC*. Macdonald noted: 'No copy of this edition, if it was ever published, seems to be known.' As Noyes had already noted, the item was published, and it is not Mulgrave's *Essay* of similar title. It is now possible to reassess the item for relevance before including it in a new bibliography of Drydeniana.

The criteria for inclusion of other new items in an expanded bibliography of Drydeniana will need to be made very explicit. Macdonald was occasionally tempted to include source-books for Dryden's works (e.g. 190a and b) but quite frequently excluded them explicitly (e.g. *Absalom's Conspiracy*, p. 214). Imitations and sequels, too, tend to be seductive. Just how far can imitation of Dryden's style (especially if prefaced by allusions to his work) be taken as an 'allusion' to Dryden? The fine distinction between the man and his work is very hard to draw.[56] Burlesques of *Ovid's Epistles* (194a–b, 195a–d) managed to pass Macdonald's scrutiny. Parodies without direct allusion to Dryden are easier to reject, but touchstones such as Tutchin's *Tribe of Levi* (1691) can be identified for help in determining the criteria for inclusion or exclusion.

Contemporary allusions to Dryden will, of course, be of great value to Dryden's biographer, so the development of a more comprehensive, chronological listing of Drydeniana published before 1700 seems fully justified. The use of short-title catalogue entries with minimal bibliographical augmentation according to the ingressive principle needs less justification than for an author bibliography. The need for a bibliography of posthumous Drydeniana may be more difficult to justify, as its major use would be for discussing Dryden's posthumous reputation. It would be very much less relevant to a biographer than a posthumous author bibliography.

A POSTHUMOUS AUTHOR BIBLIOGRAPHY

Should there be any essential difference between an author bibliography confined to the author's lifetime and a posthumous one? Posthumous publication of items that had not already appeared in the author's lifetime will have the same or similar interest as those published during his lifetime, but entries for material of this kind will not be frequent. The author's *reputation* will be of great interest, and the recensions of his text by editors and booksellers will be another topic of special bibliographical interest.

In what form was Dryden's work transmitted at particular times during the eighteenth century? The broad panorama of collected editions of his works is easily discerned, but year-by-year details of separate editions of particular works or of inclusion of particular items in other people's works or in anthology-like publications is not so easily discovered, and a rational display of such information would serve a useful purpose. After his death Dryden's works were available in a large three-volume work (D0386966 and 7394). In 1716 appeared a six-volume duodecimo containing his poems and those of his contemporaries that were not available in contemporary collected editions (D0387222). In 1717 a six-volume duodecimo edition of his plays (D0386854) appeared, and was reprinted at various dates thereafter. No collected edition of his prose appeared before 1800, when Malone's edition of the prose works (D0-386801) began the movement to bring all three major forms of Dryden's work to the public. In 1800, the drama was represented by a 40-year-old collection (D0386870) and the poems by a new reprint of Johnson's *Works of the Poets of Great Britain* (J0130207).

But what was the situation, for example, in mid-century? For the year 1750, our primitive bibliography contains only an edition of Dryden's 'Parallel between Painting and Poetry', an edition of a revived *Secular Masque*, a Dublin edition of *All for Love* and of *King Arthur*, a Glasgow and a London edition of *The Indian Emperor*, and possibly an edition of *Absalom and Achitophel*. The most recent edition of his dramatic works was seemingly in 1735. The most recent edition of his poems was 1743. Expansion of the bibliography may correct or confirm the impression of neglect that these observations imply. To explore possibilities, let us once more pay attention to the plays.

What particular plays of Dryden endured in popularity? A glance through our primitive annalistic bibliography seems to give the impression that *All for Love*, *Amphitryon*, *Oedipus*, *The Spanish Fryar* and perhaps *Don Sebastian* were those by which Dryden was judged. But this simple count of separately published items may be misleading. What is needed is a reliable guide to the bibliography of the collected editions of the plays, editions appearing in general collections of plays, and the interrelationship with separate editions of individual plays.

Macdonald lists editions of the dramatic works in six volumes dated 1717 (109ai), 1718 (109aii), 1725 (109b), 1735 (109c) and 1762 (109d), and mentions (p. 153) a 'made-up set (B.M. G.18725–30) of 1735' which contains plays dated 1735, 1750, 1762, 1763, 1768. *NUC* lists editions of 1717–25 (D0386855), 1725 (60), 1735 (62), 1735–[63] (68), 1762–63 [70] which provide a little more evidence of a 50-year period of various combinations of parts of the six-volume sets. A future bibliography ought to provide information that would help to identify more accurately the publication patterns of this recension of the texts reputed to be edited by the man to whom Dryden wished his laurels to descend – William Congreve.

A copy of volume V in the University of Western Ontario library consists of a title-page dated 1735, *Troilus and Cressida* (1735), *Spanish Fryar* (1753), *Duke of Guise* (1735), and *Albion and Albanius* (1735). In the School of Library and Information Science of the same university is a collection of disbound items that may have been part of a copy or copies of Congreve's edition. Neither Macdonald nor *NUC* is of much help in identifying these broken sets. They all have volume numbers in the signature line of the first leaf in each of the 12mo gatherings, so it is surprising to find that *Amphitryon* (1735) (G1–K12) and *Marriage-a-la mode* (1735) (I1–M12) with 'Vol. VI' and 'Vol. III' respectively still retain evidence of having been bound within the same volume. Were individual parts of the Congreve editions of Dryden also issued as parts of other dramatic collections? If we are to believe *NUC* D0387687, *The Spanish Fryar* (1753) was a separate edition (sheets A–D^{12} in the University of Western Ontario copy). This could have been substituted in an issue of the 1750s (still dated 1735) for a 1735 edition (D0387685) of the play which was an integral part of the original issue of vol. V.

In Lee's *Works* (1734), volume II, at the end of the text of *Mithridates*, is advertised *The English Theatre* in four parts, Part 1 in eight volumes, Part 2 in six volumes, Part 3 in six volumes, and Part 4 in six volumes, 'Being the Select Plays of the most celebrated authors'. Dryden is represented by three plays in Part 1, four in Part 3, and (possibly) one in Part 4. This 104-play collection dated 1731 and 'Printed for W. Feales' is extremely rare[57] but may have been very common during the eighteenth century. It was followed by several later editions, with title pages dated 1762, 1765 and 1769, and was continued as *The New English Theatre* in competition with *Bell's British Theatre* from 1776 to the early years of the nineteenth century.

The kind of bibliographical description needed for recording these collections in our primitive bibliography is quite a problem – a problem dismissed in rather cavalier fashion by Bowers in the following words: 'The matter is more one of convenience than of bibliographical concern. The bibliographical history of the parts is the only point of primary importance.'[58] Bowers tries to cut through the problem, when discussing 're-issues', by leaning heavily upon the distinctions implicit in a change in title-page. However, scholars interested in publishing history will frequently find that the *collocation* of the parts is of equal or even greater importance than the parts themselves, and that the title-page used to cover the collected parts is irrelevant.

Because each of the 'parts' (whether separately issued or not) could so easily be bound up with other issues of similar 'parts' to form other kinds of aggregate issue,[59] some form of identification of the separable parts of Dryden's collected plays would be useful. If the Library of Congress entry for Dryden's *Dramatick Works* (1735) in *NUC* (D0386862) is examined, it will be seen that sixteen lines are devoted to describing the contents (Macdonald is silent on the subject). This information in truncated form, if augmented with information identifying the leaf[60] on which each false or true title-page is printed, would be very useful for identifying broken sets, and sets in which editions of 'parts' of later dates were substituted. (The later editions would be found in the appropriate annal.) The ingressive principle thus mandates a new kind of bibliographical note. For example, in the 1735 annal would appear:

Do386862 735
DRYDEN, John
The dramatick works
[6 vols] Vols I–VI
London:
For J. Tonson
1735
12mo 311, 465, 456, 466, 407, 525pp

False title-pages in Vol 1: WG A2; RL E2; IQ I2; IE L2
In Vol 2; SL A3; SirM E2; Temp I2; EL N2; TL S2; In
Vol 3: Almanzor & A A3; 2nd part E2; Ma-la-m I2; Assig
N2; Amb R2. In Vol 4: S of I A3; A-Z D2; A for L H2;
Limb N2; Oed R2. In Vol 5: T&C A3; SF F2; D of G K2;
Vind. N11; Albion & A Q2. In Vol 6: Don S A3; Amph
G2; Cleom L2; King A Q2; LT T2.

In the 1753 annal would appear:

Do387687 753
[see description in NUC]
Found in later issues of Dramatick Wks, 1735

In the 1731 annal would appear:

E0132423 731
[see description in NUC]
Part I: A for L & Oed in Vol 2, SF in Vol 7. Part III: IE and
A-Z in Vol 2, Don S in Vol 3, Amph in Vol 6. Part IV:
Temp in Vol 6.

The note would be completed after the Folger Library copy had
been examined.

Separately published editions of some of the plays dated 1735
were also published (e.g. *Amphitryon*, Do386657 735) as would
appear in the 1765 annal:

E0132425* 50
[description not yet on file]
IU
Vol I: Amph 1735; Vol 2: A for L from Dramatick Wks, 1735

For 'parts' or broken sets, the annotation to *Dramatick Works* (1735) makes it fairly simple to decide whether a particular part might have belonged to the original issue.[61]

In the 1769 annal (one of several entries for the 1769 *English Theatre*) would appear:

E0132429* 50
[   ]
The English Theatre
8 vols Vols I–VIII
London,
For T. Lowndes
1769
12mo
General title pages
ICN
Vol I: Amph 1771; vol 2: A for L 1768

Bibliographical analysis on a grand scale will be necessary before hidden reprints can be identified. Because of the degressive principle, and because aggregations like *The English Theatre* are rare, few eighteenth-century editions of Dryden's collected works have been analysed.[62]

When our primitive bibliography has been suitably expanded, the problem of dating individual entries and of rearranging the 'annals' into true chronological order will arise. Forward or backward cross-references will help to establish relationships between 'parts' and 'aggregate issues'. Annotations on the collections of plays or anthologies of poems will permit the biographer to draw conclusions about Dryden's reputation for a century after his death and will facilitate the literary historian's work.

In sum, the method of putting together a bibliography by creating the 'lowest common denominator' of identificatory cataloguing and augmenting it according to the ingressive principle from existing bibliographical work should permit the bibliographer to decide whether one or all four of the proposed bibliographies of Dryden and Drydeniana ought to be developed and how much they should be developed. If, when the California edition is approaching completion, there is a call for a 'serious' new biography, the particular kinds of annotation needed will become clear, original bibliographical and biographical research will be justified, and the results will be added to the machine-readable data already incorporated into the primitive form of the bibliographies. Books and pamphlets will be selected for full-scale bibliographical analysis on the basis of biographical need; they will not be given equal treatment because of a largely doctrinaire desire to relate *every* finished article to the means of production. The very useful degressive principle will be transmuted into an even more useful ingressive principle. Even though the bibliographies will contain entries in various stages of augmentation, new augmentations can be added easily to the machine-readable data base, thus allaying the fear that computers will foster only the lowest common denominator of cataloguing, and making it possible to choose where the results of sophisticated bibliographical analysis should be published, other than in an 'ideal intensive bibliography'. Such a 'definitive' bibliography, even for Dryden's writings before 1700, would be of such large extent that it would be impractical to publish and of dubious value as a replacement for the corresponding pages of Macdonald's (still useful and highly economical) biobibliographical reference book.

NOTES

1 Hugh Macdonald, *John Dryden A Bibliography of Early Editions and Drydeniana* (Oxford, 1939).

2 *The Times Literary Supplement* (1966), 604.

3 William B. Todd, *A Bibliography of Edmund Burke* (London, 1964).

4 *The Times Literary Supplement* (1966), 716.

5 ibid., 781.

6 Fredson Bowers, *Principles of Bibliographical Description* (Princeton, N.J., 1949), viii.

7 ibid., ix.

8 ibid.

9 ibid., 363.

10 ibid., ix–x.

11 An entertaining summary (somewhat unfair to Bowers) may be found in the 'Epilogue' of Paul Dunkin, *Bibliography: Tiger or Fat Cat?* (Hamden, Conn., 1975), 111–6.

12 D. F. Foxon, *Thoughts on the History and Future of Bibliographical Description* (Berkeley, Calif., 1970), 8.

13 The practice of referring to a leaf and to the recto of the leaf by

the same symbol or group of symbols is a case in point. The practice of quasi-facsimile transcription of title-page information is another.

14 Foxon, 23.

15 ibid., 25.

16 D. F. Foxon, *English Verse 1701–1750. A Catalogue of Separately Printed Poems with notes on Contemporary Collected Editions*, 2 vols (Cambridge, 1975).

17 Foxon, xi.

18 Specifically, Pollard and Redgrave, Wing, and Pantzer, i.e.:

    (a) A. W. Pollard and G. R. Redgrave, *A Short-title Catalogue of Books Printed in England, Scotland, and Ireland and of English Books Printed Abroad 1475–1640* (London, 1926).

    (b) Donald Wing, *Short-title Catalog of Books Printed in England, Scotland, Ireland, Wales, and British America and of English Books Printed in Other Countries 1641–1700* (New York, 1945–51).

    (c) A. W. Pollard and G. R. Redgrave, *A Short-title Catalogue . . . 1475–1640*, 2nd edn, edited by W. A. Jackson and F. S. Ferguson, completed by Katherine F. Pantzer (London, 1976), II, (I–Z).

19 James M. Osborn 'Bibliographical Article. Macdonald's Bibliography of Dryden', *Modern Philology*, 39 (1941–2), 313–9.

20 James M. Osborn 'Bibliographical Article. Macdonald's Bibliography of Dryden: An Annotated Check List of Selected American Libraries', *Modern Philology*, 39 (1941–2), 69–98, 197–212.

21 Osborn, 317.

22 Criteria for adequate description, derived from Osborn's criticism of the bibliographical aspect of Macdonald's work, can be deduced, thus:

    (a) photographic reproduction of title-pages should be substituted for quasi-facsimile transcription of title-page data

    (b) if quasi-facsimile must be adopted, certain kinds of information (e.g. Latin quotations on title-pages) should be supplied in addition to the usual information provided

    (c) pagination should be supplied as well as collation

    (d) rules on a half-title should be noted

    (e) a consistent numbering system for individual entries should
       be supplied
    (f) location of copies described must be cited.

23 Fredson Bowers 'Variants in Early Editions of Dryden's Plays',
    Harvard Library Bulletin, 3 (1949), 278–88.

24 Osborn distinguishes an issue of 68b which he calls 68biii; a
    third 1696 edition of 69i and k which he calls 69j; and another
    1669 edition of 70b which he (inconsistently) calls X and Y. He
    notes a possible cancel in 71b; and a variant state of sheets in
    73a which Griffith thought might warrant a separate entry
    (73ai and 73aii). He distinguishes another issue of 74a; notes
    cancels in 76e; supports Macdonald against Griffith in not
    distinguishing two issues of 78a; is equivocal as to whether a
    defective sheet H in 80a constitutes a separate issue; quotes
    Dobell on a variant imprint of 80g; calls a variant title-page of
    86a 'a trial printing'; notes a variant imprint of 86e and a 1717
    edition not mentioned by Macdonald; seems to favour dis-
    tinguishing two issues of 87d; notes two issues of 88a (Griffith
    suggesting 88ai and 88aii to label them); and distinguishes two
    issues of 91aii.

25 A 1670 edition of *The Indian Emperour* (cf 69c and d) and a 1669
    edition of *Secret Love* (cf. 70b).

26 75b and 84b.

27 Of 74e.

28 This began with *The Works of John Dryden. Poems 1649–1680*,
    vol. I (Berkeley and Los Angeles, 1956). At time of writing
    vols I–IV (Poems), vols VII–XI (Plays), and vols XVII–XIX
    (Prose) had been issued.

29 e.g. 3di and ii.

30 Macdonald, viii.

31 James M. Osborn, *John Dryden: Some Biographical Facts and
    Problems*, revised edn (Gainesville, Fla., 1965), viii.

32 Charles E. Ward, *The Life of John Dryden* (Chapel Hill, N.C.,
    1961).

33 A bibliography of Father Louis Hennepin has been used to
    explain how this computer-based system can be applied in the
    field of French Canadiana. See William J. Cameron, *The HPB
    Project Phase IV: The French Canadian contribution to the develop-
    ment of a western hemisphere short-title catalog (WHSTC) of*

Spanish, French and Portuguese language books printed before 1801 (London, Ont., 1980).

34 William J. Cameron 'Lodes of French-Canadian Gold in U.S. Libraries', *Canadian Journal of Information Science*, 5 (1980), 116.

35 The construction of such a list of addresses is explained in *The HPB Project Phase IV*, Appendix A, Manual A.

36 *The National Union Catalog: Pre-1956 Imprints*, 754 vols, in progress (London and Chicago, 1968–).

37 It would thus correct one of Macdonald's major deficiencies by referring the user to the list of library holdings in *NUC*.

38 The problem of what bibliographical unit should be included in a separate entry in a bibliography or catalogue has never been satisfactorily resolved. A partial solution for the HPB project was the concept of 'bibliographically distinct volume' (see W. J. Cameron, *Bibliographical Control of Early Books* (Bangalore, 1978), 8–11).

39 The cataloguing rules developed over the years of experiment will be found in *The HPB Project Phase IV*, Appendix A, Manual D.

40 The two facts in square brackets had to be inferred from Macdonald's description. The copy of the book at McMaster University has the B reading on T1^r; the C version of U1^r, and the B version of U1^v.

41 Bowers, *Harvard Library Bulletin*, 3 (1949), 279.

42 ibid., 281. Bowers does not mention a misprint noted by Macdonald (Prauls for Pauls) nor one observed by Osborn (Pnuls for Pauls).

43 e.g. Tonson's name appears first in imprint in the following issue: and Swall's name appears first in the previous issue.

44 The value of such book-lists has been demonstrated for an eighteenth-century bookseller. See W. J. Cameron, 'John Bell (1745–1831): A Case Study of the Use of Advertisement Lists as Evidence in Publishing History', *The Humanities Association Review*, 26 (1975), 196–215.

45 Ward's *Life*, 134, is an example.

46 It could even be argued on the bibliographical evidence that *Miscellany Poems* (1684) may have grown from an interrupted plan to issue a separate edition of Dryden's satires dated 1683.

47 It was advertised in *The London Gazette*, 16–20 February 1688.

48 See Narcissus Luttrell, *A Brief Historical Relation of State Affairs*, 6 vols (Oxford, 1857), I, 430.

49 The false title-pages of the latter two poems were dated 1692.

50 Tonson may have made some special arrangement with Herringman in 1688 to issue his Charles II aggregation. Not until the 1692 editions of Shadwell's *Libertine*, Howard's *Five Plays*, and Dryden's *All for Love*, *Aureng-Zebe* and *Indian Emperour* did the phrase 'and are to be sold by R. Bentley, J. Tonson, F. Saunders, and T. Bennet' begin to appear in Herringman imprints. Joseph Knight and Francis Saunders had taken over Herringman's retail business between 27 July and 23 November 1683, if signatures in the Stationers' Register are to be taken as evidence. Knight's name last appears as Herringman's vendor in Orrery's *History of Henry the Fifth* and *The Tragedy of Mustapha*, both in 1690. Bentley had been sole vendor for Herringman of some of Shadwell's plays, although James Knapton was as frequently employed as Herringman in the early publications of Shadwell. Knapton joined Saunders as Herringman's vendor during 1691, and it is possible that he was the one from whom both Bentley and Tonson obtained their copyright shares.

51 Osborn, *Modern Philology*, 39 (1942), 315.

52 161b, 165b,c,d,e,f,g,h, 166b, 167b,c, 171b, 172b, 179aii, b, c, 181b, 184b, 186b, 188b, 190b, 192b,c,d, 194b, 195b,c,d, 201b, 205b, 207ii, 208b, 212b, 218 (β), (γ), (δ), 219ii, 241b, 243b, 246b, 248b, 250b, 256b, 257b, 266b, 275b, 284b, 289ii, 302b,c.

53 313b, 315b.

54 James Thorpe (ed.), *Rochester's Poems on Several Occasions* (Princeton, N.J., 1950).

55 George deF. Lord *et al.* (eds), *Poems on Affairs of State. Augustan Satirical Verse, 1660–1714*, 7 vols (New Haven, Conn., and London, 1963–75).

56 cf. Ecclestone, 192a,b,c, and d.

57 Only one copy (in the Folger Shakespeare Library) is mentioned in *NUC* (E0132423).

58 Fredson Bowers, *Principles of Bibliographical Description*, 99.

59 The term 'aggregation' can be used for separately published items brought together within one binding to form a 'collected' edition or issue, or a new combination of old parts. The term

'aggregate issue' can be used to describe a purposive reissue of 'parts'.

60 The recto symbol is omitted (*pace* Foxon!).

61 For instance, 1735 'parts' separately bound in the McMaster University collection are easily identified as *The State of Innocence* from vol. IV, *Spanish Fryar* from vol. V, and *King Arthur* from vol. VI.

62 Resetting of individual formes or sheets has not been noted, for instance. Two copies of *Miscellaneous Works* 1767 (Do-387194) at McMaster University differ in the outer forme of sheet B of volume III. The resetting can be detected by noting a different set of type ornaments on B1^r and by noting that the press figure '3' occurs on B8^r in one copy and on B2^v on the other.

A LIST OF THE
PUBLISHED WRITINGS
AND THE RECORDINGS OF
HAROLD F. BROOKS

Compiled by Antony Coleman

For books, the place of publication is London unless otherwise stated.

I PRE-SHAKESPEAREAN

The Dream of the Rood, translated from the Old English, Dublin, 1942.
Chaucer's Pilgrims: The Artistic Order of the Portraits in the Prologue, 1962.

2 SHAKESPEARE

Assistant editor of the Arden Shakespeare 1952–8.
Currently joint general editor of The Arden Shakespeare since 1958.
A Midsummer Night's Dream (ed.), The Arden Shakespeare, 1979.
'A notorious Shakespearean crux: *Midsummer Night's Dream* V.i. 208', *N&Q*, n.s. 17, 4, April, 1970, 125–7.
The Tempest: what sort of play? Annual Shakespeare Lecture of the British Academy, 1978 and in *Proceedings of the British Academy*, 1980 (forthcoming).
'Themes and structure in *The Comedy of Errors*', in J. R. Brown and B. Harris (eds), *Early Shakespeare* (Stratford-upon-Avon Studies, 3), 1961, reprinted with revisions 1967, 54–71, and in

Kenneth Muir (ed.), *Shakespeare: the Comedies*, 1965, 11–25.

'Two clowns in a comedy (to say nothing of the dog): Speed, Launce (and Crab) in *The Two Gentlemen of Verona*', *Essays and Studies* collected by S. Gorley Putt, 1963, 91–100.

'*Richard III*: antecedents of Clarence's dream', *Shakespeare Survey*, 32, 1979, 145–50.

'*Richard III*, unhistorical amplifications; the women's scenes and Seneca', *MLR*, LXXC, 4, 1980, 721–37.

'Shakespeare and *The Gouernour*, bk. II, ch. xiii. Parallels with *Richard II* and the *More* addition', *Shakespeare Quarterly*, XIV, 1963, 195–9.

'Shakespearean phrases in English life and writing', *Unesco Features*, 449, 4 December 1964, 9–11.

Foreword and errata in S. P. Sen Gupta, *Some Aspects of Shakespeare's Sonnets*, Calcutta, 1967.

Appendices contributed to the Arden Shakespeare

'Ravenscroft on *Titus*, and Cowley on the posthumous Folio editions of Beaumont and Fletcher, Jonson, and Shakespeare', appendix (a), *Titus Andronicus*, ed. J. C. Maxwell, 1961, 131–3.

'Chiron and Demetrius as Rape and Murder', appendix (b), *Titus Andronicus*, ed. J. C. Maxwell, 133–4.

'Act III. sc. i and *The Mirror for Magistrates*', appendix A (d), *Cymbeline*, ed. J. M. Nosworthy, 1955, 212–16.

'Had I so lavish of my presence been . . .', appendix vi, *1 Henry IV*, ed. A. R. Humphreys, 1960, 200–1.

'Why doth the crown lie there . . .', appendix vii, *2 Henry IV*, ed. A. R. Humphreys, 1966, 241–2.

'Conjectural rearrangements of verse', appendix D, *Pericles*, ed. F. D. Hoeniger, 1963, 183–8.

2 JOHN OLDHAM

Abstract of the complete works of John Oldham, edited with an introduction and notes (privately printed), 1939.

A Bibliography of John Oldham the Restoration Satirist, Oxford, 1936. Reprinted from *Proceedings and Papers of the Oxford Bibliographical*

Society, v.i., reprinted with additions and corrections, Kraus Reprint, Nendeln, Liechtenstein, 1969.

'The chief substantive editions of Oldham's poems, 1679–84: printer, compositors, and publication', *Studies in Bibliography*, XXVII, 1974, 188–226.

'The poems of John Oldham' in Harold Love (ed.), *Restoration Literature: Critical Approaches*, 1972, 177–203.

'John Oldham', *The Times Literary Supplement*, 12 July 1934, 492.

'The family of John Oldham', *N&Q*, 167, 14 July 1934, 30.

'The family of John Oldham the poet', *Miscellanea Genealogica et Heraldica*, September, 1934, 1–4.

[With F. H. G. Percy and W. D. Hussey] 'John Shepheard, Master of Whitgift School when John Oldham the poet was undermaster', *Notes and Queries for Somerset and Dorset*, XXX, 1979, 435–44.

'Oldham and Phineas Fletcher: an unrecognised source for "Satyrs upon the Jesuits"', *RES*, n.s. XXII, November 1971, 410–22; XXIII, 89, February 1972, 19–34.

'Authorship of "Britannia and Rawleigh"', *N&Q*, 179, 9, 31 August 1940, 146; but see Godfrey Davies, 'The date of "Britannia and Rawleigh"', *Huntington Library Quarterly*, IX, 1946, 311–18.

'John Oldham: some problems of biography and annotation', *Philological Quarterly*, 54, 3, summer 1975, 569–78.

'Editing the poems of John Oldham (1653–83): desiderata', *N&Q*, n.s. 21, 5, May 1974, 180–1.

3 RESTORATION LITERATURE

Articles

'The "Imitation" in English poetry, especially in formal satire, before the age of Pope', *RES*, XXV, April 1949, 124–40.

Rump Songs: an index with notes, 1939. Reprinted from *Proceedings and Papers of the Oxford Bibliographical Society*, v.iv, 283–304.

'Contributors to Brome's *Horace*', *N&Q*, 174, 12, 19 March 1938, 200–1.

'When did Dryden write "MacFlecknoe"? – some additional notes', *RES*, XI, 41, January 1935, 74–8. Reprinted in H. T. Swedenberg (ed.), *Essential Articles for the Study of John Dryden*, 1966, 165–9.

'Dryden's *Aureng-Zebe*: debts to Corneille and Racine', *Revue de Litterature Comparée*, XLVI, 1972, 5–34.

'Dryden's Juvenal and the Harveys', *Philological Quarterly*, XLVIII, January 1969, 12–19.

'Dryden and Cowley', *The Times Literary Supplement*, 10 April 1957, 245.

'Some notes on Dryden, Cowley, and Shadwell', *N&Q*, 22, 9 February 1935, 94.

'The date of Rochester's "Timon"', *N&Q*, 174, 22, 28 May 1938, 384–5.

'Attributions to Rochester', *The Times Literary Supplement*, 9 May 1935, 301.

'Gift to Samuel Butler', *The Times Literary Supplement*, 6 July 1940, 327.

'A Satyricall Shrub', *The Times Literary Supplement*, 11 December 1969, 1426.

'The Dictionary of National Biography', *Bulletin of the Institute of Historical Research*, May 1941, 135–6. (Additions and corrections to entries on Samuel Butler, Jonathan Goddard, John Oldham, Sir William Petty, Walter Pope and Thomas Sprat.)

Reviews

G. S. Alleman, *Matrimonial Law and the Materials of Restoration Comedy*, RES, XIX, 76, October 1943, 424–6.

H. G. Wright (ed.), *Ghismonda*, RES, XXIII, 90, April 1947, 174–5.

John C. Hodges, *William Congreve the Man*, RES, XXIV, 94, April 1948, 159–62.

André de Mandach, *Molière et la Comédie de Moeurs en Angleterre*, ibid.

Hugh Macdonald (ed.), *Elkanah Settle, The Preface to Ibrahim*, op. cit., 170.

Kathleen M. Lynch, *A Congreve Gallery*, RES, n.s. IV, 16, October 1953, 385–7.

D. M. Vieth, *Attribution in Restoration Poetry: a study of Rochester's 'Poems' of 1680*. *N&Q*, October 1965, 396.

4 NINETEENTH AND TWENTIETH CENTURY LITERATURE

'*Lord Jim* and "Fifine at the Fair"', *Conradiana*, III, i, 1970–1, 9–25.

[With Jean R. Brooks] 'Dickens in Shaw', *The Dickensian*, May 1963, 93–9.

'*Pygmalion* and *When We Dead Awaken*', *N&Q*, n.s. 7, 12, 1960, 469–71.

'Shavian sources in the notes to *Queen Mab*', *The Shaw Review*, XX, 2, May 1977, 83–4.

'Judgement and the life to come: Shaw's new play (*The Simpleton*) and its message', *The Inquirer*, 7 September 1935, 413–14.

'Shaw's "Geneva"', *Time and Tide*, 13 August 1938, 1153.

'W. B. Yeats: "The Tower"', *Durham University Journal*, December 1980, 9–21.

'*Four Quartets:* the structure in relation to the themes', in Graham Martin (ed.), *Eliot in Perspective*, 1970, 132–47.

'Between *The Waste Land* and the first Ariel poems: "The Hollow Men"', *English*, XVI, 1966, 89–93.

'*The Family Reunion* and "Colombe's Birthday"', *The Times Literary Supplement*, 12 December, 1952, 819.

[With David Cook] 'A room with three views: Harold Pinter's *The Caretaker*', *Komos*, 1, 2, June 1967, 62–9.

5 ON CRITICISM, AND TEXTUAL SCHOLARSHIP

'The editor and the literary text: requirements and opportunities', in A. T. Milne (ed.), *Librarianship and Literature: essays in honour of Jack Pafford*, 1970, 97–121.

The use and abuse of literary criticism, inaugural lecture delivered at Birkbeck College as Professor of English Literature in the University of London, 1974.

'The name of action', *Komos*, 2, 2, November 1969, 37–49.

'Guide to further reading', in Una Ellis-Fermor, *The Frontiers of Drama*, (2nd edn), 1964, 154–8.

6 RECORDINGS

(a) The following recordings were made at the Audio-Visual Centre, University of London, and are available on cassette.

The use and abuse of literary criticism.
What is dramatic?
An introduction to *Piers Plowman*.
Piers Plowman: the wild way.
Sir Gawain and The Green Knight: an appreciation.
Love and lovelessness in Shakespeare.
Troilus and Cressida.
Dryden: "Mac Flecknoe".
The Restoration comedy of manners.
Shaw the Victorian.
Shaw and the European revolution in drama.
Bernard Shaw: his kind of drama.
Bernard Shaw: *Major Barbara.*
Yeats: "Sailing to Byzantium".
T. S. Eliot, *The Waste Land:* poem of hope.
T. S. Eliot, *The Family Reunion.*
Virginia Woolf: a new sort of novelist.
Virginia Woolf's Nine Ages of Man: *The Waves.*
On *The Tempest.*
Yeats, *The Tower:* an exposition.

(b) Sussex Tapes
[With Alan Sinfield] Bernard Shaw, *Major Barbara*, *Heartbreak House*, *St Joan*.

Some few short pieces have been omitted from this list which has been prepared (in reasonable departure from customary practice) to illustrate Harold Brooks's achievement in several diverse fields and the scope of what has been described as 'his rich and subtle scholarship' (Frank Kermode (ed.), *The Tempest*, The Arden Shakespeare, 1958, ix).

INDEX

acting style, 21–2
acting troupes, 13, 21, 157–68
adultery, 80, 82, 85–6, 88
Age of Reason, 99
Alleyn, Edward, 64
antiquarianism, 151
anti-Spanish feeling, 70–1, 72
Aristotle, 98, 102–3, 114, 177
   Poetics, 97
Armada Triumph, 66
Armistead, J. M., 174, 180
Armstrong, William A., 47–59
Arrowsmith, Joseph, 137
Ascham, Roger
   Toxophilus, 47
Auden, W. H., 42
audiences, 16
   Tudor, 13
   'Vice', 20, 25–6, 27–8
   working-class, 14

Bachelors, 60, 61
Bacon, Francis, 112
Bale, R., 18
Barker, Harley Granville, 10
Beaumont, Francis, 157
Bedlam, 173
Behn, Aphra, 137
   plays, 165
Bell's British Theatre, 224
Bentley, Richard, 216–17
Betterton, Thomas, 168, 188
Bevington, David
   From 'Mankind' to Marlowe, 13, 28
Bible, 102
bibliographical description, 201–2, 203,
   207, 209
bibliography, 200–4
   posthumous, 222
   short-title catalogue practice, 203,
     210, 221

Bion, 127–9
Birkbeck College, 4, 6, 8, 10
Blackfriers' playhouse, 158–9, 161,
   164
Blake, William, 5
Bodleian Library, 7, 114
Boileau, Nicolas, 113, 119, 124, 140
Bondsman, The, 160, 162
book trade, 138
Bowers, Fredson, 201–4
   Dryden bibliography, 205–6,
     224
Bradbrook, M. C., 60–75
Brecht, Bertolt, 14, 17
Brett-Smith, H. F. B., 5
Bridges Street Theatre, 163
British Academy, 10, 12
British Library, 203
Brome, Richard
   Horace, 118, 124
   plays, 162, 165
Brooks, Harold, 1, 9
   criticism, 3–4
   early life, 1–6, 10
   'Imitation', 110, 139–40
   Oldham, 113, 144, 151
   scholarship, 7, 9–12
   teaching, 6, 9–10
Brooks, Jane (Jenny), 1–3
Brooks, Joseph Barlow, 1–2, 4, 5, 6
Brown, John Russell, 33
Buchanan, George, 110
Buckingham, George Villiers, Duke of,
   95–6
Buffalo Bill, 17
Bunyan, John, 99, 101, 105, 106
   Pilgrim's Progress, The, 104
Burnet, Gilbert, 93–4
Butler, Samuel, 99, 105, 106
   Elephant in the Moon, The, 106
   Hudibras, 92, 93, 96, 101

Calvinism, 103
Camden, William, 64
Cameron, W. J., 200–32
Caroline theatre, 158, 164, 168–9
Carter, John, 200–1
Case, A. E., 200
Catholicism, 100
Catullus, 111, 117–18, 129
censorship, 103
Cervantes, Miguel de, 92
Chaplin, Charlie, 15, 17
Chapman, George, 70
Charles I, 74, 101, 168
  as crown prince, 71
Charles II, 99, 100, 104, 167
Chaucer, Geoffrey, 100
  Canterbury Tales, 8
  Wife of Bath's Tale, 84
Chekhov, Anton, 14
Chorus, role of, 74
Christmas, Gerard, 72
Cibber, Colley, 157
circus clowns, 21
Clark, William Andrews, Library,
  210–11
class differences, 84–5
classic plays, 159, 164
classical literature, 110, 137, 151–2
classical society, 151–2
cloth trade, 69
  pageantry, 61
clowns, 17, 21
Cockayne Project, 69–70
comedians, modern, 21
comedy, 186
  'Vice' in, 26, 27
comedy of manners, 37, 156
commedia dell' arte, 15, 17, 22, 28
Commonwealth, the, 174, 178
Congreve, William, 223
  Double-Dealer, The, 188–90, 191–2
  Love for Love, 190, 191, 192
  Mourning Bride, The, 192–4
  Old Batchelour, The, 190
  Shakespearean influences, 186–95
  translations, 127, 137
  Way of the World, The, 38–9, 187, 191,
    192
Cook, David, 32–46
Cotton, Charles, 106
court drama, 18
court masques, 67, 68, 71
Covent Garden Theatre, 55

Cowley, Abraham, 95, 186
  plays, 163
  translations, 111, 113, 139, 140, 151
Craik, T. W., 186–99
Creech, Thomas, 136–7, 145
crib translation, 139, 140, 151
criticism
  American, 90
  Harold Brooks, 3–4
  theatre, 13
Cromwell, Oliver, 18, 101, 105
Crown, the, 65, 73
Cushman, L. W., 17, 21

Daunt, Marjorie, 8
Davenant, Sir William, 158, 168
  plays, 159, 160, 161, 162, 166
  Preface to Gondibert, 91–2
  theatre company, 158–65
    repertory, 159–62, 165, 166–7
Declaration of Indulgence, 100
Dekker, Thomas, 62, 63–4, 65–6, 68, 74
  Troia-Nova Triumphans, 67
Dennis, John, 116–17
Devil, role of, 17, 19, 21
Dissenters, 100
Dixie, Sir Wolstan, 63
Dobell, P. J., 200
doggerel, 147
Donne, John, 96, 103, 104, 118
Dorset, Charles Sackville, Earl of, 95
Dorset Garden Theatre, 168
Dover Wilson, John, 54, 55
drama historians, 156, 169
Drapers, 61, 66
  trade crisis, 69–70
Drapers' Triumphs, 69–71
Dryden, John, 8, 10, 99, 101, 111–12,
    176, 186
  Absalom and Achitophel, 95, 96, 215,
    222
  Annus Mirabilis, 92–3, 97, 215
  biography, 206–7, 226–7
  Discourse Concerning Satire, 90
  Dramatick Works, 224–6
  Fables, 100, 136
  Hind and the Panther, The, 96, 104, 105,
    210, 211–12, 215
  MacFlecknoe, 96, 105, 125, 191, 215
  Medal, The, 96, 105, 215
  Of Dramatic Poesy, 111, 113–14
  Parallel Betwixt Poetry and Painting, 97
  parodies, 221

plays, 165, 166, 167, 168, 216, 222–3
  with Lee, 173
poetry, 92–3, 97–8
religious poems, 104
satire, 90, 92, 95, 102–3, 105–6
Satires, 95
Sylvae, 145, 215
translations, 110, 113–14, 116, 119,
  128, 130–1, 136–8, 140–1, 143–51
Dryden bibliography, 200, 204–9
California edition, 206, 211, 226
dating information, 214–18
first editions, 210, 211, 214
Hind and the Panther, The, 210, 211–12,
  215
methods, 210–14
Miscellany Poems, 215
posthumous editions, 222–6
Troilus and Cressida, 212–14
Dryden collections, 208–9
Drydeniana, 204
bibliographies, 207, 218–20
new editions, 220–1, 226
Duke, Richard, 137
Duke's Company, 158
repertory, 157, 160–1, 162, 163–4,
  166, 167–8
Durfey, Thomas, 106
Dutch Wars, 101, 105

East India Company, 67
education, 138
Edwardian melodrama, 17
eighteenth century, 99
Eliot, T. S., 8, 10–11, 12
Four Quartets, 11, 12
on Middleton, 76, 82, 85, 88–9
Elizabeth I, 63, 65, 66, 100, 104
Elizabethan drama, 8, 156
Elizabethan language, 195
Elizabethan London, 61
Elizabethan society, 51, 58, 103, 174
Elizabethan translation, 140, 146
Elliot, Robert C., 96, 103
Ellis-Fermor, Una, 9
English society, sixteenth-century, 14,
  17
English syntax, 147, 150
English Theatre, The, 224, 226
enthymemes, 100
epic poetry, 91, 93, 98–9, 102
Essex, Robert Devereux, Earl of, 103
Euripedes, 98

Evelyn, John, 137
execution, 51
extramural classes, 1, 6

faith, Restoration and, 90, 99, 100–2,
  104–6
family honour, 79, 81
Fellowes, E. H., 5
Fifth Monarchy Men, 101
Firth, Sir Charles, 5–6
First World War, 4, 12
Fishmongers' Triumph, 70
Fitz-Alwin, Henry, 66
Fitzgerald, Robert, 195
Flatman, Thomas, 106
Fletcher, John, 157, 161, 162
Fletcher, Phineas
  Locustae, 110
Folger Library, 225
folk drama, 14, 17
folk origins, 17
folk rituals, 16–17
fool, role of, 17, 21
Ford, John, 162
Foxon, David, 203
Freehafer, John, 159
Freeman, Rosemary, 6, 8
French writers, 140
Fulwell, U., 18

Garrick, David, 55
Garter, T., 18
Glorious Revolution, 101
Gill, Roma, 86
Globe Theatre, 48, 49, 54, 55
Golding, Arthur, 140, 146–7
Good Old Cause, 100
Gore, Sir John, 71
Goudlad, J. S. R., 16
government
  City of London, 65, 70, 73
  Restoration, 174, 176
Great Tradition, 14
Greece, 151, 176
Greek, classical, 110, 138, 145
Greek civilization, 137
Greek literature, classical, 111
Grey, Zachary, 101
Guildhall, 60
Gunpowder Plot, 68

Haberdashers, 61, 71
Hall, Joseph, 103, 110

Halliday, Sir Leonard, 66, 68
Hammond, Antony, 173–85
Happé, Peter, 13–31
Harbage, Alfred, 166
Hardy, Barbara, 6
Hardy, Thomas, 3–4, 8
Harlequin, 22
Harlequinade, 17
Harper, Sir Thomas, 62
Harvard University Library, 211, 213
Hazlitt, William, 11
Heinemann, Margot, 79
Henry, Elector Palatine, 67
Henry, Prince of Wales, 68, 71, 73
Henry VII, 62
heraldry, 62–3, 64–5
Herbert, George, 104
Herbert, Sir Henry, 158, 164
Herringman, Henry, 216
hero, flawed, 174–5
heroic drama, 115, 156, 168
    themes, 174–5
heroic imagination, 99
heroic poetry, 91, 92, 93, 103, 106
heroism, 174
Heywood, John, 18, 22
    Love's Mistress, 160, 162
Hibbard, G. R., 81
Higden, Henry
    Modern Essay on the Thirteenth Satyr of
        Juvenal, 121
Hobbes, Thomas, 111
    concept of literature, 91–2, 98
    Leviathan, 101, 142
Holden, Arthur, 4
Holinshed, Raphael
    Chronicles of England, Scotland and
        Ireland, The, 56
Holmes, David M., 88
Homer, 95, 102–3, 106
    Margites, 103, 106
    Pope's translation, 137
Hood, Robin, 66, 70
Horace, 95, 96, 103, 106
    Ars Poetica, 113, 118, 151
    Odes, 137
    translations, 111, 112, 113, 119,
        122–7, 136, 137, 144
Horowitz, David, 33–4, 39
Howard, James, 166
Howard, Sir Robert, 165, 166
    Surprisal, The, 164
Howard family, 167

Howerd, Frankie, 16
Hume, Robert D., 156–72, 176
Hunter, Robert Grams, 33

Ibsen, Henrik, 14
'Imitation', 145, 152
    development, 110, 136, 139–40
    Oldham, 110–35
    see also translation
incest, 76–7, 78, 79, 80–1, 88
Italian opera, 168

Jacobean drama, 82, 156, 158
Jacobean London, 61
James I, 62, 63–4, 65, 66, 70, 71, 100, 104
    death of, 74
    rebellions against, 101
James Bond films, 17
Jenkins, Harold, 9
Johnson, George, 1
Johnson, Jane, 1–2; see also Brooks, Jane
Johnson, Kathie, 1, 5, 9, 10
Johnson, Lillie, 1, 5, 9, 10
Johnson, Dr Samuel, 110, 132, 186–7,
    191
    Works of the Poets of Great Britain, 222
Johnston, Arthur, 1–12
Jonson, Ben, 64, 66, 103
    Bartholemew Fair, 70
    classicist, 111–12, 117, 124, 129
    Every Man out of his Humour, 68
    Masque of Blackness, 67
    Masque of Queens, The, 68
    plays, 157, 161
    Triumphs, 67, 68, 69, 71, 74
Jung, C. G., 5
Juvenal, 95, 96, 106
    translations, 111, 113, 118, 119–20,
        136, 137, 144

Keally, Joseph, 194–5
Keller, Sir Godfrey, 105
Ken, Thomas, 100
Ker, W. P., 11
Killigrew, Thomas, 162, 164, 165, 167
Killigrew, William
    Selindra, 164
Killigrew's Company, 160, 161, 163
    repertory, 158, 166–7
Killigrew family, 167
King's Company, 157–8, 160–2, 163
    repertory, 164–5, 166, 167
King's Merchant Venturers, 69

King's Players, 64
Kittredge, G. L., 48

Lacey, John, 167
Laclos, Pierre Ambroise François
    Clauderlos de, 79
Lamb, Charles, 84
Langland, William, 8
Latin
    translation from, 110, 124, 132, 138,
        140
    syntax, 141–6, 150
Laurel, Stan, 21
Lawrence, D. H., 37
Lee, Guy, 142
Lee, Jean Rylatt, 9
Lee, Nathaniel, 173
    Caesar Borgia, 174, 175, 180
    heroic drama, 174
    Lucius Junius Brutus, 173–84; *see also*
        separate listing
    Massacre of Paris, The, 176
    published plays, 173
    Rival Queens, The, 114, 174–5
    Sophonisba, 174–5
    Venice Preserv'd, 183
    Works, 173, 224
leisure, 138
Leman, Sir John, 62
Lewis, Jerry, 21
library cataloguing, 202, 203
Library of Congress, 211, 224
Lincoln's Inn Fields Theatre, 163–4, 166,
    168
literacy, 138
literature, seventeenth-century view, 98,
    151
Little Tradition, the, 14
Littlewood, Joan, 14, 17
Livings, Henry, 16, 17
Livy
    History, 176
Loeb, James, 148
London, city of, 70
    government, 65, 73
    power, 60–1
    seventeenth-century, 138, 151
    symbolized, 64, 66
London Stage, The, 156, 157, 165
Lord Chamberlain, the, 156, 157, 158,
    160–1, 175
Lord Mayor of London
    heraldry, 62–3

pageant of, 60–4, 66
Lord Mayor's Show, 70
Lord Mayor's Triumphs, 62, 66–74
    route, 60–1
Love, Harold, 136–55
Low Countries, 69
Lowndes, T., 226
Lucian, 106
Lucilius, 112
Lucius Junius Brutus, 173
    banned, 175
    plot, 177–82
    political position, 175–6, 177–8,
        183–4
Lucretius, 136, 137, 145
Lumley, Sir Martin, 71
Lupton, T., 18
Luttrell, Henry, 214

Macbeth, 40, 168
    editors of, 53–4
    First Folio, 54
    symbolism, 47–8, 56
        cauldron, 53–4
        darkness, 48–55
        light, 48
        owl, 51, 56–7
        taper, 54–6
Macdonald, Hugh
    John Dryden, 200, 204–7, 208, 210–11,
        213–21, 223, 227
Machiavelli, Nicolo, 85
    Discourses, 176
Macmanaway, J. G., 9
Madan, Falconer, 201
Manilius, 136
Mares, F. H., 17
Marlowe, Christopher, 131–2
marriage, Restoration drama and, 37, 39
Marston, John, 66, 103, 110, 118
Martial, 111, 113
Marvell, Andrew, 94, 96, 205–6, 118
    Dryden and, 220
    Rehearsal Transpos'd, The, 105–6
Massinger, Philip, 165
medieval art, 53
medieval Church, 27
medieval literature, 8
Merbury, F., 18
Mercers, 61
Mercers' Maid, 61
Merchant Taylors, 61–2, 63, 71
    Triumphs, 66–9

Merton College, Oxford, 5
messenger, role of, 17, 21
    classical, 74
Methodism, 1–2, 4, 5
Methodist New Connection, 2, 4
middle classes
    literature, 138
    rise of, 100
Middlebrook, Sydney, 5
Middleton, Thomas, 76
    Changeling, The, 76, 160, 162
    Game of Chess, A, 71
    pageants, 64, 68–9, 71
    plays, 162
    Women Beware Women, 76–89; *see also
        separate listing*
Milhous, Judith, 161
Milton, John, 74, 95, 99, 101, 106, 111,
    138, 150
    Lycidas, 100
    Paradise Lost, 100, 104–5, 220
    Paradise Regained, 105
    Tenure of Kings and Magistrates, The, 74
mimesis, 98
Miner, Earl, 90–109
monarchists, 177, 178, 181
monarchy, 183
morality plays, 14, 17, 27, 69
Moschus, 127
Moseley, Humphrey, 158, 166
Much Ado About Nothing, 194
    as comedy of manners, 37, 38–9
    characters
        Beatrice and Benedick, 32–3, 36–9,
            42–3, 45
        Claudio and Hero, 33–7, 39, 41–5
        Don John, 33, 39–40, 42
        low life, 40–1
    main themes, 34–5
    problems of plot, 32–4, 45–6
Muir, Kenneth, 48, 76–89
Mulcaster, Richard, 62, 64, 66
Mulgrave, John, Earl of, 94–5, 221
Munday, Anthony, 62, 63, 69
    Triumphs of re-united Britania, The, 66
murder, 79–82, 86
Myddleton, Sir Thomas, 69, 70
mystery cycles, 14, 15, 17

narrative poetry, 91, 92, 105
Nashe, Thomas
    Terrors of the Night, The, 48
nature, Restoration view of, 92, 97, 98

neo-classicism, 112
Netherlands, United Provinces of the,
    65
New Arden Shakespeare, 9–10, 11
New English Theatre, The, 224
Newcastle Literary and Philosophical
    Society, 2
Newgate gaol, 51
NUC, 208, 210, 213, 219, 220, 224

Old Fortunatus, 28
Oldham, John, 5–6, 7, 10, 12, 96, 106,
    140
    'Imitations', 110–11, 112–13, 127–9,
        137, 151
        Catullus, 117–18
        Horace, 118–19, 122–7
        Juvenal, 119–23
        Ovid, 113–17, 118, 129–32, 143,
            146
    on Ben Jonson, 111–12
    Poems and Translations, 110
    'Satyrs upon the Jesuits', 5, 110, 113,
        118, 119–21, 132
    Some New Pieces, 110, 113, 118
operas, 168
Orrery, Earl of
    plays, 167
Osborn, James M., 204–5
    Dryden bibliography, 205–7, 211,
        214, 217, 218–19
Otway, Thomas, 137, 216
    Don Carlos, 114
Ovid, 103
    Amores, 130–2, 139, 141, 146
    Epistles, 113, 137, 144, 221
    Metamorphoses, 113, 137, 139, 146, 147
    poetic mode, 140
    translations, 111, 113–17, 129–32,
        140–52

pacifism, 2–3, 4
Palmer, John, 37
panegyric, 93, 98, 102, 105, 106
pantomime, 16
    English Christmas, 17
Parliament, 65, 73–4
Peele, George, 63
Peele, James, 63
Pepys, Samuel, 160, 162–3, 164, 167–8
Persius, 95, 136
Phillip, J., 18
Pickering, J., 18

Pindar, 111
pindaric mode, 140
Piscator, Erwin, 14
plague, the, 74, 169
plays
    new, 163, 164, 165–8
    revivals, 161–2, 163, 164, 167–8
    rights to, 157–62, 166
    translated, 165–6
playwrights, professional, 156–7, 168–9
Pliny, 51
Poems on Affairs of State (POAS), 219,
    220–1
poetry
    Aristotle on, 102–3
    Dryden on, 97
    English idiom, 141–3, 147, 150
    epic, 91, 93, 98–9, 102
    Hobbes on, 91–2, 98
    narrative, 91, 92, 105
    religious, 104–6
    satiric, 91–2, 94
political science, 174
Pope, Alexander, 7
    Dunciad, 111
    'Imitations', 110, 125, 132, 137
Popish Plot, 101, 118, 120
popular theatre, 14–16, 17
    the 'Vice' in, 19, 27–8
Port of London, 67
Preston, T., 18
Pritchard, Mrs, 55–6
Protestant succession, 68, 73, 100
Punch, 15
    Punch and Judy show, 17
Puritanism, 69, 71, 100
Puttenham, Richard
    Art of English Poesie, 93

Queen's University, Belfast, 6, 10

Radcliffe, Alexander, 126
*Raillerie à la Mode Consider'd: or the
    Supercillious Detractor* (Anon.), 93
Ralegh, Sir Walter, 70
rape, as theme, 78, 85
Rawlinson, Thomas, 114
received wisdom, 99
Redfield, Robert, 14
regicide, 58
religion, Restoration, 90, 99, 100–2,
    104–6
religious poetry, 104–6

Renaissance, 180
    art, 53
    drama, 158
reopening of the theatres, 156
repertory, 157–68
Republicanism, 176, 180, 183
Restoration, 99–100
    concept of literature, 98
    concept of nature, 92, 97, 98
    political concerns, 138, 174, 176, 184
    religion, 99, 100–2, 104–6
    satire, 90, 98–9, 102–3, 105–6
Restoration comedy, 147
Restoration drama, 37, 114, 125, 156,
    166
    marriage theme, 37, 39
    political, 174, 184
Restoration literature, 6, 114, 118, 173
    translations, 136–9, 150–2
Restoration London, 138, 151
Restoration society, 147, 151–2
Restoration theatre, 163, 164
    companies, 157–68
rhetoric, 93, 94
Rhode's troupe, 159, 160, 162
Rochester, John Wilmot, Earl of, 93–4,
    96, 99, 106, 121–2, 128, 132
    Poems, 220
    translations, 112–13, 118, 124, 125,
        129–30, 136–7, 151
    Ovid, 141–4, 146
Roe, Sir John, 62
Rolland, Romain, 14
Roman civilization, 137, 151–2
Roman poets, 111, 113, 150, 152
Roman satires, 118, 152
Roman Triumph, 60
Rome, 151, 176
Roscommon, Earl of, 124, 145
    Essay on Translated Verse, An, 137
Rowley, William, 162
Royal Society, 111
rural society, 14
Rye House Plot, 101

St John's College, Oxford, 62
St Paul's School, London, 64, 66
St Simon and St Jude's Day, 60
Sandys, George, 140–1, 146–7, 149, 150
satire
    concepts, 90, 91–5
        Dryden's, 90, 92, 95–7
    origins, 90

satire – *contd.*
  religion and, 103–5
  Restoration view, 90, 98–9, 103–4
  subjects, 102, 105–6
scenery, 161, 163, 164–5, 169
Scudéry, Madeleine
  Clelia, 176
sea Triumphs, 72
Second World War, 6, 12
secularization, 100
sedition, 103
Sedley, Sir Charles, 132
  translations, 131, 137
seduction, dramatic theme, 78, 85–6
Selden, Raman, 110–35
Settle, Elkanah, 165
  Empress of Morocco, The, 114
seventeenth century, 90, 132, 136
  drama, 156
  ideas, 148–9
  literature, 136–9, 150–2
  politics, 138
Shadwell, Thomas, 125
  Dryden, 219
  plays, 165
  translations, 140, 144
Shakespeare, William, 8, 9, 64, 111, 138,
    173, 181
  As You Like It, 194
  Comedy of Errors, 9
  Hamlet, 187–8, 189, 191, 194, 195
  influences Congreve, 186–95
  Julius Caesar, 194
  King Henry IV, 183, 187, 189–90, 194
  King Richard III, 9, 10
  Love's Labour's Lost, 37, 38–9, 40, 189,
    194
  Macbeth, 47–58, 168; *see also separate
    listing*
  Measure for Measure, 41, 44
  Merchant of Venice, The, 32, 37, 43
  Merry Wives of Windsor, The, 194–5
  Midsummer Night's Dream, A, 10, 11,
    40–1, 42, 190, 194
  Much Ado About Nothing, 32–46, 194;
    see also separate listing
  Othello, 42, 44, 188, 189, 194, 195
    role of Iago, 39, 77
  production of plays, 157, 159, 161,
    163, 168
  Romeo and Juliet, 32, 44, 82, 180, 189,
    192–3, 194
    role of Juliet, 41, 43

Taming of the Shrew, The, 37
Tempest, The, 10, 12
Twelfth Night, 10, 28, 194
Two Gentlemen of Verona, 9, 42
Winter's Tale, A, 42, 45
Shaw, Eleanor, 5
Shaw, George Bernard, 3, 8
  Major Barbara, 11
  Man and Superman, 38
  You Never Can Tell, 10
Shaw, Harold Watkins, 5
Shepherd, John, 7
Sheridan, Richard Brinsley, 55
Sheriffs, 60
ship pageant, 61, 68
Shirley, James, 165
Siddons, Mrs, 55–6
Sidney, Philip
  Apology, 93
sixteenth century, 14, 17
  social structure, 16–17
socialism, 5
society
  classical, 151–2
  divisions, 14
  Elizabethan, 51, 58, 103, 174
  hierarchy, 92
  Restoration, 147, 151–2
  sixteenth-century English, 14, 17
Soho Bibliographies, 200
soliloquy, 25, 28
  Macbeth, 50
Sophocles, 98, 129
Sorelius, Gunnar, 156–7, 159, 161
sovereignty, 174
Spain, 70–1, 72
Spenser, Edmund, 44, 95, 129
Spivack, Bernard, 17
Sprat, Thomas, 113, 118, 124
Spurgeon, Caroline
  *Shakespeare's Imagery and What it Tells
    Us*, 47
stage business, 25, 53, 55–6
stage directions, 19–20, 22–3
  Macbeth, 48, 49, 50, 53, 56–8
stage practice, Elizabethan, 49
Staple of News, The, 28
Stratford-upon-Avon, 81
Strindberg, August, 14
Stuart dynasty, 58
Suckling, Sir John, 186
Swall, Abel, 212
Swedenberg, H. T., Jr, 146

Swinnerton, Sir John, 67
syllogisms, 99
syntax, 141, 147, 150

Tate, Nahum, 137
Term Catalogue, 214, 216
Thames river, 67
theatre
  Caroline, 158, 164, 168–9
  development, 168–9
  Jacobean, 82, 156, 158
  modern Western, 14
  political, 14, 17, 173–4
  popular, 14–17
  Restoration, 157–68
  scenery, 161, 163, 164–5, 169
  social impact, 14
  see also plays
theatre historians, 156
Theatre Workshop, the, 14, 17
theatres, reopening, 156
Theocritus, 136
Thorn-Drury, George, 200
Tillotson, Geoffrey, 6, 8
Times Literary Supplement, The, 200–1
Todd, William B., 200, 201
Tonson, Jacob, 136, 138, 210, 211–12,
  215–16, 225
Tooley, Nicholas, 71
Tories, 177
trade rivalry, 69–70
tragedy, 173
  heroic drama, 175
  nature of, 91, 98
Traherne, Thomas, 104
translation
  language of, 141–50
  modes, 139–42
  paraphrase, 140, 142, 144, 151
  seventeenth-century, 136–9, 150–2
  see also 'Imitation'
triumphal arches, 64–5, 74
Triumphs, 60–2, 66–74
Troynovant, 66, 72, 74
Twayne's English Authors Series, 173
Twelve Great Companies, 60–1, 68, 70
twentieth-century literature, 11
Tudor drama, 8
  popular, 13
Tutchin, John, 127
  Tribe of Levi, 221

unemployment, 5, 12

seventeenth-century, 69, 70
Unitarianism, 5
United Provinces of the Netherlands, 65
Universal Magazine, The, 55
University of London, 6
University of Texas, 210
University of Virginia, 211
University of Western Ontario, 207, 223

Vanbrugh, Sir John, 168
Varenius, 110
Vaughan, Henry, 104
'Vice', the, 13–31
  character, 19, 25–6
  dramatic entrance, 20–1
  examples, 18, 19, 20–2
  origins, 17–18, 26–7
  performance, 20–5, 26, 27–8
village communities, 14
Virgil, 95, 151
  translations, 111, 129, 136
Virgin Mary, 61
virginity symbolism, 44

Wager, L., 18
Wager, W., 18
Walker, Sir Hovendon, 221
Waller, Edmund, 186
Ward, Charles E., 207
Wapull, G., 18
Watson, George, 95, 96, 97, 102
WEA (Workers' Education
  Association), 1, 6
Webster, John, 40, 62, 63, 68, 71, 74, 162
Weinbrot, Howard, 140
Wesleyanism, 4
Westerns, 17
Wever, R., 18
Whigs, 175–6, 177–8, 183
White, Sir Thomas, 62
Whittaker, W. G., 1
WHSTC (Western Hemisphere
  Short-Title Catalog), 207–8,
  211–12
WHUC (Western Hemisphere Union
  Catalog), 208, 218, 219
Wilkinson, C. H., 6
William and Mary, 100
Wilson, John
  Cheats, 166
Wilson, Robert
  *Three Lords and Three Ladies of
  London, The*, 66

Wisdom, Norman, 21
Wise, T. J., 200
Withington, Robert, 17
Woolf, Virginia, 8
  Waves, The, 11
women, literacy among, 138
Women Beware Women
  adultery, 80, 82, 85–6, 88
  chess scene, 76, 81, 84
  incest theme, 76–7, 78, 79, 80–1, 88
  masque scene, 79–81
  murder, 79–82, 86

  role of Bianca, 82–7, 88–9
  role of Isabella, 78–80, 87–9
  role of Leantio, 82–4, 85
  role of Livia, 76–9, 82, 85, 87, 88–9
working class radicalism, 2, 4
Wycherley, William
  Plain-Dealer, The, 168

Yates, Mrs, 55
Yeats, William Butler, 3, 8
  theatre, 14